The PALEOASTRONOMY SERIES: Volume 5

I0425980

BLOOD & INCEST
The Unholy Beginning of the Universe

TIMOTHY J. STEPHANY

ISBN-13: 978-1492191438
ISBN-10: 1492191434

Printed in the United States of America by Createspace

http://www.timothyjstephany.com

To Michael Wood,
for feeding my love for Anthropology

books by TIMOTHY J. STEPHANY

The Paleoastronomy Series:

The Eden Enigma: A Dialogue

Roar of the Tempests: A Dialogue

The Death of King David: A Dialogue

The Zodiac Mysteries

Blood & Incest: The Unholy Beginning of the Universe

The Gilgamesh Cycle

Enuma Elish: The Babylonian Creation Epic

The Holy Bible Revealed I: Genesis through Kings with Sources

The Holy Bible Revealed II: Compositional History

The Yahweh Document: The Holy Bible's First Edition

The Levi Document: The Earliest Biblical Source

The Sources Bible: Genesis through Kings (ASV)

BLOOD & INCEST

Persons of the Dialogue: *Soleos, Epitheus, Thaeo, & Phaedo*

CHAPTER 1

Soleos: One, two, three, four, but where then is the fifth member of our party?

Thaeo: If you are speaking of Phaedo, Soleos, I did see him heading off in a hasty flight with Arturius, but I presumed only for a brief confab; though we would have to imagine that he might be away from us for a time but that he will be rejoining us presently.

Soleos: This is unfortunate, since in not being here he is unable to regale us with some hoary antediluvian tale, something which could perhaps initiate some discourse to occupy us for the remainder of the day. Unless there is anything which is already on anyone's mind.

Epitheus: I think, Soleos, that with you here with us again that we might entreat you to disclose to us the matter we were discussing just a year ago, for I have been quite eagerly awaiting the disclosure of it ever since, and have been rapt with desire to hear it.

Soleos: Good enough, and I am more than prepared to do so. Yet before addressing this I would like to approach, as something of a preamble, what might be related concerning the very first moments of the creation of the universe. And, as it is, that we could well associate this with the present moment, by which I mean our festival of the year which we celebrate on this day.[*] Through I have heard that in years past such recollections of the dawn of time were considered suitable enough both to memorize and recite in generations past, but that this practice has erstwhile fallen into disuse. Yet I see no reason why we might not use this opportunity to do so for ourselves, if that is to our liking, as I think it might provide a most opportune chance for me to disclose something of what I have discovered concerning the matter which Epitheus speaks of.

---

[*] Presumably Easter

Thaeo: Surely. But what would you then have us speak of, Soleos, concerning the creation?

Soleos: What I suggest is that we disclose something of the very first days at the start of the universe, and in doing so too recount something of the advent and rise of man, as it is told. And for this I think we might merely call upon our own collective recollections, for there are many of them which could be disclosed, and amongst us we have those who surely know them best, apart from Phaedo, the masterful recounter of them. But as to the manner in which our disclosure of them might be suitably accomplished, I put this question to our young friend Epitheus.

Epitheus: Well, I should think, Soleos, that we ought to ask everyone to provide one which is known to him, in turn, and as such by the time we have finished perhaps we can rely upon Phaedo's return.

Soleos: A requisite suggestion, Epitheus. And we may fashion our hopes that when Phaedo does return into our presence that he might himself provide one of his own with which to regale us. But I think, given things as they are, that we ought to start our telling of tales by following Thaeo's example, who having made an ample study of them through his years, and who remains a keen student of them likewise presents them in his own inimitable style, which we have in the past found so agreeable.

Thaeo: Thank you greatly, Soleos. And though I would never declare myself to yet share the breadth of the illustrious Phaedo, I would be glad to be the one to start us off on our literary expedition. And among those I am familiar surely the one given by Hesiod strikes me as the foremost among them, and likewise which is of particularly good craft and presentation. So this is the one I will relate to you, when it begins in speaking of the earliest times; and these are his words,

> "Come hither, O daughters of Zeus, to bestow some words of pleasing song
> A poem which speaks of that divine race of gods, the everlasting immortals,
> Being those engendered from Earth, fathered by the star-filled firmament
> Also of foreboding Night, and others born from Pontos, the salt-filled sea
> Relate how came, in the foremost of times, the gods and the earth into being,

4

So too of cascading rivers and the vast oceans venting their violent spume,
Tell too of the glimmering stars, and the true span of the sky's vault above,
Speak of the divine beings, the granters of gifts, who were born from them,
How they came to divvy up their stocks of riches, and bestow their honors,
How they first came to possess the deeply ridged dome of Mount Olympus
Make these things known to me, O Muses, who stir your tea upon that peak
Tell it all from the beginning and who from among them was the first to be."[1]

And the Muses then give their reply,

"So hear then, that first among them to come into being was wayward Chaos
Then came Earth, with her wide-spread chest, being the substrate to bear all:
Those in dreamlike immortality who occupy the snowy peaks of Olympus,
So too of gloomy Tartarus which is deep within the bosom of broad Earth,
And Eros, love personified, whose splendor is unsurpassed among the gods,
Who causes the limbs to quiver, menacing every thought with unwise facets
Seeming firm-bound reason flees, instilling torpor to divine or mortal being
It was out of Chaos that grew into form dark Erebos and obfuscating Night,
She lay in sexual union with Erebos which gave rise to the delivery of a pair,
Thereby Night became the mother of her two children, Aether and Hemera,[*]
While Earth gave birth to her first child, one equaling her in span of space
Being the star-filled firmament, wide Ouranos, who roofed her every reach
And served as the unswerving abode for the holy gods who inhabit heaven."[2]

Soleos: Magnificent, Thaeo. And here the existence of Chaos comes prior to the arising of the Earth, who becomes the mother of all those who did not emerge directly from Chaos. These being identified here as the pair Erebos and Night, who are beings of darkness, and likewise their own offspring Aether and Hemera. And you will well recall that we once spoke, though now some while ago, concerning the creation which is spoken of by the Northern people (Scandinavians). But there is more than one recounting of these events, and so I will tell a different account now than then,

Listen you, both nobles and serfs; hear me all you holy ones, the children of Heimdall. Father of the Slain, you sought me to speak of the earliest times, of both mortals and gods. You wished to know of things I recall from the very foremost of days. Since I myself was the offspring of giants, I do well recall, even in those

---

[*] God of the sky and goddess of the day

early years, who were my providers. I remember the nine worlds and the nine giant women and the almighty Measuring Tree which was set deep within the bowels of the earth. Tender were the years when Ymir settled in his place, where yet there was neither sandbank nor sea, and the chilling waves did not yet lap languidly upon the shore. There was yet no earth nor sky, just an immense tumultuous brew, with not even a blade of grass to tread upon.

The first act performed was done when the sons of Bor raised up the earth; it was these glorious gods who brought the world into form there in the mid-space. Then, when the sun beamed down from the southern realm upon that rocky base, the dirt sprouted with every sort of green leaf. And the sun, that southern friend of the moon, grasped with her right hand the very cusp of heaven. Yet the sun had no idea where her proper place lay, the stars had no idea where their homes might be, while the moon was yet unaware of his own profound persuasion.

Then it was that all the powerful ones, the holy gods, went to the seat of Fate, and deliberated amongst themselves before assigning names to Night and to her children: Morning was so named, and Noon, and Afternoon, and Evening, who were to be measures of time. Then the Aesir gods gathered together upon the plain of Idavoll, and there they constructed for themselves high altars and erected temples. And they built their smithies and forged many worthy things, bending tongs and fashioning other tools. Out upon the grass they played their board games and spent their time in rapt enjoyment, not even being in want of fortunes in gold; that is, until there came three potent and bewitching giant women out of Giantland.

Then it was that all the powerful ones, the holy gods, went to the seat of Fate, and there they discussed amongst themselves: which one of them should be given the task of making the Dwarf Lord from the blood of Brimir and the body of Blain? From this decision did Motsognir become the highest among the race of dwarfs; and Durin was made, and along with them a multitude of other manikins were formed, being the dwarfs who dwell within the earth, whose diverse names were recounted by Durin.

Then it was that all the powerful ones, the holy gods, went to the seat of Fate, and there they deliberated amongst themselves:

6

while the dwarfs had made their homes beneath the earth there was yet no one to inhabit the upper realm. Such was the situation until three gods, both formidable and kind, went from among the gods' plentiful host to walk upon the earth. And there they found upon the ground Ash and Embla, unable to act and as of yet with no in-dwelling destiny. They had not yet received living breath, there was no spirit within them; they had no manner of being, nor essential spark of life or ruddy cast. Thus was breath given by Odin, while Haenir provided them with souls; and the profound spark and a ruddy cast were bestowed by Lodur.[3]

And this is how it is told. But there is more to be said concerning it, for here has been portrayed only part of the story; whereas the one we spoke of before describes the very first moment when life was engendered from out of the mixing of fire and ice, from which arose the breath of life,

At the beginning of time was a world which is called Muspell, located at the southern fringe of the world, which both glowed and was charged with a blazing heat. The entire region was all a sea of flames and every acre of it burned with hellfire, making it impenetrable by those who were not of its native kind but had come from some other land. The sentry of this country was a giant named Surt ('soot') who, as guardian of the borderland, acted as the realm's defender, wielding his sharp, fiery blade.

It was also long ages before the formation of the earth that Niflheim came into being, which held at its very core the spring Hvergelmir; the source of eleven rivers, one being the Gioll which coursed near the gates of Hel.[*] It was these rivers, together called the Elivagar, after their waters had flowed a far distance from their source, that provided the noxious slurry which turned into slush and froze there into hard ice; so that when the ice solidified and no longer flowed, the poisonous vapor which arose from the venomous mixture crystallized upon the surface; and, in that same direction, became a layer of frost. This frost built up layer upon layer until it spanned the entire distance across the

---

[*] The other ten rivers are named Svol, Gunnthra, Fiorm, Fimbulthul, Slidr, Hrid, Sylg, Ylg, Vid, and Leiptr

vast chasm called Ginnungagap.   And thus the span of Ginnungagap which was towards the north felt the full heaviness of this ice and frost, and from here a cold wind swept in towards the midpoint; while the surface approaching the southern end of Ginnungagap was left bare from the rush of hot sparks and embers which erupted from out of Muspell.

Since the world of Niflheim gave rise to a biting cold and enveloped everything in shadow, so did what was near to the world of Muspell experience a harsh heat and fiery glow; while in contrast the space of Ginnungagap was as moderate as is any space undisturbed by wind.   And here, where the flow of frost came into contact with hot currents, it melted, giving rise to a trickle of melt-water.   It was the stimulus arising from these circulating drips, imbued with energy from that fiery source, which gave rise to a human form, being the giant called Ymir.

Ymir lay there sleeping, and as he slept he sweated, so that beneath his left arm there arose a male and a female, while his two legs acting in conjunction gave rise to a boy; and from these came many offspring who are known as the frost-giants. Moreover, these circulating drips of melting frost coalesced into the form of a heifer called Audhumla, and from the udder of this cow flowed four rivers of milk which acted as succor for Ymir. Her tongue licked the blocks of ice, which were impregnated with salt.   And after a day of her licking upon these blocks by evening there emerged the hair on a man's head, upon the second day there came the full head of a man, but by the third day there appeared a man's entire form, whose name was Buri ('father').

The appearance of Buri was attractive, both large and strong, and he gave rise to a son named Bor ('son').   His son took for himself a wife by the name of Bestla, who was the daughter of Bolthorn the giant, who together had three sons as offspring: the first named Odin, the second named Vili, and the third named Ve. It was these sons of Bor who slew the giant Ymir.   And when he was felled there came such a flow of blood from the wound that its deluge brought about the demise of the entire population of frost-giants.   All but one of them was drowned, since only one survived with all of his family, and this was the giant Bergelmir. It was he with his wife who rode out the flood and was thus

8

saved, and it is from this couple that the entire population of frost-giants descended.[4]

So consider the possibility, as it appears, that Ymir and Buri are somehow identified with one another. For here we have two giants who emerge from out of the ice: one formed from the merging of fire and ice and the other licked out of the ice by the cow Audhumla. And this could suggest too why it is that there are two means of generation from Ymir: one being from the sweat of his arms and the other being from his two legs.[*]

Thaeo: Yes, and the first of these certainly is alike to what is said of Kali, who is to have produced two humans from the sweat of her arms.[5]

Soleos: But likewise there are similarities between this conception and that of the Hindus, for they speak of the arising of the 'breath' from out of heat, when it says,

When there was neither existence nor nonexistence, when there was neither spans of space nor a further atmosphere. What inhaled, and where, and in whose dominion? Was there water fathomlessly deep? No death was there but then neither was there immortality. Nothing existed to differentiate day from night, but just the one who breathed; and not from wind but through its own power. Apart from that nothing was to be found in any direction. There was but dark obscured by dark in the very first moments, with nothing which might differentiate, but only water everywhere. But the power of life which was obscured within that void, this one emerged through the power of heat. And in these very first moments there came 'want', which was the first grain of thought. It was the wise sages who looking into their hearts with profound thought identified what tied existence to absence, and this strand of theirs bridged the distance. But could anything be below? Could anything be above? There existed the seed-givers (males) and powers magnified. There was a

---

[*] This son is described as having six-heads. ('Vafthrudnismal' 33; see Larrington 1999: 45)

9

generative force (female) below and an outpouring above. But can anyone truly say? Who could say for sure? From where did it come? From where did it gain existence? For the gods arose after this, at the time the universe came into being. Thus who would be aware of how it was made? So where did this creation come from? Maybe it brought itself into being, but maybe it didn't; only the one that gazes upon it from the heights of heaven, he would be the only one who would know for sure; but perhaps even he does not know.[6]

And here we find that the first instance of life was the emergence of a pure breath from the mechanism of heat, which is precisely the way in which it occurs with Ymir.

Thaeo: Well done, Soleos, yet I am even more greatly struck by how Ymir rather resembles Gayomard. For in the Persian telling the Evil Spirit was immobile when Ormazd created the universe. And when he undertook this creation he did so by first making the firmament, second the water, third the earth, fourth the plant, fifth a Bull white as the moon, and sixth the mortal Gayomard bright like the sun. But likewise we find that one of the great gifts given to Gayomard was the boon of sleep.[7] But I too somewhat recall the particulars of the occurrence when he gave rise to a pair of humans, just as in the case of Ymir, when it says,

> There came a sickness unto Gayomard so that he fell down upon his left side. And death came to Gayomard's body through his left side, such that until the coming of Frashegird, that death is experienced by all mortal beings. But as he passed, Gayomard ejaculated semen, and this semen was made pure through sunlight. And of this two-thirds was guarded by Neryosang and one-third was taken up by Spendarmad and it was kept within the earth for forty years. When forty years had passed Mashya (Mahre) and Mashyanag (Mahryane) sprouted from the soil as the *rivas* plant; having one stem with fifteen leaves, so that their hands sat upon their shoulders and they were connected together, but otherwise were of the same height and form. Afterwards their plant bodies developed into human form, and the wonder of the soul entered into them without being seen. And from them came

six sets of twins, each male and female, thus being brothers and the sisters who became their wives…Of these six pairs of twins one was a man and woman named Siyamak and Vasag and to them were born a pair of twins, the male being named Fravag and the female Fravagen. From these were fifteen sets of twins born, and each of these pairs grew into a race of mankind, so that they engendered the entire population of the earth.[8]

Soleos: Splendid, Thaeo.

Epitheus: Yes. And I have always found it interesting to consider what might be meant by this emphasis upon sleep, since we find that Adam too is put to sleep when God takes his rib to create the woman, as likewise when Ymir is sleeping when he produces his offspring. And that Ymir gives birth to children beneath his arm is likewise strikingly similar to Adam, wherein Eve was made from his rib; or, as it says, that each one was born out of the other's side.[9*] And it is likewise Adam that was viewed to be a being of huge proportion,[10] and likewise to be the first moral to be buried, even before Abel,[11] and this matches what we might regard is so with Ymir, where his body becomes the basis for the world.[12]

Soleos: Quite so, as likewise is Apsu made the base of the world.[13]

Epitheus: And it says of Adam:

> Surely a singular being is the 'man of the mountain', who is called Adne Sadeh or more simply Adam. His shape is just like that of a human, yet he is joined to the earth through an umbilical cord which he requires to live, for if this string were ever broken he would perish. And this being gains his sustenance from anything which can be drawn from the ground around him, limited by the space he might crawl by his cord. So no being might undertake to enter into the space delimited by his tether, since he grabs and consumes whatever he can get his hands on. And as it is impossible to approach him, the only way to kill him

---

* Similar to the Hindu couple Daska and Aditi who are said to have been born from one another. (Rig Veda 10.72; see O'Flaherty 1981: 39)

11

is to break the umbilical cord from a distance with an arrow. Then he would die with dire moaning and groaning.[14]

But the appearance of Ymir sleeping has caused me to wonder whether it is possible that this was inspired by some true occurrence.

Soleos: Please go on, Epitheus.

Epitheus: I think it is possible that the notion of such a creation could actually have arisen from the eye-witnessing by people of human bodies melting out of the ice, by which I mean those who had died and been trapped in the ice during the glacial period (Ice Age). Then as the glaciers melted there would have emerged from it frozen bodies which still looked rather lifelike, coming from out of the ice as if they were only sleeping.

Soleos: Splendid, Epitheus; that is indeed an interesting thought. And as Ymir was to have arisen from the meeting of heat with ice and born out of the running melt-water, he likewise appeared in the form of a sleeping giant.

Epitheus: Yes.

Soleos: And then perhaps too other animals would have been emerging from the melting ice which could have given rise to the notion that at the time of creation such beings were being spawned from the very ice itself. And it would not have been known that these beings had been trapped in the distant past, but rather that they were engendered from out of the mixture of heat and cold, and born from the dripping melt-water.

Epitheus: Yes. But what I am not sure of, despite its plausibility, is if there remains anything which might serve to indicate that this story actually hearkens back to such a time, which we would have to imagine would be at least 10,000 years ago.

Soleos: Truly, but if such creatures emerged from the ice, and we presume that they would have been identified as giants, it might too make sense, given the way it is recorded, to have been an entire family. And it would also be expected that there would be found children under his arms or huddling near his feet, precisely where we would expect to find them, which matches the description of Ymir's children.

Epitheus: Indeed so.

Soleos: But likewise we would know that after these beings had been exposed to the sun that their bodies would begin to atrophy rapidly; and then we might assume that, if it was seen by human beings, that the bodies would soon be seen riddled with maggots, which is also contained in the description as having emerged from Ymir's flesh to become the dwarfs.[15]

Epitheus: Yes.

Soleos: Thus without any other explanation it would appear to them that such a being could be identified with the conception of a giant which had existed at the beginning of time from which the world was made.[*]

Epitheus: Thoroughly.

Soleos: So this might merely have provided subsequent detail to an initial mythical conception, which was that a giant had emerged from the ice at the dawn of time. And although such a thing could have occurred at any time when the heat of the sun melted glacial ice, if it specifically dates to when the glaciers were in a period of gradual withdrawal, then perhaps hundreds of ice-entrapped carcasses could have been brought to light.

Epitheus: Truly, it is an interesting notion.

Soleos: Just so, but then do you yourself, Epitheus, have a creation myth you would be prepared to share with us?

---

[*] Is it possible these creatures identified as giants could be Neanderthals?

Epitheus: Yes, indeed, Soleos, I have been thinking diligently about it. And although I might recount again one with which we are already well familiar (Genesis), I have decided instead to relate another, which is one I know of by the merest chance because of my eager interest in the matter, and the details which are provided here surely supplement the other. And although it is closely related to that one it also expresses matters rather differently.

For it was upon the first day that he made the skies above, along with the lands and the seas, and every one of the spirit-beings which act as his servants: angels of the signs; angels of the sacrifice, angels who are the spirits of fire; angels who are the spirits of wind; angels who are the spirits of cloud and shadow, of snow, sleet, and ice; angels of echoes, thunder, and lightning; angels of the cold and warmth; and of the seasons of winter, spring, harvest-time, and summer; and every one of the spirits of the creatures of his which inhabit both heaven and earth. Then he made the deep chasms and gave rise to darkness, both of dusk and of night; as well as light, both of dawn and of day; which were planned from the seat of wisdom held deep within his thoughts. And he looked upon his creations and we then blessed him and went before him with praises because of what he had made; because upon that first day he had created seven wondrous things.

Then it was upon the second day that he raised the vault of heaven within the waters; and upon that day the waters too were separated, so that one half was set aloft of and the other half was set below the vault of heaven, to lie midway so that it covered the surface of the entire earth. And this was the only thing which he made upon the second day.

Then it was upon the third day that he did to the waters as he had proclaimed: "Let them recede, no longer to be in contact with the entire earth, but gathered to one place so that the dry land might be seen." And the waters did as he had spoken; they moved off from over the surface of the earth and gathered to a single place, even beyond the heaven's vault, so that the dry land was seen. And upon that day he made upon it every one of the inland seas at each of the locations where they accumulate, and every one of the rivers, and the places where the waters accumulate upon mountains. And also within the entirety of the earth, and every single pond and pool, and widespread dew upon the ground; and every kind of seed which is sown. And all which is consumed, and the fruit tree and even more trees, and so too the garden of Eden which is in Eden–and of great abundance–and all others as such. These four magnificent things the Lord made upon the third day.

Then upon the fourth day he created the sun and the moon, along with the stars; and he placed them within the heaven's vault so as to provide light for the entire earth, and to hold dominion over the day and the night, and keep separate the light from the darkness. And the Lord made the sun to be a vital indicator upon the earth for days, *sabbaths*, months, seasons, years, *sabbaths of years*, and *jubilees*, along with every one of the notable days of the year; and to keep separate the light from the darkness, so that all things which arise and grow upon the earth might flourish. These three things he created upon the fourth day.

Then upon the fifth day he made the great sea monsters which were set within the cradle of the seas–as they were fashioned with his hands to become the first full-bodied creatures–and every one of the fish which swim within the waters, and every bird which takes wing, and every one of their species. So the sun made its path aloft of them that they might flourish, and so too aloft of all that now inhabit the earth, and all things which arise from within the earth, and every fruit tree, and everything else of substance. These three things he created upon the fifth day.

Then upon the sixth day he made every one of the wild beasts of the earth, and every one of the domestic animals, and all things which travel upon the earth. Only after every one of these was made did he create man–both male and female he created them– and he granted him oversight over all things which inhabit the earth, of those which were within the seas and of those which take wing; and over both the wild beasts and domestic animals, and all other things which move upon the earth or range aloft of the entire land; over every one of these he gave him oversight. These four things he created upon the sixth day, and this made a total of twenty-two fine things. And he completed his creation upon the sixth day, of all that was in the sky or on the earth or in the seas to the fathomless deep; and both within the light and the darkness and in every other place.[16]

Soleos: Well done, Epitheus, and here comes Phaedo just in time.

Phaedo: Hello my friends, I have finished my business with Arturius and on my return I noticed from some distance that you were already engaged in something which was holding your undivided interest. And so I am sorry to have missed what has thus transpired.

Soleos: By all means join us then Phaedo, for we commenced in your absence upon the matter of the beginning of time. And although at first we were hoping that you might be here to lead us in our endeavor, you have yet come at an opportune moment. For already have Thaeo, Epitheus, and I each recounted one story of the events of creation, being in turn the Greek, the Nordic, and the Hebrew. Thus we are all ready to delight in another that you, Phaedo, might be willing to tell.

Phaedo: Thank you, Soleos, and indeed I will have no difficulty doing so myself as well, since I could well relate to you the account of the Egyptian creation. And the record of this is made of the words spoken by the Eternal God of Egypt (Nebertcher) after he himself arises into existence, when he says,

> "I am the creator of everything which exists. I am the one who arose into being as the god Khepera in the very first moments of the very earliest time. I arose in the shape of Khepera and I gave rise to everything which has existence; which is to say that I made myself from out of the primal element, and formed and shaped myself from out of the matter present at that foremost time. I have the name of Ausares (Osiris), being the primal element of primordial matter, and I have exerted my will in everything which is upon the earth. I have spread myself across its length and secured it within my grasp. Then I was the One and Only, for the other gods had not hitherto come into existence, and I had not yet given rise to Shu and Tefnut. But my own name emerged from my own lips, arising from powerful spells; and I immediately manifested through those things which comprise and are part and parcel of the form of Khepera.
>
> I emerged from out of the primal element, and from the very first I held within myself the numerous things which have come

16

into existence; and the things which I created, once I was manifest; that formed from my words were a great many. The sky had yet not been made, the earth had not come into being, and the offspring of the earth and the things which scurry over land had not yet gained form. At that time there was nothing at all upon the earth, but if anything was made I was him who made it. Because I was yet alone, the One and Only, and where I was there were no other beings who might serve as my partner. And there was yet no place where I might rest my feet, so I did my work through the strength of a spell which was held within my thoughts, and with it established a foundation close by through the placement of Maat (foundation), and thereafter I created everything which was to come into being.

So I began the planning of things within my own thoughts and I created them and they gained shape as I had envisaged them, through the exertion of the Holy Spirit (Soul-God). These, at that time, I brought into solid form from out of the Nu, wherein they had no substance and no ability to act upon their own. These were the diverse things of Khepera, and so too the descendants of these arose from the very offspring which they themselves had given birth to. I made sexual union with my own fist, and took my own shadow as a wife, and my will was exerted through my own hand; and the seed touched my lips and from me there came the shape of two gods, Shu and Tefnut. And after I gave rise to Shu and Tefnut, thus I went from being the One and Only to thereafter being three gods, and I now gained physical substance upon the earth. So it was that these two gods gained their physical form upon the earth from me. Shu and Tefnut were then raised up from out of the lifeless Nu where they had been hitherto.

Then my father Nu informed me that my Eye was being obscured by them within the billowy clouds which they kept hidden behind them. Then two months (*hen* periods) after they had emerged from me, sure enough they conveyed to me my Eye (sun). And after this I brought together my limbs, being part of my own body, and I cried over them; and from these tears shed from my Eye grew both men and women. Then both plants and crawling creatures of every kind arose from out of the divine *Rem* (tears of Re), from the tears which flowed from me. Then I gave my Eye an *uraeus* (divine cobra) of fire, but it was angry with me when it discovered that another Eye (moon) had taken its place. And the dynamic force of this one (the moon) exerted itself upon the plants, those very plants which I had seeded, and it became their master; whereupon I gave it a portion of the brightness which had hitherto been reserved for the other Eye (sun); then I gave it a place upon my face from where it holds dominion over the entire earth. And when those noteworthy times came around, following the appearance of billowy clouds, I would restore to them what they had lost, appearing myself from within those clouds. Then Shu and Tefnut gave rise to Geb and Nut, and Nut gave birth to the quintuplets Osiris, Horus, Set, Isis, and Nephthys,[*] born in that order, and they have left a great many descendants upon the earth."[17]

Soleos: Formidable indeed, Phaedo.

Phaedo: Thank you. And we also find that according to Plutarch that the Egyptians believed that the body of the earth was sprawled out towards the east, where they presumed its head to be.[18] And I would not think this to be mismatched with other conceptions where a giant's body is established to become the foundation of the earth.

---

[*] In another version, Shu and Tefnut give rise to these five gods.

CHAPTER 2

Soleos: Well done.   Thus we have completed four, so shall we perhaps go another round, Thaeo?

Thaeo: Surely, but I will have to think for a moment, because I would wish to tell one which is far different than the one I gave before.   So I will speak of the ancient Persian creation, which has more recently become known to me.

> Hear now of what Zardusht recalls of the birth of Ormazd and Ahriman, at a time when nothing had yet been created: not yet heaven, nor yet earth, nor were there any other beings alive in heaven or earth.   There was only Zurvan ('Time'), the Almighty God, whose name means 'fate' or 'destiny'.   For a thousand years he made sacrifices that he might potentially gain a son, who would be named Ormazd, and who was predestined to create the heaven and the earth and everything else found within them.   For a thousand years he made his sacrifices and thought to himself, "Will these sacrifices ever bring me what I wish for, and there will come to me a son named Ormazd, or is this all done in vain?" But even while he thought such thoughts Ormazd and Ahriman were yet conceived within the Womb.   Ormazd grew from the sacrifices which he had made, but Ahriman grew from his lack of faith.   When he discovered this, Zurvan proclaimed, "Behold, there are twins within the Womb, and the one who appears first before my eyes will I crown king."   Knowing his father's intentions, Ormazd told this to Ahriman; and with this knowledge Ahriman severed the Womb and emerged, making his appearance before his father.   Seeing him but not knowing who he was, Zurvan asked, "Who are you?"
>
> And he answered him, "I am your son, of course."
>
> So Zurvan replied, "But my son is full of light and sweetness, while you are full of darkness and foul-smelling."   And as they spoke in this manner, Ormazd, full of light and sweet-scented, was born in his proper term, appearing before Zurvan.   Seeing him, Zurvan recognized at once his own son, Ormazd.   Then the staffs used in the sacrifices, which he held in his hand, he gave over to Ormazd, saying, "Before now I've been the one making

sacrifices for your sake, but from now on you'll be the one making sacrifices for my sake."

But as Zurvan passed the staffs to Ormazd with blessings, Ahriman, who moved nearer to Zurvan, proclaimed, "Did you not make a vow, stating that 'whichever of my two sons first stands before me I will crown king?'"

Thus, so as not to breach his pledge, Zurvan replied to Ahriman, "O you villain, you imposter! You will indeed receive the kingship but for only 9,000 years, when Ormazd shall then become your lord. For after 9,000 years Ormazd will reign and act in whatever way he judges best." After this Ormazd and Ahriman set about making every one of the different species of animals, but those made by Ormazd were tall and good, while those made by Ahriman were bent and evil.[19]

Soleos: Superlative. And I have another I myself could tell, which is a variation of the creation from the Hindus, which begins,

It was a time when this world lay in fathomless darkness, where nothing was yet to be seen: existing as a featureless void; beyond conception, beyond words, and enveloped within an all-pervading quiescence. At that time the self-born Lord came into being, the formless bringing form to this world through the initial creation of the basic elements, and it was through an exertion of his will that he cast aside the enshrouding darkness. It is this One–who exists where no eye can see and where no ear can hear; he who cannot be apprehended; he who is invisible, incorporeal, and everlasting; who holds within himself all substance; who cannot be comprehended–he is the one who emerged alone in brilliance.

All his thoughts were preoccupied with the will to give rise to all the myriad of beings which were to spring from out of his body. First, he brought into form the waters, and into this matrix he discharged his fertile seed which took the shape of a golden egg with the radiance of the sun; within which he brought about his own self-birth as Brahma, the ancestor of every world. Nara is the name given to these waters, and all waters might surely be referred to as the children of Nara. And because his first abode was within these waters, he has from time immemorial been called 'Nara-yana'. It was that very source, incorporeal and everlasting, which held within itself both the nature of the manifest and the unmanifest–and the male being born out of it is revered the world over as Brahma.

The Lord, being incubated within that egg for the duration of a year through the influence of his own body caused the shell to fracture into two pieces, and from these halves he fashioned the vault of the heavens and the foundation of the earth; a middle space which was left between; the eight directions; and the basins, which have been filled with water ever since.

So too he discharged from out of his own body the Mind, which holds within itself that which is physical and that which is spiritual. And forth from this Mind came Awareness, as a guide to life and living; and likewise the supreme Will; along with every thing which holds within itself these three influences; and then little by little developed the five sense organs which identify physical substance. It was through the process of melding these supremely powerful six with the cells of his own body that he brought every being into existence. And as these six together in physical form are united therein, the knowledgeable have come to refer to this structure as the Body. These are penetrated by the mighty elements along with their influences; as so too is the Mind, with its own invisible atoms, the imperishable source of all things.

It was from the invisible atoms within the matter of these seven mighty male influences that the world, both the transitory and the everlasting, was formed. And traditional knowledge assigns to each element in sequence the unique quality it gains from the preceding one, and thus every element acquires a sum of qualities which is determined by its place within that sequence. And it was at this foremost time, through the Holy Word alone that he designated, for each of them, a name by which it would be known, and a specific mode of actions, as well as their assigned domains.

And the Lord brought into being a company of gods who had breath, and who possessed within themselves a motive to act; along with the lesser Sadhyas and so too the never-ending practice of sacrifice. He blended through the use of fire, wind, and sun the three eternal Vedas, comprising the Rig verses, the rules of Yajus, and the songs of Saman, which are used for the sacrifices. Then too arose Time, and the measurement of time, the constellations, the planets, the rivers, the seas, the mountains, both the plains and the hills; asceticism, language, sex, lust, and anger–these were the things he created through his Will to give rise to all the myriad of beings.

Then he differentiated actions, most notably he brought about the distinction between Right conduct and Wrong conduct, and also charged that these beings have within themselves aspects existing in opposite pairs, such as that of pleasure and pain. And along with the transient molecules of the five elements, known from tradition, the entire universe acquires its structure through patterns. Thus, as they are given birth to time and time again, every being follows its own specific behaviors which were determined at the very first by the Lord: aggression and peace, mercy and cruelty, good or evil, honesty and deception–those which he assigned to each one at the time of the creation is what resided within them henceforth. And just as with the transition of the seasons, where each has its own distinctive character, so too do these physical beings have their own specific behaviors. So too, for the proper development of these worlds did he create from out of his mouth, his arms, his thighs, and his feet; the Brahmin, the Ksatriya, the Vaisya, and the Sudra.[20]

So we now come back again to Epitheus, and have you yet another you'd like to tell?

Epitheus: It is possible, Soleos, for I could mention the only other I know well enough, although it is not quite so simple to comprehend. But I will attempt nevertheless to relate it, which you no doubt know yourselves and might be able to correct me if you believe I have related it falsely.

Once the final form of the divinities had arisen from the Infinite One, a being called Sophia was released from Pistis; and she conceived the creation of something as a semblance of the elemental light. At once her aspiration manifested itself within a heavenly form of unsurpassed magnificence, falling between the divinities and those who had yet to achieve their form, just like that which covers (firmament), acting as the boundary between men and those who inhabit the heavenly sphere.

The Aeon of Truth possesses no shadow inherent to it, since the infinite light inhabits it throughout; but beyond it there is Shadow and this is called Darkness. Generated there was a power which spread itself beyond the Darkness; and concerning the Shadow, those powers which arose after referred to this as the 'Infinite Chaos'. It was from this that every kind of divine being emerged, from one and the other and everything in-between. As a result the Shadow came after the initial creation which had already occurred, and the Abyss came into being from the Pistis mentioned before.

The Shadow recognized that there was a Force of greater influence than itself and became envious of it; and through its own self-generation it gave abrupt birth to Envy. From that time forward the manifestation of Envy has been present within every Aeon and all their worlds. But Envy was truly a miscarriage which lacked spirit, and it was like the deep shades within the vast waters. This Envy which had emerged from Shadow fell down into the realm of Chaos, and from that moment the vast waters came into being, so that what had been held within the Shadow was now released into Chaos. And in the same way that the wasted afterbirth falls from one who has given birth to an infant, just so the material substance which had arisen from the Shadow was cast. But it was not from Chaos, rather it was material which itself existed within a part of Chaos.

After this, Pistis appeared and hovered above the material within Chaos–which had been cast away like a miscarriage, since it lacked spirit–because it appeared as a fathomless darkness and a bottomless watery depth. When Pistis saw what had been brought into being from her own shortcoming, she became troubled; and this troubling manifested itself as a revolting thing which escaped so as to reside within a part of Chaos. So she faced it and gave breath to its face within the Abyss, which lies below every one of the heavens. And when Pistis Sophia wished to make that which lacked spirit into a manifest form, to be the lord of all matter and energy, then a Lord came forth for the first time from within the waters, leonine of form but lacking sexual

23

distinction, yet holding a formidable power within himself, but lacking any knowledge of how he came to be.

And when he was seen by Pistis Sophia swimming within the watery depths, she addressed him, saying, "Child, come here," which is taken to mean the same as 'Yaldabaoth'. From that time the Logos, the first law, which made reference to the gods and the angels and to men, first came into being; and the gods and the angels and men are all those which were brought into existence through the Logos. Likewise, the Lord Yaldabaoth did not know of the supremacy of Pistis; he failed to comprehend her face, but instead perceived its reflection upon the surface of the water. It was because of this voice he heard that he referred to himself as 'Yaldabaoth'. Still the Ideal Ones referred to him as 'Ariel', since he had a leonine form. Then once this being became the lord of all matter, Pistis Sophia arose again into the light.

When the Lord recognized his power he knew only of his own existence; he perceived none other but the darkness and the water. Thus he concluded that there existed none other apart from himself, and his thoughts gained corporeal form through the Logos, manifesting as a wind going hither and thither over the surface of the waters. When this wind emerged the Lord drew apart the watery mass to one place and the dry mass to another place. From the one mass he formed a place for himself which he called 'heaven', and from the other mass the Lord made for himself a footrest, which he called 'earth'.[21]

And so from here it becomes very like the one we are well familiar with.

Phaedo: Well done. And your story, Epitheus, reminds me of another, which comprises part of the Finnish creation story, which I will now relate in part,

There was one daughter of the atmosphere
Just a lass, a fine child of Nature's world
For a long while she had retained her purity
She was yet an untouched virgin of a girl
But there in the sky's broad fields
There upon its expansive pastures

She became lonesome, her life was empty
Since she was always by herself, a maiden
There in the sky's broad fields
There in the vast empty spaces
And so she allowed her foot to drop lower
She let herself down within the sea waves
Upon the rising ocean surge, the vast way
And a raging wind blew, an eastern storm
It churned up the waters into frothy spume
It stirred up the waters into a lofty spray
The airstream made her helpless,
The crests tossing her to and fro,
Upon the surface of the deep blue
And the upon bubbly white-caps
The breeze blew into her womb, filling her
The amusement of the sea bloated her belly
So that her middle became great
It was not an effortless pregnancy
It was seven-hundred long years
It was nine full life-spans of man
And yet there came about no birth
There was no being that emerged
The girl was tossed, like a mother of water
She went to the east, to the west
She swam north-west, and south
Going to the very ends of the sky
There were agonizing birth-pangs
She was beset by her heaviness
And yet there came about no birth
There was no being that emerged
All she could do was cry to herself,
Or rather to only speak to herself:
"What cruel fortune I experience
Unlucky girl, how life besets me
For this is now my only existence
Always will I flop beneath the sky
To be blown helpless by the wind
To be tossed to and fro upon crests
Upon the expanses of the deep blue

On the bosom of vast wave-crests
It surely would have been far better
If I had remained as a girl of the air
Then to be tossed, like a mother of water
This water I lie in is much too cold
So dreadfully I am made to tremble
Within the rising surge where I live
Within the waters where I do totter
Hear Old Man, highest of the gods,
You who do hold aloft the heavens
Please assist me when you're called
Make your way to me when I plead
Help out a girl who is in dire straits
Aid a lass who suffers in pregnancy
Make haste, attend with all speed
Do most where you're most needed!"
Then some time went by, a moment passed,
When there arrived a duck, an ordinary bird,
Flying around, searching for a roosting place
Somewhere to nest, a suitable spot to dwell
It coursed to the east, it coursed to the west
Yet still there was not a place to be found
There was not even a bad location for a nest
And not a even a single spot to make a home,
So it just continued its soaring and gliding
Then it thought to itself, mulling in its mind:
"Is it possible to put my house upon air gusts,
To set my dwelling place upon sea waves?
For will not the wind blow my house apart
Will not the sea waves take away my home?"
Thus it was that the mother of water,
So too this girl of the atmosphere,
Lifted up her knee from the waters
Lifted up her back from the ocean
Providing the duck a roosting place
A plot of temperate land to dwell
So the duck, an attractive creature,
Swooped down and flew above it
Espying the knee of that mermaid

There set within the cerulean sea
It looked to him like a green hill
Just like a band of grassy growth
So it both flapped and fluttered
As it alighted upon the kneecap
And there it laid some gold eggs
There were six fine golden eggs
The seventh being rather of iron
Then it set about brooding them
To raise warmth upon the kneecap
And one day there was a hatching
Then a second hatched, and a third
When this happened the mermaid,
That daughter of the atmosphere,
Then felt like her skin was burning
That her flesh was igniting on fire
It seemed as if her knee was alight
And all her muscles were erupting
So then she pulled away her knee,
She jostled both her legs and arms,
Causing that egg to fall into the sea
To be drowned in billowing waves
And the shell was soon pulverized
It was dashed to pieces in the whirl
But the pieces failed to descend into the mud
The many fragments stayed within the waters
All these remains became wondrous
The bits left floating were glorious
For the egg's bottom became earth
And the egg's top became heaven
The part of the top which was yolk
This then became the shining sun
And the white part of the egg top
This grew into the glowing moon
And that part which was speckled
This then became the stars of night
And the part which was shadowy
This then became the air's clouds

Then ages of years and more years passed
The new sun gleams, the young moon glows
And yet still the mother of water is floating
The daughter of atmosphere on the calm sea
The girl of the air set within the misty waves
Afore is only soft water, abaft is empty sky
Then in the ninth year, in the tenth season,
She lifted up her head from within the sea
Raised aloft her chin and started to create
To put together all of the beings she sought
There upon the billowing ocean, the vast sea
At the spot where her fingers were spread
There were mounted up the high headlands
At the spot where her toes touched beneath
There were impressed the basins fit for fish
And anywhere she churned up the waters
There she carved out the yawning grottoes
When she shifted herself towards the land
Then she created the broad sandy beaches
When her feet were extended towards shore
Then she dug out the many dens for salmon
And when her head rested upon the coast
Then she shaped the several bays into form
She then moved herself out from the land
And stayed there for a time, making reefs
There too were erected the rocky ridges
Holding disaster for ships
To be a bother for sailors
After this many islands were laid down,
As great cliffs rising from within the sea
Then the pillars of the sky were erected
And the lands and continents borne up
Ridges were scored upon these rocks
Clefts were chiseled upon craggy faces
Even then Vainamoinen did not come
That immortal singer would not show
Steadfast and ancient Vainamoinen
Merely tumbled in his mother's belly
For as many as thirty summers and winters

In that calm sea, within those misty waves
Pondering to himself, thinking for a time,
How might he exist, how should he exist
Within this shadowy haven
Within this close-fitting home
Having no view of the moon,
Being unable to see the sun,
Then he spit out words to say,
Sounds came from his mouth,
"Moon release and sun liberate,
And reveal a path, Great Bear,
Release me from odd trapdoors
Free me from unfamiliar gates
Out of these too tight lodgings
From within this confinement!
Set a weary wanderer on soil,
Bring a child of man outdoors,
So that I might gaze upon the sky's moon
That I might view and wonder at the sun
And to see the motions of the Great Bear
That I might make a study of astronomy!"

Yet still as the moon did not heed his plea
Nor for that matter did the sun take action
He became lonesome, he grew perturbed,
So he forced these fortress gates to shift
He used his ring finger, set free the lock,
Using his left toe, with his nails he came,
Spilled forth over the entry,
Fell from his knees through,
And flew headlong into the shapeless sea
With his hands forwards he fell seawards
But he was kept within the waves' cradle
And he became a man of the billowy main
There too he was tossed for five full years
For five, then six, seven years, then eight
Before he finally made his way to shore
Reaching a limb of land of no designation
Upon a continent that had no grown trees

And shifting his knees he turned himself
Pushing with his arms he raised his chest
So that now he might gaze upon the moon
That he might view and wonder at the sun
And to see the motions of the Great Bear
That he might make a study of astronomy![22]

So this I would compare to the other, as I am wondering if it has become apparent to everyone how this very event, the birth of Vainamoinen, so clearly resembles that of Yaldabaoth, in that both are formed within the sea; the other by Sophia in heaven without a father and here by a daughter of the atmosphere from the strong wind which impregnated her.

Epitheus: Yes, it is curious, Phaedo. But then this is also similar to the story of the creation with a world that was yet without form and empty, with darkness upon the face of the Abyss, and where the wind of God moved over the surface of the waters.

Soleos: Indeed so, Epitheus, for we find here that the foremost event of generation arises from a wind stirring up the sea; and where we might well presume that as the wind constitutes the male element that the primal ocean itself is the female; being the enigmatic and unpersonified 'Womb' which was referred to earlier by Thaeo.

Epitheus: But so too this method of generation is precisely that found in relation to the Son of Man, who is said to have been born in this manner,

Once seven days had passed I had a dream during the night, and saw that there came a wind from over the sea which gave rise to many waves. As I looked at it, know that this wind caused something, which had the shape of a man, to rise up from the depths of the water. As I looked, know that this man rose up into the clouds of the sky, and where he looked everything which fell under his gaze was shaken, and when he spoke from his mouth everyone hearing his voice melted, just as wax melts when it feels the heat of the fire.

30

Then I looked again, and know that a great number of men had collected there from the direction of each of the four winds of the sky to declare war upon this man who had arisen from out of the water. And I looked, and know that he chiseled for himself a tremendous peak of rock and rose up to settle upon it. And I looked to see if I could identify the lands where the mountain had been chiseled, but I was unable to.

I gazed out again, and know that all those who had collected there to oppose him, to make war upon him, were very frightened, but still they were prepared to do battle. And know that when he witnessed the charge of the coming army that he did not raise his hand nor did he lift a spear or any other weapon of war; but rather I only saw him emit from his mouth something like a torrent of fire; a fiery breath which issued from his lips, and a flurry of sparks that ejected from his tongue. These joined together: the torrent of fire, the fiery breath, and the tremendous flurry; and they descended upon the charging army which was ready to do battle, and it consumed them all in flames, so that the great number was swiftly reduced to a pile of burnt ashes and a pall of smoke. And when I perceived this I was left awestruck.

Following this, I watched this man descend from his rocky peak and summon to him another great crowd, and these were peaceful. And there followed many others which gathered around him, some joyous but others troubled; some of them were in chains, while some brought along these others to offer them as sacrifices.[23]

Thaeo: What you say appears entirely comparable to the notion that the wind over the water generates a third material which is a composite of the two,[*] and this is precisely what we find in the birth of the goddess Aphrodite from the sea foam, when Hesiod says,

> Vast Ouranos, bearing night's spangled shroud, came yearning for sweet embraces and spread out fully over Gaia to accept her love. But from his hiding spot his son extended a stealthy hand which grasped him. In his clenched right fist the hard-bladed

---

[*] In other words, foam is viewed to be a composite substance of air mixed into water. (see Rig Veda 10.72; O'Flaherty 1981: 39)

weapon with sharp serrations was wielded with accurate aim, swung strongly so that he severed off his father's outstretched members, which were tossed away with discourteous abandon. But not for nothing were they discarded from his hand, for the drops of blood saturated the breast of Gaia. And after due term she bore the potent Furies; and the gigantic Giants, girded with light-gleaming armor, wielding formidable sharp spears in their grips; and also the celebrated nymphs known the world over as the Ash-tree Nymphs.

Once Cronos had hacked the members off with his flint knife, he flung them from the mainland into the churning basin of water, where they floated for quite a time upon the vast sea; and from this godly flesh there amassed an encircling white foam within which grew a maiden. Bringing the girl first to blessed Cythera, and from there she found her way to the wave-lapped shores of Cyprus, where the shy but stunning goddess stepped lightly upon the sands, and wherever she stepped with her enchanting feet tender shoots of grass did spring. Both gods and men refer to her as Aphrodite, and the 'foam-born goddess' and 'richly wreathed Cytherea'; because she had grown within the sea-foam, and 'Cytherea' since she came to Cythera; and 'Cyprogenes' since she was born upon the wave-lapped Cyprian shore; and 'Philommedea', for she had been engendered from out of members ('medea').[24]

Soleos: Well done, Thaeo. And this view of the wind moving over the waters, which through turbulence so ignited the creation of the 'self-born one', is similar to the description of the arising of Ymir.

Thaeo: Yes. And as Ymir's name truly means 'hermaphrodite' we find that Aphrodite gave birth through Hermes to a hermaphroditic son called Atlantius, who is also called Hermaphroditus,[25] as Ovid recounts,

In Mount Ida's caves the Naiads cared for a young boy,
Who was the son of Hermes and the Cytherean goddess
His face showed resemblances to both father and mother
And his name, Hermaphroditus, combined theirs together
When fifteen years had passed, the young man left Ida,

The mountain of his rearing, striking out for new vistas,
Traveler's ways were made light for him by his wonder
And sights of unseen places brought him great pleasure[26]

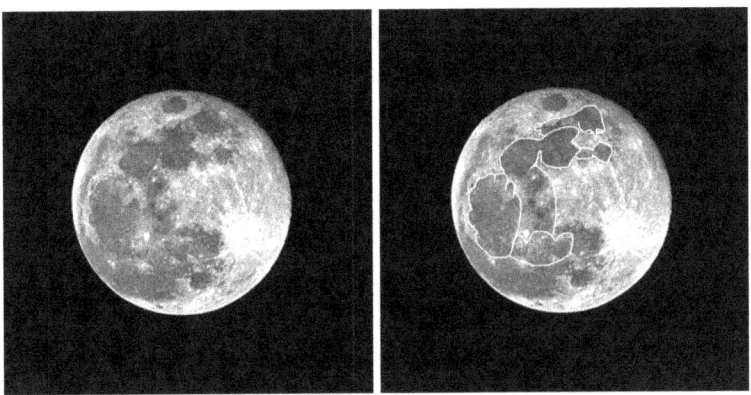

**Aphrodite rising out of a shell from the sea
could arise from this moon image.**

Epitheus: But I too am aware of such a one as this, which is mentioned again as a continuation of the myth I spoke of before, when it goes on to say,

The Rulers then acquired what was necessary for the creation of man. But Sophia Zoe, who stands next to Sabaoth, foresaw what would happen and was amused at their short-sighted decision, for in their ignorance they molded him opposite of themselves and then had no idea what to do next. So she devised a plan to create her own man beforehand, so that he could tell their molded body how they had been condemned to live, and thereby he would act as their savior. The birth of this 'instructor' came about in this manner: Sophia threw a modicum of light and it bobbed upon the water, and at once a man came into being who was androgynous. That modicum initially shaped the water into a female body, but after this it shaped itself inside the body of this mother image, which had become visible, and there it completed its term in twelve months. And an androgynous man was born, which is the

33

one the Greeks call 'Hermaphrodites'. The Hebrews refer to his mother as 'Eve of Life' which means 'bringer of life', and it is her son who is the begotten one called 'Master'. After this the Rulers named him 'the beast' (Satan) so as to deceive their molded bodies, but the word 'beast' is truly taken to mean 'instructor', because he was far more wise than the rest of them.[27*]

---

[*] According to the Gnostic perspective, the character of Satan brought knowledge (*gnosis*) to man and thus served a beneficial role against the false god Yaldabaoth (Yahweh).

CHAPTER 3

Soleos: But we also might recognize how Aphrodite could have given birth given the especial nature of Hermes, as we are aware. And being hermaphroditic would suggest he might likewise represent the first mortal being, and thus be equivalent with Ymir. And this mortal being we could recognize as a combination of elements: the first being a goddess born out of foam, which is a mixture of water and wind; and of Hermes, who is some manifestation of heavenly fire.[*] And this then seems to make perfect sense, given that foam itself is identified with the fertile seed which brings life into existence.

Thaeo: And as of yet it remains a matter of conjecture as to whether the tale of Ymir and the cow Audhumla recalls the melting of a human body and auroch from out of the glacial ice, though its mythic origin might still be found if we look to the realm of the sky. And thus there too, given the divine origin of Aphrodite and Hermes, we have also to include the conception of a heavenly cow and progenitor giant, which we could identify with the constellations of *Taurus* with *Gemini* and *Orion*.

Soleos: Indeed. Or likewise, as we have seen, the constellation of the 'Summer Triangle' representing the cow and *Pegasus* representing the hermaphroditic being.[†]

Thaeo: And there remains no question concerning the consistency of this image, for just as we have the myth of the giant Ymir and the cow Audhumla, so too the mortal Gayomard is associated with the primeval bull, as does the Hindu Purusa likewise have his primeval cow. And all of these appear to have arisen from out of an original mythic conception. But likewise we find too that Aphrodite was identified with the Egyptian goddess Hathor, who was shown in cow form.[28]

---

[*] See *The Zodiac Mysteries*
[†] See *The Zodiac Mysteries*

Phaedo: What you say, Thaeo, is also compatible with the *Gemini* stars being identified as Nergal, who is the Babylonian god equivalent to Ymir, as god of the underworld.[29]*

Soleos: And if there are two separate accounts given, in considering Ymir and Buri to be essentially the same, this could likewise be taken to mean that it was not the three sons of Bor who slew Ymir but rather that Ymir was slain by his own sons.

Epitheus: What you say, Soleos, would then well equate with the three sons of Noah, whom we imagine did castrate and then behead their father.[†] And, after performing this, his sons then cover him with a blanket, which we figured could represent the surface of the earth. And Noah is said to have been in a drunken and prophetic state prior to this.

Thaeo: And so too from the wrestling match between Zeus and his father Cronos, which leads to Zeus's victory and gave him supremacy over the gods of Olympus, caused Cronos to be sent beneath the earth or banished to the Isle of the Blessed, from where he prophesied.

Soleos: Just so. As likewise we find Mimir continuing to imbibe his mead at the Well of Fate, which is also considered to be the brew of immortality.

Thaeo: While Aphrodite was not only a goddess of the Star,[‡] but likewise was known as the eldest of the Fates, and associated with romantic love and brides, and thus with the moon.[30]

Phaedo: But when we say this I cannot help regarding a similarity of this with the circumstance of King Oedipus, who received a prophecy that he would come to murder his own father, which caused him to flee his adoptive father's kingdom and end up instead

---

* Nergal descends down into the underworld starting at midsummer and then rises again prior to midwinter. (White 2008: 125)
† See *The Zodiac Mysteries*
‡ The Etruscan Aphrodite was called Astghik meaning 'little star', which is the planet *Venus*.

36

in Thebes, which was the kingdom of his true parents King Laios and Jocasta. And here Oedipus unknowingly both slays his own father and then weds his own mother. As it says,

He is a blind man who now can see, he is a beggar who now has wealth, and he will go into a foreign land and graze with his staff the ground which lies before him. And he shall be known as both father and brother of the children he plays with, husband and son of the woman who gave him birth; who inherited his own father's bed and shed his own father's blood.[31]

Thaeo: And it is this incest which was found to be responsible for the affliction which beset the city of Thebes, over which he ruled. For it says,

When Laios commenced his reign he took Jocasta, the daughter of Menoiceus as his queen. But a divine oracle had made known to him that he ought not to have a child, since it prophesied that his own son would be his murderer. However, once when he was especially inebriated with wine he had sex with his wife and from this a son was born to them. Then after three days, so as to prevent the fate of the oracle from being fulfilled, he took the child and had his ankles pierced with pins to hold him fast and then gave him to one of his herdsmen to take up to the Cithairon Mountain and there leave the baby to die alone in the wilderness, which was an accepted practice then known as 'exposure'. After he had left him there one of the herdsmen of the Corinthian king, named Polybos, found the infant and took him back to the queen, who was named Periboia. She made as if he was her own son and after his ankles had healed he was given the name of Oedipus, which means 'swollen foot'. But when he grew up he was of far greater strength than any other boy his own age, but he could not learn from Periboia anything concerning his parentage so he went to the Delphic oracle and received in reply from the god that he must not return to his homeland, for if he did he would be the murderer of his father and have incest with his mother.

Upon receiving this, but thinking that his adoptive parents were his true parents, he attempted to do as the oracle suggested by moving away from Corinth. Then when he was passing through Phocis in his chariot he came upon his father Laios in his chariot, not knowing who he was. It was a narrow way they were both attempting to traverse and so Laios's herald, named Polyphontes, called out to Oedipus that he ought to clear the way. But when Oedipus was not quick to comply Polyphontes killed one of his horses, and this angered him to such a degree that he killed both Polyphontes as well as his master Laios the king, before continuing on his way to Thebes.

After the burial of King Laios, the son of Menoiceus, named Creon, became king of Thebes. And during his reign Hera sent upon them the creature known as the Sphinx, a dreaded daughter of Typhon and Echidna, who had a woman's face but the body and tail of a lion and the wings of a falcon. Having learned a riddle from the Muses she sat upon Mount Phicion and posed the riddle to the people of Thebes. But each time they were unable to provide the proper answer the Sphinx would capture one of them to consume. After many of the people were lost, including King Creon's own son Haimon, the king declared that anyone who could provide the proper solution to the riddle would receive his kingdom and queen in return. Oedipus heard this declaration and provided the solution to the riddle, and in hearing the correct answer the Sphinx reacted by leaping down from atop the Acropolis to her death. Oedipus thereby gained the kingdom for himself and, without knowing it, took his own mother Jocasta as his wife. However, when it was learned that he had done this Jocasta hanged herself and Oedipus tore out his own eyes and was then exiled from Thebes, after which he went to Colonos in Attica where he was kindly received by Theseus, though he was not fated to live long after his arrival there.[32]

But most of all the consequence of his actions was that during his reign the city of Thebes suffered greatly from famine and plague, and the sterility of both women and animals, and such is why he was banished from his homeland.[33] And while it is said that he had sons and daughters by Jocasta it is also said that as a result of their sterility Oedipus and Jocasta were unable to have any children.[*]

---

[*] Apollodorus records that Oedipus had two sons by Jocasta named Polyneices and Eteocles, along with two daughters named Ismene and

Soleos: And as Oedipus was abandoned upon a mountain before being found and adopted by the queen of Corinth, as such his abandonment in the mountains resembles somewhat that of Moses.

Thaeo: Then there is the story of King Echu, who had intercourse with his own daughter, who then gave birth to a daughter herself who was given to some herders so that she would be left out to be consumed by savage beasts. But she was then rescued and eventually became wife to Eterscelae and through him had a son who is Conaire the Great.[34][*]

Soleos: And the story of Moses being set in the river Nile is likewise similar to that of King Sargon of Akkad (Agade), whose illegitimate birth caused his mother to hide him and put him into a reed ark which was set upon the River Euphrates. The baby was saved from exposure by a poor peasant who then took him and reared him as his own son. As it relates,

> My mother was a priestess, and she gave birth to me furtively
> Then placed me within a reed ark, sealing it around with gum,
> And set me to drift in the river, from which I could not escape
> But the currents took me to the feet of Aqqi, the water bearer[†]

Thaeo: And they too resemble those who survived the Flood, having been set within a box which we identified before as the 'Great Square' (of *Pegasus*), who are Noah, Atrahasis, Manu, and Bergelmir. But this is also true of Abraham who we before equated with Atrahasis.[‡]

Epitheus: Yes. And I cannot help but think that what you are speaking of brings some meaning to the brief but pointless episode wherein Abraham travels to a king with his wife Sarah, where it says,

---

Antigone. Although he says some give their mother as Euryganeia, the daughter of Hyperphas.
[*] Conaire the Great is a legendary King of Ireland
[†] Aqqi is an appropriate name for a water bearer, being related to 'aqua'.
[‡] See *Roar of the Tempests: A Dialogue*

There came a famine in the land, and so Abram traveled down into Egypt to remain there for a time, for this famine was very severe throughout every land. And as he was just about to enter Egypt, he said to his wife Sarai, "Since you are a very beautiful woman to the eye, I know that when the Egyptians look upon you that they will say to me, 'She is your wife', and then will kill me but take you alive. So instead tell them that you are my sister, so that no mischance might befall me because of you, that I will not be killed for you."

When Abram came into Egypt the Egyptians saw that she was very beautiful indeed. And when the princes of Pharaoh looked upon her they spoke such praises of her before Pharaoh that she was immediately brought into Pharaoh's palace.[*] Thus he benefitted Abram because of her, so that he gained sheep and oxen, he-asses, servants and maids, she-asses, and camels. But Yahweh inundated Pharaoh and his household with severe afflictions because of Abram's wife Sarai.

So Pharaoh summoned Abram, saying to him, "Why have you done this to me, and not told me that she was your wife? Why instead did you tell me, 'She is my sister,' so that I took her to become my wife? So then, here is your wife, take her and be gone." And Pharaoh gave orders to his men pertaining to him, and they set him on his way, with his wife and all his possessions.[35]

And likewise,

Going from there Abraham went into the southern territory, camping between Kadesh and Shur, then went on to stay in Gerar. There Abraham said of Sarah his wife, "She is my sister." And King Abimelech of Gerar sent for her and had Sarah brought to him.

But God appeared to Abimelech in a dream at night, saying to him, "Know that you are a dead man, for the woman you have taken for yourself is another man's wife."

---

[*] This pharaoh is named Pharethothes (i.e., Pharaoh Thoth) in 'Fragment 1' of Artapanus preserved in Eusebius, '*Praeparatio Evangelica*' 9.18.1. (see Charlesworth 2009, Vol. 2: 897)

Abimelech had not yet touched her, so he replied, "Lord, will you decimate a people who are innocent? For did he not himself tell me, 'She is my sister'? While she herself said, 'He is my brother.' But with a forthright heart and unimpeachable hands did I do this."

Then in the dream God said to him, "Truly I am aware that you did this with a forthright heart, and I made sure that you did not come to sin against me; thus I would not allow you to touch her. So now give this man back his wife, for he is a man of God, and he will offer prayers for your sake so that you might live. But if you fail to return her, realize that you will undoubtedly die; you and everything which is yours."

So Abimelech arose early in the morning and summoned together all his servants and told them everything which he had experienced, and his men were left in tremendous awe. Then Abimelech summoned Abraham, saying to him, "What is this you have done to us? Is there any harm I have done to you that you have brought upon me and my kingdom this great misfortune? What you have done to me is something which ought never to be done." Abimelech then said to Abraham, "What were you thinking that made you do this?"

And Abraham replied, "I did so because I had concluded that there was no fear of God anywhere here, and that they would kill me for my wife. Moreover she is truly my sister, being my father's daughter but not my mother's daughter, yet still she is my wife. When God caused me to leave my father's house I told her, 'Do this for me for my own good, that wherever we might go tell them of me, He is my brother.'"

So Abimelech gathered sheep and oxen, and male and female slaves, and presented them to Abraham, and returned his wife Sarah to him. Abimelech then said, "Know that all my land is at your disposal, stay anywhere you would like."

And he said to Sarah, "Know that I have given your brother a thousand silver coins to serve as proof of your virtue in the eyes of anyone around you, so that in their view you will be absolved."

Abraham then prayed to God and God restored health to Abimelech, and also restored health to his wife and female slaves so that now they bore children, for Yahweh had sealed the wombs of the household of Abimelech due to Abraham's wife Sarah.[36]

And there is an identical episode concerning Isaac, which is enough like the latter to hardly be worth repeating.[*] But the name of the king which Abraham or Isaac meet here is Abimelech, which means 'Father King'. Thus the king he confronts could be the Underworld King and thus be the same as Lugalira ('Mighty King') and also Molech ('King'),[†] whose names are likewise related to Loki, the Nordic god of fire and earthquakes.

But so too it rather seems to me that this is entirely equivalent to the story of King Oedipus too, where the affliction in Thebes is due to Oedipus having killed his father and married his mother; for we find here likewise that a plague in Gerar arises due to the sin of Abimelech concerning Sarah, leading to the inability of any of his household to bear children. Thus equating one with the other, the king identified here as Pharaoh or Abimelech could be the father of Abraham, who would also be responsible for slaying his own father and then taking his father's wife, who is his own sister. Although it seems the specifics of the matter have been reworked somewhat, the residual details yet permit us to recognize that it shares the salient features of the story of King Oedipus.[‡]

Soleos: Very astute, Epitheus, and from what you say we might see Abimelech as a hermaphroditic giant who, like Ymir, is King of the Underworld. And this is very like the situation where we found a hermaphroditic being giving birth to Hephaistos and Athena;[§] which is interesting too, for when we were speaking before of the giant who survives the flood, we also considered him to be identical with Isaac and likewise with Abraham, who act as progenitors of mankind.[**]

---

[*] Genesis 26
[†] The name Molech arises from the substitution of the vowels from 'bosheth', meaning 'shame', which was written when a thing was to remain unspoken; thus the original name was Melech. (Asimov 1981: 162)
[‡] The two sons of Oedipus were to have slain one another according to Pausanias (ix 25.2; see Levi 1979, Vol. 1: 360). This is at least similar to what Rebekah says to Jacob: "Why should I lose both of you in a single day?" (Genesis 27:45).
[§] See *The Zodiac Mysteries*
[**] See *The Zodiac Mysteries*. This figure too brings with him in his craft both the formative plant and animal, and in one instance from Nias Island

42

Epitheus: That is indeed true, Soleos, so we might regard that after giving rise to Sarah and Abraham that this hermaphroditic giant then took Sarah, his own daughter, as his wife, and undertook to dispose of his son. But this son somehow survives and returns to his father and slays him, then takes his own sister for himself.

Thaeo: Yes, and I would venture that this could also be true of Gawain and the Green Knight, for Abraham clearly says that Sarah is his half-sister, when he says, "in fact she is my sister, because she is the daughter of my father but not of my mother, and yet she is my wife."[37] And it occurs to me that this would also be true of Gawain, the nephew of Arthur, who himself is the half-sister of Morgan Le Fay, who is the wife of the Green Knight. Thus if we were to substitute Arthur for Gawain, who confronts the Green Knight, we already find Morgan Le Fay is Arthur's half-sister just as Sarah is the half-sister to Abraham.

Soleos: And in this case we would have to presume that the Green Knight would take the role of the father and Underworld King.

Thaeo: Indeed so.

Epitheus: But then what should we make of Abraham's attainment of a second wife named Hagar, who then gives birth to Abraham's first-born son Ishmael?

Thaeo: If we consider that through Sarah that Abraham gave rise to the god Isaac, could we then think of Hagar as being the mother of men? Consider the name of Ishmael, for this could be taken to mean 'divine son of Ma' (*ish-Ma-el*), where 'Ma' is the name of the universal mother goddess, known as Ninmah or Mami (in ancient Mesopotamia), who is also known to have given rise to humankind. And thus Ishmael could well be a divine ancestor of man, and clearly he is given such a role.[*]

---

there can be seen upon his head an owl and a serpent; these two likewise being similarly symbolic of Athena and Hephaistos.

[*] Genesis 17:20, 25:12-18

Epitheus: But is it possible that these two wives may have arisen from entirely different episodes, for Isaac is clearly made a progenitor figure of the Israelites, being the father of Jacob?

Thaeo: Yes. And so then might we identify from this rather a consistent sequence of three generations: with the first being the primordial being, a second being the race of giants, and a third being the race of gods? For if we took the Greek story with the primordial giant as Ouranos, then the giants would be the Titans, followed third by the Olympian gods.

Soleos: And so too of Ymir followed by Thrudgelmir and Bergelmir; and Buri followed by Bor and the gods Odin, Vili, and Ve. But then too if we were to equate Buri with Bestla's father Bolthorn, then Bor and Bestla would be siblings, who then give rise to the three gods.

This is just as we have here, with Abraham and Sarah being the two children of Abimelech, but not strictly siblings but through the term of calling them 'half-sister' and 'half-brother' as a means to accommodate that they had not arisen from two different mothers but from the same hermaphroditic being. And in this sense, it would seem, through two distinct births; as we find with Athena who sprung from the head of Zeus and Hephaistos who was born fatherless from Hera.

Epitheus: Just so.

Soleos: And having both emerged from the same being, could we honestly call them anything other than brother and sister?

Epitheus: Surely not.

Soleos: Yet at the same time, these events seem to have been somewhat confounded.

Epitheus: In what way, Soleos?

Soleos: I mean that in regards to how it might be considered that there would only be one progenitor figure, and that each of these: Adam, Noah, Abraham and Lot, Isaac and Ishmael, and Jacob and

Esau, I suspect represents a line of descent with each having his own specific creation story; and where each too is given the role of father of humanity. Although here they have instead been given the role of fathering the finer divisions of humanity, so that only Adam and Noah still retain the role of the father of all mankind, where Noah's sons are the fathers of the three continents;[*] with Lot as the father of Ammon and Moab, Ishmael as father of the Arabs, while Esau is the father of the Edomites as is Jacob the father of the Israelites.

Epitheus: Truly so.

Soleos: Then we should seek to clarify this through a further investigation so as to determine how they might have initially been equivalent, and in doing so we must likewise seek to show how the various episodes might come to have been reworked. And in doing so to identify which arrangement was foremost among them.

Epitheus: I would very much like to do so.

Soleos: And as we have determined, prior to the father of humanity there existed a hermaphroditic giant; and this holds for the most part, except in the case when it is said that Aphrodite and Hermes give rise to a hermaphrodite; where we saw that it is Ouranos who gives rise to Aphrodite in the sea foam, which is comparable with an insemination of the sea, and as for Hermes himself we well comprehend.[†]

Epitheus: Indeed so.

Soleos: This then would be similar to both the slaying of Ymir and too the circumstance of Cronos, whom we suspect suffered a similar fate. But likewise, as you suggested before from inference, that King Abimelech was slain by his own son Abraham. And this would fit in with the conception of the Great Flood, which is associated with the slaying of Ymir.[38] Although we would have to presume that the three generations from Aurgelmir (Ymir), Thrudgelmir, and

---

[*] Asia, Europe, and Africa
[†] See *The Zodiac Mysteries*

Bergelmir are, as we surmised before, comparable with the generations of Buri, Bor, and Odin.[*] So that if we were to consider the man, woman, and son produced by Ymir as two instances of the same creation, the son would then have to be Thrudgelmir in order to make it consistent with Ymir giving rise to the Frost-giants, of which only Bergelmir and his wife are said to survive.

Epitheus: Truly, and so too we are aware of a similar situation concerning Noah, who escaped in a box from a land populated by angels who, we are told, had intercourse with the daughters of men.[†]

Thaeo: Indeed. And likewise the first generation of humanity are said to have been females, and as it says in the Sibylline Oracles,

> Cronos, Titan, and Iapetos ruled, who were the finest children of Gaia and Ouranos, called the Earth and Heaven by men, who were given names because they were the first ones to give speech to men. There were three regions of the earth, corresponding to each one's individual portion; and each one ruled his own share and there was no conflict among them because their father had caused them all to swear oaths, and the apportionments were made fairly. But when the entire period had passed and their father became old, he died, leading his sons to a grim breach of their oaths, and thus conflict arose among them concerning which of them should gain the throne and rule over all men. Cronos fought against Titan; but Rhea, Gaia, crown-fond Aphrodite, Demeter, Hestia, and beautifully braided Dione, caused them to make peace.
>
> Bringing together all the kings, relations and brothers, as well as others who were born of the same mother, thus all having come from the same lineage; they elected Cronos as king to rule over them all, because he was the elder and of the goodliest appearance. However, Titan caused Cronos to swear profound oaths that he would not give rise to any males, so that he might reign in his place when Cronos had himself come to an old age and met his end. So as Rhea was giving birth, the Titans

---

[*] See *The Zodiac Mysteries*
[†] Genesis 6:1-4

remained nearby, and they ripped every male child to pieces but permitted the females to live and be raised by their mother. When Rhea started giving birth to the third batch of children, Hera emerged first; and when they noticed that it was a female the savage Titans returned home. But after this Rhea then gave birth to a male, whom she then immediately dispatched in secret, and under the oaths of three Cretan gentlemen, so that he might be reared, without being noticed, in Phrygia. Thus he was named Zeus by them, since he had been thus dispatched. And in like manner she sent Poseidon away in secret.

Moreover Rhea, a wonder among women, upon the third instance, gave birth to Pluto when passing Dodona, where the watery way of the River Europus coursed, and its waters dumped into the sea along with the River Peneius which they call the Stygian. But when the Titans had learned that children were being kept in secret, who were children that Cronos had had with Rhea, Titan collected together sixty of his sons and had both Cronos and his wife Rhea put in chains and confined beneath the ground, and had them guarded in their forced confinement. So naturally when the sons of mighty Cronos heard of this it provoked a formidable war, and the clamor of conflict was raised to challenge him. And this was the commencement of all wars to be found among mortal men, because this marked the first war of mortal men.

So compare this birth of Zeus then with Moses, who is born while all other male children are thrown into the Nile. And here the Pharaoh who condemns the sons of Egypt would parallel Cronos, and Moses likewise with Zeus. And this survival of Zeus is very like that of Dionysos, who was stolen away by Hermes and taken away to Mount Parnassos to be raised as a girl.[39] And when Rhea escapes with Zeus and gives birth to him, a flood arises which could be the very same one which wiped out the race of giants.[40]

Epitheus: Indeed, Thaeo. And Noah after the Flood is lying exposed when his two sons (Shem and Japheth) cover him. And it could be due to the actions of the third brother (Ham), who is said to have looked upon his father's nakedness.[*] For how much more would they have reacted if he had instead castrated their father, by which then Noah would become even more like Ouranos, so that his blood and semen could then have seeded the earth and given rise to women and men.[†]

Thaeo: Yes. And we find the instance of the castration of Ouranos gave rise to the ash tree Nymphs; and are not human beings also referred to as the 'ash-tree folk?'

Soleos: Rightly so. And thus we could compare Noah with Zeus and Moses, or with Cronos and Ouranos, so that somewhere along the line we encounter a race of giants, a race of gods, and the race of humanity. So it might serve us to organize these according to the three generations following the primeval giant, who gives rise to a pair of giants, who give birth to the gods, who then give rise to humanity?

Thaeo: Indeed, we could, and the arising of humanity might be considered in terms of either a direct birth from a divine being and from a line of descent, or else that they were rather created by the gods, but that within this mortal being is to be found the divine spirit of life. And just such is true of Erechthonios, being himself the product of both earthly and immortal combined within a single being, himself of serpentine form; and who could also have been the progenitor of the human race.

Epitheus: Just so.

Thaeo: And we could well associate a serpentine form with the ultimate progenitor of humanity, as we would find if we considered Leviathan to be the father of humanity and perhaps the female Leviathan as mother of the world, like Gaia. And, as we considered, Moses could have been born from out of Leviathan upon the Nile; and the flood story would also have us believing that Noah, Abraham, and Isaac are distinct progenitor figures, where Noah is

---

[*] Genesis 9:22
[†] See *The Zodiac Mysteries*

48

equivalent with Nahmizuli, Abraham with Atrahasis, and Isaac with Bacchus.[*]

Epitheus: That is almost certainly so. But we might take this even further, as the father of Noah is Lamech, while we noted before that Abimelech could have been the father of Abraham. And Noah's wife is named Emzara which means 'mother Zara',[41] so perhaps then we might consider it entirely the same as 'mother Sarah'.

Source	Progenitor	Giants	Gods	Offspring
Hesiod	Ouranos-Gaia	Cronos, Rhea	Olympian gods	mankind
Ovid	Ouranos	Hermes, Aphrodite	Hermaphroditus	-
Apollodorus	Zeus-Hera	Hephaistos, Athena	Erechthonios	Tros[†]
Hesiod	Chaos	Erebos, Nyx	Aether, Hermea	(Thalassa)[42][‡]
Edda	Buri/Bolthorn	Bor, Bestla	Odin, Vili, Ve	mankind
Edda	Ymir	man, woman	-	Frost-giants
Veda	Purusa	-	-	humanity
Persian	Gayomard	-	-	humanity
Bible ('Y')[43]	Abimelech	Abraham, Sarah	Jacob, Esau	Israelites
Bible ('L')[44]	Abimelech	Isaac, Rebekah	Jacob, Esau	Israelites
Bible ('P')	Lamech	Noah, (Emzara)[45]	Shem, Ham, Japheth	mankind

Mythical generations from progenitor to the arising of humanity.

Soleos: Well done. But here too we can recognize the insertion of an extra generation, so that Abraham does not give rise to the gods himself but to a son who then fathers Jacob and Esau, with Jacob becoming Israel from whom the Israelites are descended. And so too

---

[*] See *Roar of the Tempests: A Dialogue* and *The Zodiac Mysteries*
[†] Ancestor of the Trojans (*Iliad* xx)
[‡] Thalissa, equivalent to Amphitrite, is the personified sea, and according to Diodorus Siculus (*Library of History* v, 55.1) she gave rise to the people of Rhodes.

if we consider Abraham and Isaac to be parallel progenitors, then they both gave rise to sons who might be considered gods themselves, who then give rise to humanity.[*]

Thaeo: And I believe your distinctions hold true as well for Erebos ('shadow'), the son of Chaos, the primordial giant; who was wedded to Nyx ('night') his sister, and who gave rise to Aether (sky god) and Hemera (day goddess), as we were speaking of before.

Soleos: Just so. And what we have identified here might well provide a solution to a concern which would surely have emerged in the human mind, which is simply the question of how the first man and woman might have come into being? For they would have to have arisen without leading us into an infinite regression, where each pair of male and female must themselves have two parents and so on.

Epitheus: Indeed not.

Soleos: Likewise, given the advent of a single man and woman, they would have to consider how the threat of incest could be avoided? But the line of descent we have found achieves such a resolution, because the gods are allowed to have incestuous relationships with one another. For we find the situation where a number of notable dualities occur, although it is not entirely certain how they might all have arisen; one aspect which does pervade is that what is denied to humans is something identified as being reserved for the gods, which seems to be the very reason why there are so many brother-sister relationships amongst them, and thus permissible to them, and *essentially* forbidden to mere mortals.[†]

Epitheus: Yes.

---

[*] See *The Zodiac Mysteries*

[†] The Egyptians have such male-female gods Amen and Ament, Tem and Temt, Nu and Nut, Hehui and Hehet, and Kekui and Keket. We also have Jove and Juno among the Greek gods; as well as Frey and Freyia, Berchta and Bercht (Berchtolt), Frigg and Frikko, Nerthus and Niord, Fairguneis and Fiorgyn, Geban and Gefion, and Hruodo and Hreda among the Norse.

Soleos: Thus by the time humans appear, in such a manner of decent from the gods, incest only arises prior to the emergence of humanity, and thus exists only where it remains permissible; that is, only among the gods, as with Yami and Yama or Gaia and Ouranos.

Epitheus: Undoubtedly.

Soleos: Yet when the gods create man artificially by some other means they might likewise form more than one pair, as do Deucalion and his wife Pyrrha, who create men and women from out of stones.

Epitheus: Yes.

Soleos: But there is one other option available, which is that humans are descended from some species of animal; and as such that sibling relationships would be permissible for them. Whereas it was only after this that identifiable human forms arose into being. And this could be precisely behind what is said of humanity having descended from serpents or a serpentine being, who is not himself human and thus was not required to forgo the practice of incest, which likewise is true of the giants and the gods.

Epitheus: I understand what you are saying. But then let us not forget the story of Lot and what is said concerning himself and his two daughters, for it is said that,

> Abraham set forth at dawn to the place he had been standing with Yahweh, gazing out to where Sodom and Gomorrah were situated and the land which lay below in the valley. And as he looked out before him there was a great plume rising from off the land like a smoking furnace. Thus it was when God obliterated the cities situated in the valley that he remembered Abraham and so sent Lot away from the center of the destruction when he obliterated the cities in which Lot had lived. And Lot left Zoar and went to live up in the mountains with his two daughters, since he was reluctant to remain in Zoar. So he made his abode within a cave to live there with his two daughters. And the elder said to the younger, "Here our father is old, but there remains not a man upon the earth who will come into us as is the way of the world.

So let us go and cause our father to consume wine; then we will lie with him so that, through our father, we might have descendants." So that night they caused their father to consume wine and the elder daughter went in and lay with her father, but he was unaware of when she came and when she went. Then upon the following day the elder said to the younger, "Know that I spent the night with my father, so let us cause him to consume wine again tonight so that you might also go in and lie with him that, through our father, we might have descendants." So that night likewise they caused their father to consume wine, and the younger went in and lay with him, but he was unaware of when she came and when she went. Then both of the daughters of Lot became pregnant by their father: and the elder gave birth to a son named Moab, and he is considered the father of the Moabites even now, and the younger also gave birth to a son, named Ben-ammi, and he is considered the father of the Ammonites even now.[46]

So here we must regard the behavior of the two daughters of Lot as strange, for they surely would not have found any men there in the mountains, but must have believed that no other men existed upon the entire earth. Thus we would have to presume that this situation is precisely what would arise in a situation where Sodom and Gomorrah were the only cities on earth. So that after the loss of his wife Lot came to dwell in a cave with his two daughters where they give birth to the generations of humanity; which are reduced here to Moab and Ammon (Ben-Ammi), the progenitors of the Moabites and the Ammonites.

Thaeo: So too I would think it is possible that Lot's own story is the same as that told by Ovid, for in the former case Lot and his wife met two travelers and gave them lodgings for the night, which had been denied them by the other inhabitants of these two corrupted cities. Thus too when they come to destroy humanity they allow Lot and his family to survive the destruction. And you will see such a circumstance is very similar to the story told of Philemon and Baucis.

There in the depths of the Phrygian hills stands an oak tree
By its side is a linden tree, with a modest wall encircling both
This location I saw for myself, for Pittheus caused me to go
Pelops, his father, ruled in Phrygia before coming to Troezen
And nearby to that location there is an uncultivated fenland
But still one which in times past had been cultivated by men
Now, however, it's home to wild water foul and reed beds
Jupiter had cause to go there once, taking on a mortal visage,
With his father came wingless Mercury, grandson of Atlas,
Still he kept at his side that miraculous wand, his *caduceus*
They knocked upon a thousand doors looking for sanctuary
At a thousand doors they found no place, being sent away,
But there was one simple house where they found a haven
It was one roofed with a simple mat of grasses and straw
Within that shack there lived a very old woman, good Baucis
And living at her side was Philemon, just as aged as she
After they had married when young they chose this shack
And there too they had grown old, contented in their poverty
They thought it neither an indignity nor a curse not to hide
There was no question as to who was slave and who master
With just two of them, they acted as both master and slave
So that when these two gods of heaven came into their home
They had to duck down because the lintel of the door was low
And the elder gentleman put out a bench upon which to sit,
After he'd dutifully spread upon it a coarse homespun cloth
The burning coals of their former fire Baucis fanned anew
To this she added a collection of dry leaves, and bits of bark
And bent down, using all of her lung power to ignite flames
Then having done this, beneath the roof she gathered tinder
Both branches of wood and dry twigs, and split them in two
So that they then could be fit beneath the modest copper pot
She prepared a cabbage from their garden cut by Philemon
While her husband took a tined pole to stab a slab of bacon
Which hung high among the smoke-blackened rafter beams
Then cutting off a small piece of the carefully guarded pork
He placed it deftly into the pot of boiling water to let it cook
Meanwhile, to pass the time, they engaged in cheery banter
And at the same time they chattered everything was readied
Taking out their couch which had a frame and legs of willow

53

Which was kept by them especially for important feast days
Upon it was set a cushion which had been stuffed with grass
Over which they spread an unexceptional old cloth covering
So the gods seated themselves, while Baucis set up the table
Having tucked her skirt at the waist, hands shaking with age,
The wonky leg was simply set right with an old pottery shard
Slipped beneath the short leg to shimmy it, to make it straight
Then Baucis rubbed the table with a spray of fresh mint leaves
And then the fruit which is loved by clever and wise Minerva,
Black olives, and cherries kept since autumn soaking in wine,
Lettuce leaves, radishes, cottage cheese, lightly cooked eggs,
Each of them being served within simple earthenware dishes
And in the same manner, a bowl with wooden cups for wine
With the nicks of time pasted over with hardened bees wax
The concoction prepared in broth was served from the hearth
And new wine was set out, with room made for the last dish
Nuts, figs, and dates, with grapes plucked fresh from the vine,
With baskets brimming full with an array of aromatic apples
Amidst them all was a dish of delicate, translucent honeycomb
And abounding all the time were their ready and affable faces
But when that bowl of wine, so quickly depleted, was restored,
So as to never fail in providing portions anew of plentiful wine,
Shocked as they were by this miraculous event, became fearful
Old Baucis and Philemon put their hands together to beseech
Apologizing for the unworthiness of their scant fare and charity
So they grabbed the only goose they had left upon their land,
Who acted as defender of that modest acreage, for the deities
A spritely goose indeed, putting them through quite a gauntlet
Running them ragged, persistent to take wing and evade them
Until, as it seemed, it came for sanctuary near to the two gods
They said to Baucis and Philemon there was no need to kill it
"Yes, we are gods. But your unrighteous neighbors will find
That a severe penalty awaits them, but fear not, you'll survive
So now you must come with us, abandon your modest house
We will go to that lofty peak which lies far away over there."
So they went upon their walking sticks up the high mountain
Being just a bowshot from the pinnacle, they turned to look
But behind them now was nothing but a pervading floodplain
Covering everything but their little cabin; as the couple looked

They were astonished and left weeping for their lost neighbors
And that modest cabin, their home for so many years, even so,
Standing trivially before, was now transfigured into a temple
Rather than forked poles which had abutted against its rafters,
Now there were lofty marble pillars, and no more a straw roof
The sundry fibers had melded together into a canopy of gold
Across the old bare ground stretched a span of marble flooring
Where enshrined within the doors were carved panels in relief
Then Saturn's son, Mighty Jove, spoke to them both gently,
"Speak to me now of what gift you would wish granted to you,
For you have proven yourself a righteous man and good wife."
Philemon and Baucis talked among themselves a short while,
Before they made their decision known, and they told him,
"We would wish to be your priests, guardians of your temple,
And as we have spent many years together without discord,
We wish that when one dies the other may go that same hour
That I need never look upon the plot of land where she rests
And that she will have no need to lay my bones in the ground."
This request was granted them; they became the gods' priests
There they remained, as long as they both lived, in that temple
Until at long last, being wearied after their many years together,
One day, sitting upon those holy steps, recalling years gone by,
Philemon noticed that his wife Baucis began sprouting foliage
Baucis too noticed branches were burgeoning over Philemon
So soon each had a full tree top ascending around their faces,
Until there was no longer any way to speak through the bark
While there still was time, calling out to each other together,
"Goodbye, my devoted partner; goodbye and farewell, dear."
And the Phrygian farmers there will yet reveal these two trees
Standing aside one another, once being Baucis and Philemon[47]

Soleos: Well done, as usual, Thaeo. And this destruction you speak of we might regard too as being of quite a similar circumstance to Noah and the flood, where the beings on earth had become evil. And this is spoken of by Adam,

"No doubt you have heard, my son Seth, that a Flood will come to cleanse the entire earth due to the daughters of Cain, who is your brother and the one who killed your brother Abel from a

55

desire for your sister Lebuda, because sin was brought about by your mother Eve. Then after the Flood will follow six-thousand more years of an orderly cosmos before it will come to its end.[48]

And it is not unusual to find that famine and plague and disasters are thought to be sent due to the transgressions of mankind against the gods.[49] But more so the gods would grow restless when mankind became a source of great disturbance to the gods through their endless noise and commotion, and this is precisely the circumstance which exists within the story of Atrahasis, which, if we are not out of luck, Phaedo will be willing to tell us.

CHAPTER 4

Phaedo: Indeed, I would be glad to do so, Soleos,

When gods, not men, performed the work, bore the burdens
The weight was too great, the work too taxing, a sore plight
So the seven great Anunnaki made the Igigi to take the load
The king was their father, Anu; their counselor of war, Ellil,
The chamberlain, Nimrod; and their canal manager, Ennugi,
Taking up the container they cast lots, the gods divvied up,
So that Anu took his home in the heavens, to live in the sky
While Ellil went to make his abode among the men of earth
And astute Enki acquired for himself the entire sea's crater
After Anu was in the sky, and the Apsu gods did descend, [*]
Then the heavenly Anunnaki made the Igigi take the load
They caused the gods to carve out the many water canals
They had to open up conduits, the sustenance of the land
They caused the Igigi to carve out the many water canals
They had to open up conduits, the sustenance of the land
So the immortals carved out the channel of the river Tigris
And the divinities carved out the channel of the Euphrates
Boring a chamber at the lowest depths, setting stanchions
In the deep waters of the Apsu, beneath a covering of land
They placed braces within, situating these to raise it aloft,
Those which stand at the peaks, underlying all mountains
And they kept track of every long year that they worked
The excess water drained down to fill up the great swamp
And they kept track of every long year that they worked

It was 3,600 years in which they carried the heavy loads,
The work was burdensome; they were busy night and day
So they grumbled and blamed one another often enough,
They complained over the piles of soil they had dug up,
"We should go to the chamberlain, to our chief overseer,
So that he might bring us rest from our unrelenting labors!

---

[*] Anu is god of heaven, Ellil is god of fire and lightning, while Enki is another name for Ea, the water god who resides in the underground abyss, the Apsu.

Let us go and bring out the lord, as the supreme authority,
As the counselor of war, bring him forth out of his house,
Let us go there and collect Ellil, as the supreme authority,
As the counselor of war, bring him forth out of his house."
Among them Alla raised his voice to speak and be heard
Making a speech to his brothers, to all of the high gods,
"We've kept track of every long year that we've worked
It has been 3,600 years we have carried the heavy loads,
The work is burdensome; we remain busy night and day
So we've grumbled and blamed one another often enough,
We complain over the piles of soil that we have dug up,
We should go to the chamberlain, to our chief overseer,
So that he might bring us rest from our unrelenting labors!
Let us go and bring out the lord, as the supreme authority,
As the counselor of war, bring him forth out of his house,
Let us go there and collect Ellil, as the supreme authority,
As the counselor of war, bring him forth out of his house
So let us raise up our battle cry and bring war to the fore!"
The gods listened to every word as he made his speech,
They placed their implements in piles and set them aflame
Their troubles dispatched to the fire god, consumed in fire
When they arrived at the gate of Ellil, wise war counselor,
It was already nighttime; it was already the middle watch
His house was already encircled, but the god did not know
It was already nighttime; it was already the middle watch,
Ekur had already been encircled, but Ellil did not know it
But his servant Kalkal had the good sense to close the gate
He secured the lock and then kept an eye on the entryway
Kalkal went and woke Nusku, and they observed the Igigi,
Nusku then went to wake up his lord, got him out of bed,
"Master, you must know that your house is surrounded,
And a raucous mob has already gathered about your door!
Master Ellil, you must know your house is surrounded,
And a raucous mob has already gathered about your door!"
So Ellil had weapons he kept for his residence brought out
Ellil raised his voice to be heard, saying to his officer Nusku,
"Nusku, first you must go and suitably secure the door,
Then pick up your weapons and set yourself before me."
So Nusku went and sought to suitably secure the door,

Then picked up his weapons and took his place before Ellil
Nusku raised his voice to be heard, speaking to chief Ellil,
"My lord, behold your face has become pale as a tamarisk!
For what reason do you show such fear of your own clan?
Ellil, behold, your face has become pale as a tamarisk tree!
For what reason do you show such fear of your own clan?
Make an announcement that Anu might come to your aid,
And do so that Enki will have cause to stand by your side."
So a herald was sent with word that Anu might come to him,
And so that Enki had cause to journey and stand at his side,
So that now the king of the wide heavens, Anu, had arrived,
And so too the king of the mighty abyss, Enki was there too
Also, there gathered the great Anunnaki to be in attendance
Ellil stood up to make his case, raising his voice to be heard,
He spoke to the entire assembly of the high gods gathered,
"Have they raised up in armed rebellion so as to depose me?
Ought I now raise my weapons to go against my own clan?
For what did I behold here with my own eyes when I looked,
But that there was an angry mob assembled about my door!"

Anu raised his voice to be heard, speaking to the chief Ellil,
"Then command Nusku to go, to divine the Igigi's purpose
Have him establish the will of those gathered at your door
A word from you and this whole thing could be cleared up
To find out for what reason they have gathered at your door."
Ellil raised his voice to be heard, saying to his officer Nusku,
"Nusku, go first to open the door, then pick up your weapons
And take your place before me! Then go out among the gods
First prostrate yourself, then rise up and speak to them thus:
'Your father Anu, supreme authority Ellil, the lord Nimrod,
And the manager of your canals Ennugi, wish me to request:
Who is the one among you who is leader of this heated mob?
Who is the one among you who is organizer of this uprising?
Who among you has turned his face unto the arena of war?
Who are you that have come here hastily to the door of Ellil?'"
So Nusku went and opened the door, picked up his weapons
Then took his place before Ellil, in the presence of the gods
After prostrating himself, he rose and spoke to them thusly,
"Your father Anu, supreme authority Ellil, the lord Nimrod,

And the manager of your canals Ennugi, wish me to request:
Who is the one among you who is leader of this heated mob?
Who is the one among you who is organizer of this uprising?
Who among you has turned his face unto the arena of war?
Who are you that have come here hastily to the door of Ellil?"
Thus Nusku spoke to carry out the duty given to him by Ellil
Now Alla raised his voice to be heard, speaking to Nusku,
"Every one of the gods is ready to come to blows over this!
And we have thus stopped partaking in our endless digging,
The burden is far too heavy for us, and it was diminishing us
The weight is very great, the work too taxing, a sore plight!
And so each god sought to bring his discontent before Ellil."
Nusku hefted his weapons, turned, and came back to Ellil
"My lord, I performed my mission to disclose the situation
I went to find an answer as to why your door is surrounded
Having explicated the things you gave me charge to convey,
This then is what response they gave me in reply; they said,
'Every one of the gods is ready to come to blows over this!
And we have thus stopped partaking in our endless digging,
The burden is far too heavy for us, and it was diminishing us
The weight is very great, the work too taxing, a sore plight!
And so each god sought to bring his discontent before Ellil.'"
So Ellil listened to everything he said, and became tearful,
Ellil chose words with care, speaking to the conqueror Anu,
"Wise judge, return with this verdict to your heavenly realm
Flex your muscles before the Anunnaki gathered about you,
Declare one god from among them, allocate him to perish!"

Together with Anu, his brothers Ea and Ellil agreed that Belet-ili, the womb goddess, ought to create primitive man so that they might accept the work of Ellil, the burden of the Igigi gods.

They called the goddess, the midwife, shrewd Mami, saying,
"You are the womb-goddess, give rise to the species of man!
Give rise to a primitive human, to perform the labor of gods!
Let him be the one to bear the yoke, who does Ellil's work,
So that man will be the one who performs the labor of gods!"
Nintu raised her voice to be heard, speaking to the high gods,
"It is not best that I fashion him, this is better done by Enki

For it is by his efforts that things are made free from error
But if he provides me with clay, I will certainly carry it out."
Enki raised his voice to be heard, speaking to the high gods,
"Know that on the first, seventh, and fifteenth of the month
I will conduct a water-purification, and one god will be slain
Thus the gods will be cleansed through these holy ablutions
Then Nintu will combine the clay with his flesh and blood
So that a being, divine and mortal, will come from the clay
Then we will hear the heart-beat rhythms from henceforth
Let the spirit arise into being from out of the divine flesh,
But let her relate to man, while he is alive, of his condition
So they will never forget that the spirit is eternally made."
And all gathered in the assemblage gave their affirmation,
Of the holy Anunnaki who were the determiners of destiny
Then it was on the first, seventh, and fifteenth of the month
That he conducted a water-purification through immersion
The wise god Ilawela was chosen to be slain at the congress
Nintu combined together the clay with his flesh and blood
So that they heard the heart-beat rhythms from henceforth
And the spirit arose into being from out of the divine flesh,
Nintu related to man, while he was alive, of his condition
So they would never forget that the spirit is eternally made
Then after having done this she combined together the clay,
After she convened the high gods, both Anunnaki and Igigi
And she caused her spittle to dribble onto the heap of clay
Then Mami raised her voice, speaking to the high gods,
"I have done precisely the task that was given to me to do
And you have slain a god altogether along with his mind
Now I have brought you release from your tiresome tasks
And have caused your burdens to be shifted onto mankind
While you have given humanity the capacity for speaking
Thus I have released the bonds and brought you freedom!"
Hearing every word spoken with relief, they kissed her feet
"Until now we have referred to you by the name of Mami,
But henceforth you shall be called 'Mistress of all the Gods!'"
Then astute Enki and wise Mami went to the abode of Fate
There the womb-goddesses had already gathered together
And there he stomped upon the clay pile while she stood by
So she chanted the spells Enki, who was there, asked her to

When she had finished, she pulled off fourteen bits of clay
Setting out seven bits on her right and seven bits on her left,
And midway between the columns she set there a mud-brick
And then she slit open a stiff reed and severed the umbilical
Then called over the clever and worldly womb-goddesses,
Here, seven and seven, were seven males and seven females,
For the womb-goddesses were the determiners of destiny
So he covered each pair, Enki covered them, as she looked

Thus man learned their laws and customs from Mami,[*] and the people worked at their labors and their numbers flourished as the burgeoning societies of men are inclined to do.

Six-hundred years, not even six-hundred years went by
The inhabited land sprawled and the people grew plentiful
And the inhabited lands raised a howl like a bellowing bull
But the god was annoyed by all the noise that they made
Ellil had to put up with all of their loud clamor and clatter
Ellil raised his voice to be heard, speaking to the high gods,
"The noise which is made by man has become too great,
All of this clamor and clatter has kept me from my sleep
Therefore command an outbreak of the shivering disease
And thus the divine Namtara was summoned by the gods
Then the divine Namtara unleashed the shivering disease,
And all of the people were beset by the plague outbreak
There was one man among them who was named Atrahasis
And he heeded diligently the words spoken by his god Enki
He often communed with his god, receiving the god's reply
Atrahasis raised his voice to be heard, speaking to his lord,
"How long are we going to be beset by this terrible disease?
Is it their intention that we bear this syndrome for all time?"
Enki raised his voice to be heard, speaking to his servant,
"Bring together the elders; gather to you the men of rank
So as to instigate a rebellion within your own community!
Send out messengers to announce this within every district
And cause them to raise a loud cry throughout all lands
That you no longer will pay fitting homage to your gods

---

[*] The Earth Goddess Demeter too is known as the 'law-giver'

That you no longer beseech the favor of your goddesses
But rather find your way to the door of the god Namtara
Present him a loaf of baked bread, leave a flour offering,
And let him feel his own shame upon receiving these gifts
So that he might remove from you his discredited hand."
Atrahasis did as he was told, bringing the elders to his door
And he raised his voice to be heard, speaking to the elders,
"I have brought together the elders, and the men of rank,
So as to instigate a rebellion within our own community
Send out messengers to announce this within every district
And cause them to raise a loud cry throughout all lands
That you no longer will pay fitting homage to your gods
That you no longer beseech the favor of your goddesses
But rather find your way to the door of the god Namtara
Present him a loaf of baked bread, leave a flour offering
And let him feel his own shame upon receiving these gifts
That he might remove from off of us his discredited hand."
And the elders paid heed to his prudently spoken advice
Thus they built a temple in the city dedicated to Namtara,
Sent out messengers to announce this within every district
And caused them to raise a loud cry throughout all lands
So they no longer would pay fitting homage to their gods
So they no longer beseeched the favor of their goddesses
But rather found their way to the door of the god Namtara
Presented him a loaf of baked bread, left a flour offering,
Such that he himself felt shame upon receiving these gifts
So that he removed from off of them his discredited hand
And the shivering disease was no longer a menace to them
Then after this the gods received again their daily offerings
Though their numbers were no less, but became even greater
While the racket, their clamor and clatter, grew ever louder!

Six-hundred years, not even six-hundred years went by
The inhabited land sprawled and the people grew plentiful
And the inhabited lands raised a howl like a bellowing bull
But the god was annoyed by all the noise that they made
Ellil had to put up with all of their loud clamor and clatter
Ellil raised his voice to be heard, speaking to the high gods,
"The noise which is made by man has become too great,

All of this clamor and clatter has kept me from my sleep
Now let us make it so the humans will be denied their food!
So that growth will not be great enough to cure their hunger!
Let it be so, that in the heavens Adad will withhold his rain,
And beneath no subterranean water will gush from springs
Cause the winds to be unleashed and rage, denuding the soil
Let there be clouds aloft in the sky, but which bring no rain
So the farmers' fields will yield hardly any crop to speak of
Let Nissaba hold back the nourishing flow from her breasts
There are to be no blessings which are bestowed unto them
So that their lives will be wretched and filled with misery."
Then the gods sent messengers to Adad to withhold his rain,
To Nissaba to withhold the nourishing flow of her breasts,
And the winds were unleashed and raged, denuding the soil
There were clouds aloft in the sky, but they brought no rain
So the farmer's fields yielded hardly any crop to speak of
There were no blessings which were bestowed unto them
So that their lives became wretched and filled with misery
Atrahasis raised his voice to be heard, speaking to his lord,
"How long are we going to be beset by this terrible famine?
Is it their intention that we bear this syndrome for all time?"
Enki raised his voice to be heard, speaking to his servant,
"Bring together the elders, gather to you the men of rank!
So as to instigate a rebellion within your own community
Send out messengers to announce this within every district
And cause them to raise a loud cry throughout all lands,
That you no longer will pay fitting homage to your gods
That you no longer beseech the favor of your goddesses
But rather find your way to the door of Adad the rain god
Present him a loaf of baked bread, leave a flour offering,
And let him feel his own shame upon receiving these gifts
So that he might remove from you his discredited hand."
Atrahasis did as he was told, bringing the elders to his door
And he raised his voice to be heard, speaking to the elders,
"I have brought together the elders, and the men of rank,
So as to instigate a rebellion within our own community
Send out messengers to announce this within every district
And cause them to raise a loud cry throughout all lands
That you no longer will pay fitting homage to your gods

That you no longer beseech the favor of your goddesses
But rather find your way to the door of Adad the rain god
Present him a loaf of baked bread, leave a flour offering,
And let him feel his own shame upon receiving these gifts
That he might remove from off of us his discredited hand
To condense a misty haze that will appear in the morning,
So during the night he will go and beckon droplets of dew,
As patron, to restore the fruitfulness of the land nine-fold."
Thus they erected a temple in the city dedicated to Adad,
Sent out messengers to announce this within every district
And caused them to raise a loud cry throughout all lands,
So they no longer would pay fitting homage to their gods
So they no longer beseeched the favor of their goddesses
But rather made their way to the door of the rain god Adad
Presented him a loaf of baked bread, left a flour offering,
Such that he himself felt shame upon receiving these gifts
So that he removed from off of them his discredited hand
And condensed a misty haze that appeared in the morning,
So during the night he went and beckoned droplets of dew
As patron, he restored the fruitfulness of the land nine-fold,
So that the days of dryness passed, and the drought ended
Then after this the gods received again their daily offerings

But in less than three periods of time, then it came to pass,
The inhabited land sprawled and the people grew plentiful
And the inhabited lands raised a howl like a bellowing bull
So the gods were bothered by all the noise that they made
Ellil raised his voice to be heard, speaking to the high gods,
"The noise which is made by man has become too great,
All of this clamor and clatter has kept me from my sleep
Let it be that Anu and Adad shut the sky above their lands
Let it be that Sin and Nergal seal shut the middle region
And regarding the barrier which defines the limits of Ocean
It will be for Ea and his *lahmu*-men to assure it's kept closed[*]
So Anu and Adad went and shut the sky above their lands
Sin and Nergal assured that a seal secured the middle region
And regarding the barrier which defines the limits of Ocean,

---

[*] The word *lahmu* means 'muddy', describing the men who inhabit Apsu.

Ea and his *lahmu*-men assured that this too was kept closed
And that man of great wisdom, Atrahasis, cried every day
He would walk the riverside grass with an incense-offering
Even though there was not a murmur from the canal waters
Still, at midnight he dutifully made the sacrificial offering
And even as the lassitude of sleep was getting hold of him,
Still he spoke to the irrigation waters in the canal channels,
"May the irrigation waters carry it away, the river convey it,
Let this gift offering find its way to the feet of my lord, Ea
So that when Ea looks upon it that he will not forsake me!
So that when I sleep I might experience a portentous dream."
After this, and he'd conveyed his package upon the waters,
He sat down with his face to the river and began to weep,
And the man cried as he remained by the side of the river
There he wept while looking over the surface of the waters,
As his entreaty was making its way down into deep Apsu
And Ea heard what he had spoken, and having heeded him,
He called together his *lahmu*-men, addressing them thusly,
"Go and seek out the man who has sent this bequest to me
And when you find him, learn what plight has befallen him
Have him tell you everything which goes on in their lands."
So they journeyed across the magnificently broad oceans
Until they went the entire way to the Apsu water's shore
Conveying to Atrahasis the message they brought from Ea,
"Are you the weeping man who sent his plea into the Apsu?
Know that Ea has heard you and that we were sent by him."
And Atrahasis raised his voice, speaking to the *lahmu*-men,
"If it is true that Ea has heard me, then what did he receive?"
The *lahmu*-men raised their voices, speaking to Atrahasis,
"We know that even as you were being overcome by sleep,
The irrigation waters carried your gift, the river conveyed it,
And your offering found its way to the feet of your lord, Ea
So when Ea looked upon it he remembered you and sent us."
He lowered himself to the ground and kissed it before them
Then the *lahmu*-men went back across the waters of Ocean
Ea raised his voice to be heard, speaking to his officer Usmu,
"Go forth and seek out Atrahasis, and convey my decision:
That the state of your lands arises from the people's actions."
And thus Usmu, Ea's officer, raised his voice to Atrahasis,

"The state of your lands is the result of the people's actions
If there is no water to speak of and fields engender no longer,
This has come about because there is very little that I can do
If the gods have abandoned you this is why you are forsaken
The land is like a youth who has fallen down upon his face
And having fallen no longer gets succor from the sky's teats
The land has fallen like a fig which is lying upon the ground
The teats of heaven are closed up and are not given to stream
The waters of the Abyss below are dammed and will not flow
Thus from this have the dark plowed lands become blanched
From this the pastures lie fallow, unadorned by rising grain."
So from on high, no rain descended to fill the canal works
Below, subterranean waters no longer gushed from springs,
There was no delivery which sprung from the earth's womb
Nothing green took root and no plants grew into fruition
The folks no longer gazed over the bands of growing wheat
The black soil of the countryside had been blanched white
The landscape everywhere lay encrusted with a salty dust
For the first year they consumed any grain that was in store
For the next there was none left to take from the storerooms
In the third year they were showing the signs of starvation
So that their faces were a matrix of sores, like malted grain,
And they remained alive only by clinging urgently onto life
Their faces became sunken; they walked bent-over in public
Their shoulders, once steadfastly set, were now slouching
Their former bearing, once raised aloft, was now drooping
So they conveyed the message from Atrahasis to the gods
Setting the matter forth before the gathering of the high gods,
They convened, prepared to address the situation facing them
The words which had been sent by Atrahasis were conveyed
Setting the matter forth before the gathering of the high gods[50]

CHAPTER 5

The god Enki argued on man's behalf to each god: to Adad, and Nissaba, and to the Igigi, that the earth was becoming a desolation, so that they were persuaded to release the rains and allow the springs to stream. But when Ellil, who had planned for man's destruction, realized that the gods had let slacken their resolve, he became angered,

Ellil convened a congress, speaking to his children the gods,
"Adad caused his rain to pour down in buckets abundantly,
So streaming water was plentiful throughout the meadowland
Clouds were so numerous that they nearly blotted out the sky
They must not feed on Nissaba's grain, the comfort of man."
The god sat beset with nerves, troubled there in the congress,
Enki sat beset with nerves, and troubled there in the congress
The warrior Ellil was aware that this breach was done by Enki
And that the other gods had repealed what they had decided
And he was stomping mad from his elevated ire at the Igigi,
"Every one of us, of the great Anunna, consented to do this
The heavens were to be firmly secured by Anu and Adad,
While I was responsible for securing the earth down below,
And likewise, when Enki had arrived at his assigned place,
He was going to release the bonds and bring us liberation!
You were going to serve up an abundance unto the people!
You were supposed to take charge and manage the scales!"
Ellil raised his voice to be heard, saying to his officer Nusku
"Go and gather fifty of the *lahmu*-men here on my orders
Go and fetch them so they are standing here in front of me."
And so fifty *lahmu*-men were brought together on his orders,
Then the chief warrior, Ellil, spoke to the *lahmu*-men, saying,
"Every one of us, of the great Anunna, consented to do this
The heavens were to be firmly secured by Anu and Adad,
While I was responsible for securing the earth down below,
And likewise, when Enki had arrived at his assigned place,
He was going to release the bonds and bring us liberation!
You were going to serve up an abundance unto the people!
You were supposed to take charge and manage the scales!"

Ellil convened a congress, speaking to his children the gods,
"You are the ones who passed your burdens onto mankind
You are the ones who gave voice to man that he might speak
And you have slain a god altogether along with his mind
So you must do something about it and bring about a flood
You ought to utilize your power against your own people!
You have so far proceeded wrongly, thus do the opposite
We must give astute Enki an oath which he must swear to."
Enki raised his voice to be heard, saying to his fellow gods,
"Why on earth would you force me to swear to an oath?
Why too should I utilize my power against my own people?
And this great flood you speak of, what are you implying?
I'm confused by what you mean, is it even in my power?
Rather this sort of vandalism is something Ellil should do!
He himself should select the manner by which this happens
So that he will be the one who gets Adad to boom in the sky
With Shullat and Hanish walking ahead like chamberlains,
So Errakal will rip out every one of the pins from their bars,
While Nimrod will come on hard and breach every blockade
The Great Ones, the Anunnaki, will be required to bear torches
That they might illuminate the country with their radiant light
So when Adad comes all light will be swallowed into darkness
He will rear up and then go about trampling the terror-stricken
On the first day a tempest will rise, blowing in an awful fury,
Unleashing the dreaded Flood-weapon; and rage like a war
The explosive annihilation-weapon will descend over the people
Who will lose sight of one another in the sheets of pouring rain
Even the gods will be alarmed by the full force of their flood
They will retreat to the safety of the highest heaven of Anu
Where they will cower like dogs, kneeling by an outlying wall
There they will stay, brought to their knees, and crying tears,
Their lips will not utter and will be foaming over with spittle
Wind will rage six days and seven nights, the tempest prevail
And every man and woman will have been reduced to clay."
Then Ellil raised his voice, speaking to his children the gods,
"The words you heard Enki speak are of no significance to us,
You know the land is full, and how much they have multiplied
And how we have been so annoyed by all the noise they make
So that we cannot get any sleep from all their incessant clamor

You are the one who passed your burdens onto mankind
You are the one who gave voice to man that he might speak
And you have slain a god altogether along with his mind
So you must do something about it and bring about a flood
You ought to utilize your power against your own people!
You have so far proceeded wrongly, thus do the opposite."
And the congress decided in favor of the flood Ellil desired
Enki raised his voice to be heard, speaking to the high gods,
"This divine assembly has agreed to do something unfounded
You should not have listened to the justifications put forward
But you have made your commands strict and irrevocable,
And Ellil has achieved something horrendous for the people!"[51]

And from this decision of the gods is set into motion their actions which bring about the Great Flood upon humanity, which drowns out the entire globe and wipes out all life, but for Atrahasis and those with him aboard his craft.

Soleos: Thus the gods here deliberate as to the fate of man and make a judgement as to whether he ought to or ought not to survive. And as such, in this case, one of the gods appeals to the others concerning what they ought to do. And this could be compared to the case of Sodom and Gomorrah, if we imagine that the gods went down to save Lot, warning him of the imminent danger, while other gods remained nearby preparing for their destruction. Thus we might well regard the curious passages: "Then Yahweh rained upon Sodom and Gomorrah fire and brimstone, from Yahweh in heaven", then could be rendered to say "Then Ellil rained upon Sodom and Gomorrah fire and brimstone, from Shamash in heaven" which would make more sense.

Epitheus: Yes. And the conversation between Abraham and God is likewise the sort of plea bargaining, as between Atrahasis and Enki, which might have transpired between them, when it says,

So the men went from there and turned their eyes towards Sodom; and Abraham accompanied them to set them upon the correct path.

Then Yahweh said, "Should I conceal from Abraham what I am soon to do, since Abraham will become a great and powerful nation, so that all nations on earth will, through him, be blessed? For I have selected him and know that he will command his children and all his descendants to abide by the way of Yahweh through virtue and justice; so that Yahweh might bestow unto Abraham that which he spoke of to him."

And Yahweh said, "As the charges made against Sodom and Gomorrah are great and their misdeeds grave, I will travel down myself to determine whether or not they have done everything recounted in the charges which have come to my ears; but if not, then I will know better." And so the men turned around and went in the direction of Sodom, while Abraham remained standing by Yahweh.

Abraham then approached and asked, "Will you truly destroy the good with the evil? Considering there lived fifty virtuous men in the city, would you then wipe it out rather than spare it for the sake of the fifty virtuous men who were there? That is not a thing which you would do, to destroy the good with the evil, so that the good fare no better than the evil! You would not do such a thing! Wouldn't rather the Judge of the entire earth act rightly?"

And Yahweh replied, "If there were fifty virtuous men in the city, I would spare the entire place for them."

Abraham then observed, "See, I have determined myself to speak unto the Lord, when I am but dust and ashes. But then consider if there were five fewer than fifty, would you then wipe the entire city out for the lack of five?

And he replied, "I would not wipe it out if I found forty-five there."

He spoke to him again, saying, "Then consider if only forty were found there."

And he replied, "I would not do it for the sake of forty."

Then he said, "If the Lord will not be angered, I will speak yet again. Consider if only thirty were found there."

And he replied, "I would not do it for the sake of thirty."

Then he said, "See, I have determined myself to speak unto the Lord, but consider if only twenty were found there."

And he replied, "I would not wipe it out for the sake of twenty."

Then he said, "If the Lord will not be angered, I will speak but once more. Consider if only ten were found there."

And he replied, "I would not wipe it out for the sake of ten." Then Yahweh went on his way, after he was finished speaking to Abraham, and Abraham returned to his tent.[52]

Soleos: But so too, just as with Lot and his daughters, we end up with the very same problem after the Flood as at the beginning of time, which is that the wise man and his family are the only survivors and thus the dangers of incest again arise. And I know there is a story that addresses this told by the Benua-Jakun,[*]

They say that the ground is not altogether hard but is like a hide stretched over a vast watery abyss, and long ago the god Pirman punctured this hide so that the world would be plunged into and obliterated by a tremendous flood. Pirman had already created a man and woman and set them within a ship made of *pulai* wood, which had been entirely covered and sealed. Within this vessel the two of them bobbed and tossed for quite a while until they finally came aground. The man and woman clawed their way out through the seam and stepped out onto the dry earth. They witnessed the world we live in stretching off in every direction all the way to the horizon. Yet at this time everything was obscured in darkness because there was yet no morning or evening, as the sun had not yet been made. But when the dawn first broke forth there were revealed to them seven minute rhododendron bushes and seven clusters of *sambau* grass. And they spoke to one another, saying, "Alas, we are facing a sorry plight indeed, for we have neither children nor grandchildren!" Yet after some time the woman conceived through the calves of her legs, and there came from her right calf a male and from her left calf a female. It is for this reason that offspring from the same womb cannot marry. And every human being is descended from these two children of this very first couple.[53]

---

[*] A primitive aboriginal tribe of the Malay Peninsula in Johor

And thus here the problem is solved through the first two humans not emerging from the same womb, and thus they are not brother and sister, although there are still yet only two of them.

Epitheus: That is so, and although the story of Adam and Eve avoids incest by having them formed as separate beings rather than from the same parent, nevertheless their children could not avoid it. For although Eve is said to give birth to Cain and Abel and Seth, it is also said that marriage occurred with their sisters, when it says,

> On the first day of the fourth month Adam and his wife left the garden of Eden to live in the land of Elda, which was the place where they had been made. Adam called his wife Eve, but they hadn't a son before the first Jubilee; it was afterwards that he had intercourse with her. And he worked the soil, which he had learned to do in the garden of Eden.
>
> Then in the third Week of the second Jubilee,[*] Eve gave birth to Cain; and in the fourth Week she gave birth to Abel. And in the fifth Week she gave birth to Awan, Adam's daughter.[†] But it was at the commencement of the third Jubilee that Cain slew Abel due to the approval of Abel's offering, while Cain's own offering was rejected. He slew him within the fields, where his blood gave a cry from the earth to heaven, accusing him because Cain had killed him. And Yahweh punished Cain because of Abel, since he was the one who killed him, making him a wanderer upon earth due to Abel's blood being spilt. So he was then as one cursed upon the earth. Thus it is written upon the holy tablets, "He who strikes another man in spite will be cursed, and this will be pronounced by those who witness it. While the man who fails to disclose it after having witnessed it will be cursed along with him."[‡] Thus in setting ourselves before Yahweh, our God, we must tell him every evil which is done from the sky to the earth and which are done in the light of day or in the dark of night, or wherever they occur.

---

[*] Each Jubilee is comprised of seven 'weeks of years' or here "Weeks", each being a period of seven years.

[†] Also called Noaba or Leboda (Pseudo-Philo 1.1; see Charlesworth 2009 Vol. 2: 304)

[‡] Deuteronomy 27:24

Adam and his wife mourned for four Weeks of Years (four-times seven years) for Abel. Then upon the fifth year, in the fourth Week, they again became joyous; and Adam once more had intercourse with his wife and she gave birth to his son, which he named Seth, saying, "Yahweh has brought to us another beginning on earth, to take the place of Abel because Cain killed him." In the sixth Week Adam fathered Azura, his daughter. Then Cain took Awan his sister as a wife, and she gave birth to Enoch at the close of the fourth Jubilee; while in the first year of the first Week of the fifth Jubilee, then houses were built upon the land. And Cain established a city which he called Enoch after his son. Then Adam had intercourse with Eve, his wife, and she gave birth to nine more children.

In the fifth Week of the fifth Jubilee, Seth took Azura, his sister as a wife. In the fourth year of that Week she gave birth to his son Enos. Seth was the first one to speak the name of Yahweh upon earth.[*] In the third Week of the seventh Jubilee, Enos took Noam, his sister as a wife, and she gave birth to his son in the third year of the fifth Week, and his name was Kenan. At the close of the eighth Jubilee, Kenan took Mualeth, his sister as a wife, and she gave birth to his son in the third year of the first Week of the ninth Jubilee, and he was called Mahalalel. And in the second Week of the tenth Jubilee, Mahalalel took Dinah, his cousin, who was the daughter of Barakiel, as a wife. And in the sixth year of the third Week she gave birth to his son, and he named him Jared, for at that time the angels of Yahweh, called Watchers, had descended to earth so as to instruct the sons of men to do what was just and upright upon the earth.[54]

So here we find the very circumstance which is here unavoidable; that Cain and Seth and some of their immediate descendants likewise marry their sisters.[†]

Soleos: Yes. And I cannot help but think that this is meaningful in terms of identifying the nature of Cain himself.

---

[*] Genesis 4:26: A son was likewise born to Seth, and he named him Enosh. It was then that men began to proclaim the name of YHWH.
[†] Josephus likewise mentions the existence of daughters of Adam and Eve. (*The Antiquities of the Jews* 1.2.1 § 52)

Epitheus: But what do you mean?

Soleos: I mean that when Cain was sent away from God's presence, he is said to have had a mark put upon him, when it says,

> So Yahweh made a mark upon Cain, in the event someone might happen upon him and wish to kill him. Then he went forth from the location of Yahweh to live in the land of Nod, which lay to the east of Eden.[55]

And so precisely what are we to make of this reference to the mark upon Cain?

Epitheus: I am not sure. We do know at least that it follows the slaying of his brother, Abel.

Soleos: But from this we also might recognize something quite peculiar, for does not God say,

> "But what is it you have done, Cain? For your brother's blood is crying out to me from the very ground, thus shall your punishment be from the ground; for by your hand you have fed your brother's blood into the earth's open mouth. This wound of the ground will be a wound unto you, for when you now till the earth it will no longer give you its bounty as it has done before. And you will no longer live a settled life but will become like a vagabond upon the earth."[56]

And does this not remind us of the prior commentary which says,

> "Because you believed what your wife told you and ate from the tree from which I said you must not eat, the ground will be cursed for you and only from hard labor shall you eat of the ground for all the days of your life; briers and bramble it will provide and you will eat from among the plants of the field. Only by the sweat of your brow will you eat your bread, until you return to the ground out of which you were made, for you are dust and to the dust you will return."[57]

75

Epitheus: It does, certainly.

Soleos: Thus we must regard that each of these explains, in its own way, precisely why the labors of man are difficult; but more precisely, that these both constitute variants of the same story concerning the origin of man.

Epitheus: I see what you mean. And just as you say, that they went out from the garden of Eden to dwell in Elda, so here too Cain is claiming that once he travels beyond the protection of Yahweh he will be made vulnerable to attacks from others. So that when he leaves he might no longer anticipate that his endeavors will be free from trouble, which is precisely the problem faced in their banishment from the garden.

Soleos: Just so. But then too he is said to move to a land which is 'east of Eden', suggesting that he has set out on his journey from Eden. And, likewise, that he was under Yahweh's protection before his banishment, for Cain tells Yahweh that he cannot bear leaving the land.

Epitheus: Yes.

Soleos: So those who might kill him we could presume here to be the beasts of the wilderness, and thus the mark that was upon him provides the motive which causes wild beasts to flee in fear from man. And we find this very thing actually said of Cain, when it says,

> Yet he became fearful, that in wandering here and there that he should come to be surrounded by savage beasts, and from this might meet his end. So God encouraged him not to feel such forebodings of doom, but rather that he might travel over the entire earth without fear of what harm might come his way among the savage beasts and, putting a mark upon him that he might be recognized, bade him to go on his way.[58]

Epitheus: A similar situation surely occurs regarding Noah and his sons, where it says that every beast upon the earth will be alarmed by you and frightened by you?* And there is a similar situation in the case of Adam, when God is delivering his sentence, that the animals he had formerly controlled would become wild and uncontrollable, because of his transgression.[59]

Soleos: Very good, Epitheus. Though there is something further we might consider, for the mark of Cain has sometimes been interpreted to be a manifestation of skin disease. And we find that the (Mesopotamian) god of the moon, Sin, was also a god of skin disease.†

Epitheus: So are you suggesting the skin disease are the spots visible upon the moon?

Soleos: Quite so. And Sin, whose name also is identical to a breach of morality (sin), might have been accused of some similar crime. But the association of the moon with the spots upon his face also makes him an ideal candidate for a god of skin disease.

Epitheus: Yes. And likewise all were said to have wept during the sin of Adam but the moon, when it says,

> And it is precisely related how the moon was guilty of sin, at the time of the transgression of Adam; that when he heeded the words of Satan, who had taken the form of a serpent, because the moon was not shameful but rather she shone even more brightly (waxing), that this made God angry to the extent that he made visible her diminishment (waning).[60]

Soleos: Precisely so. And this thus relates back to what we were speaking of before, in relation to the incest of Cain with his sister; for this appears likewise in the encounter when the moon goes to visit his sister the sun in her bedroom night after night. And then, so as to identify her nocturnal visitor, she covers her hands with black

---

* Genesis 9:2
† A fragment of Alcaman (5) gives the name of the moon as Melana, which seems to provide the origin of the word *melanin*, the pigment in human skin, meaning 'dark'. Dionysos was also known as Melanaigis ('black goat-skin').

ashes so that when he comes to her that night she touches his face all over with her blackened fingers. Then upon the following morning she thereby discovers that her ravisher was her own brother. And thus the moon wears forever the mark of his sin, while he yet chases after his sister, the sun, as they course through the sky.[*]

Thaeo: And the goat-god Pan likewise claims that he kissed Luna, the moon goddess, and was thus responsible for the spots to be seen upon her face.[61]

Epitheus: And this too could explain why Cain is described as being 'shiny and bright'.[62]

Thaeo: But it seems that if we can associate Cain with the moon god Sin, we also might Abel with the sun god Bel. Certainly their story is somewhat like the Chaldean story of Belus, who divided the heaven from the earth and then had himself beheaded, having his blood then mixed with earth to produce mankind.[63] In the same way it could have been Cain originally slew his brother so as to create the earth from his body, with the blood of Abel having caused the red earth, and likewise that from his death came the product of pitiful humanity, prone themselves to mortality.[†]

Soleos: Just so, and the identification of Cain and Abel with Sin and Bel would also make them like the brothers Hod and Balder. And Nanna in the death of Balder may have filled the very same role as Awan does with Cain and Abel, so that she was the wife of whichever one emerged victorious, as the two alternated during the

---

[*] This is a myth of the Inuit Indian tribe concerning Malina and Anninga (Harley 1970: 34; Krupp 1991: 60), the Algonquin tribe (Harley 1970: 56-57), and the Caddo Indian tribe. A myth from New Guinea has the moon kept in a jar by an old woman. Some boys come to release the moon and take it with them but cannot and the moon goes free, but they leave their dirty fingerprints upon it from their attempts to catch it.

[†] Bloodshed is said to have existed plentifully at the beginning of the world according to 'The Apocalypse of Daniel' 4:6. (see Charlesworth 2009, Vol. 1: 765)

year.[*] Also these same two brothers go by Herebeald and Haethcyn,[†] where it is said that Herebeald is slain by an arrow released from Haethcyn's horn-tipped bow, and that he paid for the deed with his life.[64] And his bow too could associate Haethcyn with the moon.

Phaedo: Yes. And as far as mankind having descended from them this is certainly true, not only from reference you made to the 'daughters of Cain' being the mothers of the Nephilim,[‡] but likewise concerning what is said of the two sons of Cronos called Belos and Canaan.

> Abraham was living in Heliopolis where too resided the Egyptian priests, and he taught them a good deal. He spoke with great understanding to them concerning astrology and the other sciences, telling them that either it was the Babylonians or else he himself who had acquired this knowledge. But as for who made the initial discovery of it, this he credited to Enoch, for it was Enoch rather than the Egyptians who first became aware of astrology. Among the Babylonians they say that it was a son of Cronos, named Belos, who was the first man alive, for Cronos had given rise to two sons named Belos and Canaan. Canaan became father to the ancestor of the Phoenician people. His son was named Chus, known to the Greeks as Asbolus, and Chus became ancestor of the Ethiopians; and he was the brother of Mitsraim, who is ancestor to the Egyptians. And though the Greeks claim that Atlas is the discoverer of astrology, Atlas and Enoch are one and the same.[65]

Epitheus: So too they are like Jacob and Esau who both provide offerings to their father Isaac. And in that case a blessing is conferred upon the one who will rule over the other which likewise gives Esau the desire to slay his brother. And we must consider that

---

[*] See *The Eden Enigma: A Dialogue*. The Norse goddess Nanna could be related to Nana, the Sumerian goddess of the Evening Star who like Ishtar was called the 'Mistress of Heaven'.

[†] There even might be a remote connection with the Mayan brothers Xbalanque and Hanahpu, where each are likewise associated with the sun and moon.

[‡] 'The Testament of Adam' 3.5 (see Charlesworth 2009, Vol. 1: 994), *supra*

this provoked them into a contest which occurred when Jacob is said to have wrestled with God, but who was indeed his own brother.[*]

Soleos: And we might guess that this too is akin to the situation of the farmer and herder who are attempting to win the favor of Inanna, which we have spoken of before.[†] So these two brothers (Cain and Abel) could likewise have been seeking the favor of their sister (Awan) such that one of them created the plants of the earth and the other the animals of the earth, but that she judged the animals a better gift than the plants and thus Cain out of envy killed his brother and was then made to suffer banishment for his crime and become a nomad upon the earth.

Epitheus: So it would appear, for it is said that the contention between Cain and Abel arose because they both desired to have their only sister.[‡] And we might regard in this case that the fall of man was not due to the eating of the fruit, as in the Eden story, but was caused by the fratricide when Cain killed his brother and took his sister.

Thaeo: And there is no shortage too of stories where the initial pair are forced into incest for the sake of commencing the human line, and that these are sometimes the very pair who, like Noah, escaped the great deluge; as in the case of Deucalion, whose wife was also his sister.[66]

Phaedo: But likewise it is more often than not that wicked practices are what bring about this very calamity upon the world. And among the tribes of India it is told that after people were created from the dust that they immediately became incestuous and disregarded their creator Sing Bonga. Thus Sing Bonga was sorry that he had made man and set about to destroy them by a flood and fiery rain from out of heaven. This destroyed all but two, a brother and sister who took refuge beneath a tree. Then God repented and brought an end to the fiery rain by conjuring up the rainbow-serpent Lurbing, who raised himself up and, in so doing, held back the rains.[67]

---

[*] See *The Death of King David: A Dialogue*
[†] See *The Eden Enigma: A Dialogue*
[‡] 'The Testament of Adam' 3.5 (see Charlesworth 2009, Vol. 1: 994)

Soleos: But then we could presume that the Cain and Abel story, as we know it, must really be a combination of two stories, or two versions of the same story: that of the first men and that of the sun and moon. So that in the first the mark is put upon Cain so as to protect him from being killed by the wild animals, where he then goes on to become a father of humankind; whereas in the other the marks are put upon his face and are to be seen upon the moon. And it would seem that the similarity of these two stories led to their eventual confusion and combination into a single story.

Epitheus: Truly. But these marks we have associated too with the spots he gains from the incest he committed with his sister, which thus must have occurred subsequent to his having slain Abel, and by which Cain would have become a father of mankind. And thus it seems to me that these two might be reconciled if we were to consider that both the first man and the progenitor of mankind were both the moon. And this is essentially the same as the first man Manu or Heimdall being a divinity who is also the moon.

Man with sticks on his back, seen upon the moon, and typically viewed as a punishment for working on a Sunday.

Soleos: Perfectly put, Epitheus, but so too it is said that the figure upon the moon is that of Cain carrying the bramble which was viewed by God to be his worthless gift from the fields.[*] Likewise, it is seen as the shape of Isaac bearing upon his back the sticks for his own sacrifice upon Mount Moriah.[†] Thus we might have cause to consider an original folk tale where Abraham went willingly to sacrifice his son Isaac, but that at the last moment his son was swept away by God and placed upon the moon, where he can still be seen carrying the wood upon his back;[‡] after which a ram was sacrificed in his place.[§] And that the Hebrews were aware of this story is clearly demonstrated in the following tale,

> When the people of Israel were out in the wilderness, they discovered a man who was collecting sticks upon the Sabbath day. Those who had found him collecting sticks brought him before Moses and Aaron and the entire congregation. So they held him, because they were not yet sure what ought to be done with him. And Yahweh said to Moses, "This man must be put to death, and the entire congregation must stone him with stones at a place beyond the camp." Thus the entire congregation took him beyond the camp and stoned him to death with stones, as Yahweh had commanded Moses to do.[68]

And the man who collects sticks upon the Sabbath day is the one who is said to be seen upon the moon, and placed there by God as a punishment for his transgression.

---

[*] But tell me please, where come the dark spots
Which cover his body, which seen upon earth
Do cause men to speak of Cain in old fables?
(Dante, *Divine Comedy*, Paradise ii, 50)
[†] Philo of Byblus in his work on the Jews says:
"It was an ancient custom in a crisis of great danger that the ruler of a city or nation should give his beloved son to die for the whole people, as a ransom offered to the avenging demons; and the children thus offered were slain with mystic rites. So Cronos, whom the Phoenicians call Israel, being king of the land and having an only-begotten son called Jeoud (for in the Phoenician language Jeoud signifies "only-begotten"), dressed him in royal robes and sacrificed him upon an altar in time of war, when the country was in severe danger from the enemy." (Frazer 1998: 265)
[‡] This very same self-sacrifice is attributed to the hare seen upon the moon.
[§] Compare this with the story Athamas' offering of Phrixos and the sacrifice of the ram.

Thaeo: Yes, and thus we have established again that the two brothers are the sun and the moon, where we might regard their sister as representative of the heavens and the earth, and that their fight pertains to which of them will rule over her during the year. As likewise in the contest between Gwythyr and Gwynn, where the two of them fought every May Day, with the victor gaining the hand of Creiddylad, daughter of Lludd Silver Hand, who waited for the outcome secure within her father's house.[69]

CHAPTER 6

Epitheus: We already know that Jacob was associated with the moon, and likewise we considered too Esau to be the sun.[*] And these competing brothers are also similar to Abraham and Lot, and so too did we identify Abraham with the moon,[†] and Lot his brother could likewise be the sun. For just like Abraham and Lot, Esau also moved to a land beyond the Jordan, and in both cases because the property of each was too great for them to live on the same side of the Jordan. When it says,

> Lot likewise, who was travelling with Abram, possessed flocks, herds, and tents. But the land was not able to support them both if they continued to have nearby habitations, for their possessions were numerous, and thus they were unable to continue living near one another. And there grew conflict between Abram's cattle herders and Lot's cattle herders, so Abram said to Lot, "There shouldn't be any conflict between you and me, and between my herdsmen and your herdsmen, because we are brothers. But is not there an entire country within your range? Therefore you ought to part from me, so that were you to take what is to the left then I would go to the right; or if you were to take what is to the right, then I would go to the left."[70]

And likewise,

> Then Esau gathered together his wives, his sons and daughters, and everyone else from his household; along with his cattle, all his other animals, and every thing he owned that he had acquired within Canaan; and he went into those lands, away from the sight of Jacob, his brother. What they possessed was too large for them to live near to one another, because the land where they were could not have provided adequately owing to their cattle. So Esau came to dwell in the highlands of Seir, and Esau is the same as Edom.[71]

---

[*] See *The Death of King David: A Dialogue*
[†] See *Roar of the Tempests: A Dialogue*

84

Phaedo: Quite so. But regarding the battle of brothers over their sister, strangely too Jacob fights his adversary at night, who is dispelled by the sunrise. And the Egyptian Set was to have defeated Aphoph when the sun sank into the underworld, when Set represented the sun going into the abyss. But when Set represented the underworld he himself became the serpent attacking the sun. And thus these too likewise represent a cosmic conflict, where the battle of the brothers Horus and Set represents the conflict between heavenly light and abysmal darkness, which is no doubt one which is related to the conflict between Jacob and Esau. And this conflict between Horus and Set is told in a tale called the 'Conflict of Horus and Set', if you would like to hear it.

Epitheus: Certainly.

Phaedo: Thus the story goes:

> It happened once that there was a verdict to be made between Horus and Set. The young god (Horus) was seated before Almighty God (Re) to petition for the position of his father Osiris, while at the same time Thoth was passing the Whole Eye (*wedjat*)[*] to the lofty ruler of Heliopolis (Atum).[†] And Shu, the son of Re, speaking to the lofty ruler of Heliopolis, said, "The high seat is one of kingly authority, so when you make your declaration speak these words: 'The office goes to Horus'."
>
> Thoth said to all the Ennead, "That is unquestionably right."[‡]
>
> With this Isis gave out a great cry of inexpressible joy, and spoke in the presence of Almighty God, saying, "Fly to the west, North Wind, and carry with you this good news to Osiris."
>
> Then Shu, the son of Re, said, "He who bestows the Whole Eye expresses the Ennead's wishes."
>
> And Almighty God uttered, "Yes, but what do you mean by making this decision yourselves?"

---

[*] The 'Whole Eye' is called the *wedjat*, being the eye taken by Set and then healed by Thoth, and symbolic of the power of the sun.

[†] Heliopolis was the holy city of Re, the Egyptian sun god.

[‡] The specific definition of Ennead consisted of nine deities: Shu and Tefnut, Geb and Nut, Osiris and Isis, Seth and Nephthys, and Atum.

Onuris replied, "He will receive the Cartouche of Horus and will have the White Crown set upon his head."[*]

Almighty God kept quiet for a long while, fuming at the Ennead until Set, the son of Nut, spoke, "Let him and me be sent out and you will see me outfight him before the Ennead, for there remains no other means to divest him."

Then Thoth said, "Ought we not rather see here a pretender, for is it to be that when Osiris's son Horus yet lives that his position will be given to Set?"

At this Re-Harakhti became enraged, for Re's thoughts were that the position ought to be awarded to Set, the son of Nut.[†] Then Onuris let out an anguished cry before all of the Ennead, saying, "What are we to do?"

Atum, the great ruler of Heliopolis, said, "Let us summon Baneb-djede,[‡] the great Living God, so that he might pronounce his judgement concerning these two young men."

So Baneb-djede and Ptah came before Atum, who then disclosed to them, "You must pronounce your judgement concerning these two young men so that they might not remain in perpetual conflict."

Baneb-djede replied, saying, "We ought not exert our power without prudence, but rather let us send a letter to Great Neith,[§] mother of gods, and whatever she declares we will do."

And the Ennead answered Baneb-djede, saying, "This will be the first time they are judged in 'Truth is Supreme' court."

So the Ennead spoke to Thoth before Almighty God, saying, "Would you be so good as to write a letter to Great Neith, mother of gods, in the name of Almighty God?"

Thoth replied to them, saying, "Of course I will do so. I will do so, gladly." So he sat down and wrote out the letter, which read: "Re-Atum, your servant begs you to inform us what we ought to do concerning these two young men who have stood

---

[*] Onuris is Anhuret or Anhur, the god who returned to Re the 'sun eye'.

[†] Re was obliged to Set for warding off demons as he made his passage through the sky.

[‡] Banebdjedet is a ram-headed god whose cult center was in Djedet (Mendes).

[§] Neith is a goddess of war and hunting, whose holy city was Sais

before this court for eighty years,[*] but where there has yet come about no resolution. Please advise us as to what our proper course ought to be."

Thus Great Neith, mother of gods, conveyed her reply to the Ennead, which stated, "Give the position of Osiris to his son Horus. Do not commit a breach, which would be impermissible, for my rage would grow so great that the sky would collapse to the earth. Then convey to Almighty God that he ought to bestow great gifts unto Set, and give him Anath and Astarte,[†] his two daughters, in marriage; but inaugurate Horus into the position formerly held by his father, Osiris.

Thus the letter of Great Neith, mother of gods, was delivered to the Ennead where they were gathered together in 'Horus with High Horns' court, and the piece of correspondence was placed in the hand of Thoth. Thoth read it aloud before Almighty God and all of the Ennead, then they made a unanimous pronouncement, declaring, "The goddess is correct."

But Almighty God became angered at Horus, saying, "You are yet of an immature character, and thus the position is not suited to you, a mere boy, the odor of whose mouth is yet tainted."

At this Onuris grew supremely enraged, as did the rest of the Ennead, including the Congress of the Thirty. And divine Bebon stood up and addressed Re-Harakhti, saying, "Your temple is forsaken!"[‡]

Re-Harakhti was greatly unsettled by this slam directed at him, and he lay himself down upon his back in severe distress. Thus, after the Ennead exited, they cast harsh invectives at divine Bebon, saying, "Be off with you, for what you did is contemptible."

Thus each one left for his own dwelling, while Almighty God spent twenty-four hours reclining upon his back within his enclosure, depressed and entirely without company.

After some time the goddess Hathor arrived and came before Almighty God, her father, and lifted up the hem of her skirt to expose her privates before him. Almighty God was made to

---

[*] 5 × 80 = 400
[†] Anat and Astarte are Canaanite goddesses.
[‡] Bebon or Baba is a demon who is sometimes identified with Set

laugh in return, and he then rose up and again took his seat amongst the Great Ennead. He addressed Horus and Set, saying, "Relate to me something concerning you."

Set, the son of Nut, was the first to speak, saying, "As for me, Set is my name and I enjoy the highest potency of anyone among the Ennead, for each day I slay Re's adversary while standing upon the Bark of Infinity,* and no other god has the fortitude to accomplish this task. Thus I ought to be given the position which was formerly held by Osiris."

And they responded, saying, "Set, the son of Nut, has spoken truly."

Then Onuris and Thoth protested vociferously, saying, "Since when has an office been given to the maternal uncle when a legitimate son yet lives?"

To this Baneb-djede retorted, "Since when has an office been given to an immature boy when Set, his elder brother,† yet lives?"

The Ennead gave a passionate outcry in the presence of Almighty God, saying, "What is the value of your words when they are not even worthy enough to be heard?"

Then Horus, the son of Isis, said, "This is wrong, cheating me and denying me the position of Osiris, my father, here before the Ennead."

At which point Isis grew livid at the Ennead and swore an oath by God before them, being, "By the goddess Neith, my mother, and by high-plumed Ptah; such things ought to be judged by Atum, the lofty ruler of Heliopolis, and likewise Khepri, living upon his bark."

Then the Ennead replied to her, "There is no reason for you to become upset, the judgement will fall to the one who is most deserving, and thus all that concerns you will be duly addressed."

Thereupon Set, the son of Nut, grew in anger towards the Ennead, after they had declared this to Great Isis, mother of gods; thus he spoke to them, saying, "With my club of 4,500 *nemset*-weight will I slay one of you each day!" Then he swore before

---

* The 'adversary' is the snake Apep who attacks Re. The 'Bark of Infinity' is the boat of Re during the day, called the Manjet boat. The boat of his night journey is called the Mesket boat.
† Set is the elder brother of Horus and the maternal uncle (brother of Isis), paternal uncle (brother of Osiris) of Horus the Child (Harpocrates).

Almighty God, saying, "I refuse to attend this law court as long as Isis is present."

And Re-Harakhti spoke to them, saying, "We will convey ourselves across to Central Island and there choose between them. But warn the ferryman Nemty not to convey across any woman who looks at all like Isis."[*]

Thus the Ennead were conveyed over to Central Island and seated themselves and there consumed their bread. Isis also went and approached the ferryman Nemty while he was lounging there beside his craft, but only after she had metamorphosed herself into the appearance of an elderly woman with a shambling gait, who wore a slim golden ring upon her finger. She spoke to him, saying, "It is the proper thing to do to voyage over to Central Island and provide me passage there, for I have brought this bowl of porridge for a young boy who has been tending a cattle herd upon that island for fully five days and by now he is surely very hungry."

He replied to her, "But I have been given orders to refuse any woman conveyance to that place."

To this she said, "Only in regards to Isis have you been told to do as you have said."

Then he said to her, "And what might you offer me to gain your passage to Central Island?"

And Isis answered, "I'll give you this cake."

He said in response, "What good would your cake be to me? Should I receive a cake for your passage over to Central Island when I was given explicit orders to convey no woman?"

So she said to him, "Then I will let you have this gold ring, here on my finger."

And he said, "Then give me the gold ring."

So she handed it over to him and he, in turn, ferried her across to Central Island. And as she made her way beneath the trees there, she looked out and saw the Ennead sitting there and consuming their bread before Almighty God within his enclosure. After she had gone most of the distance and was approaching closer, Set looked up and first noticed her. But she had worked a

---

[*] Nemty is an Egyptian war god and associated with the falcon and Horus.

89

spell so as to metamorphose herself into the shape of a lovely teen of unrivaled beauty, and thus he was driven by a lustful desire to have her at once. Quickly he rose from his place, where he had been consuming bread with the Great Ennead, and went to catch up with her; while none of the others had even seen her, but only he had. Calling out to her from behind a sycamore he said, "I'm near you, lovely girl."

She turned and replied, "Show discretion, gracious lord, for concerning myself I was wife to a cattle herder to whom I gave a son. Then my husband died and the boy started to manage his father's cattle herds. But after this a visitor came who took up residence in my barn, and said this to my son when he spoke to him, 'I will smite you and take all your father's cattle herds, then I will expel you.' So now I would like for you to give him your protection."

On hearing this Set spoke to her, saying, "Since when are the cattle given to a visitor when the son of the father is yet alive? Rather this stranger's face should be struck with a stick, and he ought to be expelled so that your son might take his father's position."

With that Isis metamorphosed herself into a kite and soared aloft to perch upon the top branch of an acacia tree. Then she called out to Set, saying, "You ought to be ashamed of yourself, for you have said so with your own mouth. It is your own keen reasoning which has been your own judge, so what do you have to say now?"

And he was shamed and after this walked into the presence of Re-Harakhti, very much embarrassed, and Re-Harakhti asked him, "Why are you so perturbed?"

Set said to him, "It was that vile woman who has beset me yet again, for she tricked me by metamorphosing herself into a lovely teen girl before me. And she spoke to me, saying, 'Concerning myself I was wife to a cattle herder to whom I gave a son. Then my husband died and the boy started to manage his father's cattle herds. But after this a visitor came who took up residence in my barn, and said this to my son when he spoke to him, "I will smite you and take all your father's cattle herds, then I will expel you."' Thus is what she said to me."

And Re-Harakhti asked him, "What did you say in reply?"

Set answered him, saying, "I replied thus to her, 'Since when are the cattle given to a visitor when the son of the father is yet alive?' And then I said to her, 'Rather this stranger's face should be struck with a stick, and he ought to be expelled so that your son might take his father's position.' These are the words I spoke to her."

Following this admission Re-Harakhti said to him, "Behold, you have judged yourself by your own words, what could you possibly say now in your defense?"

Then Set replied to him, saying, "Summon the ferryman Nemty and have him suffer severe reprisals, saying to him, 'Why did you agree to convey her over?' This is what ought to be spoken to him."

So the ferryman Nemty was summoned and led before the Ennead, and the fronts of both his feet were cleaved away.* Then the Ennead were ferried over to the western lands and took their places upon the mountain.

In the evening Re-Harakhti and Atum conveyed a message to the Ennead, stating, "Why do you remain here still? Concerning your two young men, they will spend the rest of their lives in the courts of law! But when my letter arrives, you shall set the White Crown upon the head of Horus, the son of Isis, and bestow unto him the position of Osiris, his father."

But with this Set grew enraged, so that the Ennead spoke to him, "For what reason do you become so enraged? For is this not done according to the command of Atum and Re-Harakhti?"

So the White Crown was placed upon the head of Horus, son of Isis, while Set, still greatly incensed, shouted vehemently in front of all of the Ennead, saying, "Is this office to be given to my younger brother when I, the elder brother, am yet alive?" And he swore an oath, saying, "The White Crown shall be taken from off the head of Horus, the son of Isis, that he might be thrown into the water that I may do battle with him for the position of Pharaoh." And Re-Harakhti agreed to this.

Then Set spoke to Horus, saying, "Let us go and metamorphose ourselves into hippos and plunge in the deep

---

* The original adds as an aside: And thus has Nemty refused to take gold even to this day when before the Great Ennead, saying, "Due to my actions gold shall remain a hated thing within my city."

waters in the very middle of the sea. But as for him who does not emerge after three whole months, the position will not be his." Thus they both jumped into the water.

Isis sat herself down and cried, saying, "Set will murder my son, Horus." And she collected together a bundle of yarn and from this wove a cord; then collected a *deben*-weight of copper and had it molded into a harpoon barb. Tying the cord to this she threw it into the water at the very location where Horus and Set had submerged. But it was Horus who felt the bite of the copper barb, so that he cried out in a loud voice, saying, "Help me Isis, help me my mother, and plead with your copper harpoon to release me, for am I not Horus, the son of Isis?"

After this Isis shouted greatly, beseeching her copper harpoon, "Release him, for is he not my son Horus! He is my own child!" And thus the copper harpoon released him.

Then she threw it again into the water and it was Set who felt its bite. So Set cried out in a loud voice, saying, "What have I ever done to you, my sister Isis? Plead with your copper harpoon to release me, for am I not the brother of Isis?" And she felt a great tenderness for him, and Set called out to her, "Would you choose a stranger over your own brother Set?" And so Isis beseeched the copper harpoon, saying, "Release him, for is it not my own brother you have bitten?" And the copper harpoon released him.

Then Horus, the son of Isis, was enraged at his mother Isis and strode forth displaying a visage as terrible as an Upper Egyptian panther, carrying his axe weighing 16 *deben*. And he struck off the head of his mother Isis and, taking it up in his arms, climbed up the side of the mountain. Then Isis metamorphosed herself into the shape of a stone statue lacking a head.

Then Re-Harakhti said to Thoth, "What has just arrived here bearing no head?"

And Thoth replied to Re-Harakhti, "My noble lord, that is Great Isis, mother of gods, as she appears now that her son Horus has struck off her head."

Thus Re-Harakhti gave out a thunderous command to the Ennead, saying, "We must go out and exact a harsh retribution upon him." So the Ennead climbed up those same mountains that they might reach Horus, the son of Isis. But Horus had lain himself down beneath a *shenusha*-tree at the oasis, and there Set found him and grabbed him, pushing him down on his back upon the mountain. He then tore Horus's two eyes out of their sockets and planted them upon the mountain so that they might provide light to the earth. His two eye-balls were transformed into two bulbs, each of which grew into a lotus flower. Then Set went off and when he spoke to Re-Harakhti he lied, saying, "I wasn't able to find Horus," although he had found him.

Then the goddess Hathor went forth and she found Horus fallen in the desert upon his back and in great misery. So she caught a gazelle and milked it, saying to him, "Open your eyes so that I can sprinkle this milk into them." So he opened his eyes and she sprinkled the milk into them, making sure that she put some into his right eye and some into his left eye. Then she said to him, "Now open both your eyes." And he opened both his eyes, and when he looked at them he could see that they were both healed.

Then she went forth to Re-Harakhti, saying, "I found Horus after Set had torn out his eyes, but I rejuvenated him. Do you not see that he has returned?"

Then the Ennead made a declaration, saying, "Let us summon both Horus and Set so that they might receive their judgement."

So having been brought before the Ennead, Almighty God spoke to Horus and Set, saying, "You will go out again but must do as I command. You must eat and drink together so that we might enjoy peace, and end your interminable quarreling."

Set then said to Horus, "Come with me, and we shall have a celebration at my house."

Horus replied to him, "I agree, certainly, I agree."

Then following this, in the evening, a bed was made for them and they both lay down to sleep. But during the night Set stimulated his phallus to erection and then forced it between Horus's thighs. Horus put his hands between his thighs and in so doing got a handful of Set's semen. Horus then went out to relate this to his mother Isis, saying, "Give me help Isis, my mother, look at what Set did to me." And he opened up his hands and showed her Set's semen. She let out a cry, grabbed a copper blade, and severed off his two hands, which were both in the same condition. Then she went and got some perfumed oil and spread it over Horus's phallus so that it became erect, and then shoved this into a jar so that he emitted his semen down into it.

Then in the morning Isis took Horus's semen into Set's garden and asked his gardener, "What kind of plant does Set eat when you're around?"

And the gardener answered her, "He eats none of the vegetables here when I'm around, except for the lettuce plant."[*]

So Isis went and infused this with Horus's semen. So when Set came back, as was his daily routine, and consumed the lettuce plant, being his usual thing to eat. By doing so he became impregnated with Horus's semen. Then Set went and told Horus, "Come with me, that I might challenge you in the law courts."

Horus replied to him, "I agree, certainly, I agree."

So they both made their way to the law court and took their place before the Great Ennead, and were told, "Relate matters concerning you."

Set spoke, saying, "I should be given the position of Pharaoh, for regarding Horus, who is the one being judged, I have done the business of men to him."

The Ennead let out a gasp of astonishment, and they struck at and spit in Horus's face. But Horus merely laughed at them, and took an oath by God, saying, "Everything that Set has spoken is false. Have Set's semen called forth that we might see from whence it comes, and then my own be called forth that we might see from whence it comes."

So Thoth placed his hand upon Horus's shoulder and spoke, "Come forth semen of Set." And its reply came from the waters in the very heart of the bog. Then Thoth placed his hand upon Set's shoulder and spoke, "Come forth semen of Horus."

And it answered him, "How do you wish me to emerge?"

To this Thoth replied, "Out from his ear."

Then it asked him, "Are you sure it is the ear I must emerge from, given that I am divine seed?"

To this Thoth answered, "Then emerge from out of the crown of his head."

---

[*] Lettuce was taken to have aphrodisiac properties, and was associated with the fertility god Min

94

Thus it came forth in the shape of a golden sun-disk atop Set's head, and Set became greatly angered and reached his hands up to grab the golden sun-disk. But Thoth took it from him and set it as a halo upon his own head. Then the Ennead declared, "Horus is vindicated, while Set is proved wrong."

Thus Set grew greatly enraged and gave out a loud scream at the utterance that 'Horus is vindicated while Set is proven wrong.' Thus Set swore a formidable oath by God, saying, "He will not be given this position until he and I go outside and each construct a ship out of stone that we might race against one another. But as for him who wins over his competitor, he shall be the one who receives the position of Pharaoh."

Horus constructed for himself a ship made of pine, but covered it over with plaster, and then launched it into the sea during the night so that no one in the whole land saw it. Thus when Set observed Horus's boat he thought it was made entirely of stone. So he went to a mountain and sliced off the mountain's peak and made for himself a boat of stone fully 138 cubits long. Then, while the Ennead were present, they embarked each man to his own ship. But Set's boat sank in the water, so there he metamorphosed himself into a hippo and attacked the bottom of Horus's boat. So Horus grabbed some copper harpoons and threw them at Set. But the Ennead ordered him, "Do not throw those at him."

So he collected together his harpoons, placed them within his ship, and went downstream as far as Sais, to speak with Great Neith, mother of gods. He said, "Let judgement be made concerning myself and Set, given that for eighty years we have been contending within the law courts. But they have not been able to pronounce a verdict concerning us, nor has he been proven right in his case against me. Rather uncountable times have I been vindicated, each day in my statements, though he ignores every judgement the Ennead has declared. I have contested with him in the 'Way of Truth' court, and have been fully exonerated; I have contested with him in the 'Horus with High Horns' court, and have been fully exonerated; I have contested with him in 'Field of Reeds' court, and have been fully exonerated; and I have contested with him in 'Lake of the Field' court, and have been fully exonerated. Then the Ennead spoke to Shu, the son of Re, saying, "Horus, the son of Isis, speaks truly in everything he says."

Then Thoth spoke to Almighty God, saying, "We will send a letter to Osiris that he might judge between these two young men."

And Shu, the son of Re, declared, "What Thoth has spoken to the Ennead is unquestionably right."

Then Almighty God said to Thoth, "Seat yourself and compose a letter to Osiris that we might hear what he has to say."

So Thoth took his seat and composed a letter to Osiris, including these words, "Please do not fail to send to us a reply as to what ought to be done concerning Horus and Set, so that we do not exert our power without prudence."

Soon thereafter this letter came before the King, the son of Re. When it had been read aloud to him he gave out an anguished cry, but made his reply with extreme celerity; sending his message to where Almighty God was gathered with the Ennead, which read, "For what reason would my son, Horus, be cheated now when I was the one who gave you powers and I was the one who made barley and wheat so as to give sustenance to the gods and the cattle which accompany you, when no other god or goddess possessed the ability to do so?"

When the letter of Osiris arrived at the location where Re-Harakhti was seated with the Ennead, upon the White Mountain of Xios,* it was read aloud before him and the Ennead. Then Re-Harakhti declared, "Be so good as to send a reply to Osiris as speedily as possible, relating in it that, 'If you had never existed and not been born, I daresay that barley and wheat would yet exist'."†

This letter from Almighty God was read aloud before Osiris, and he sent back a reply to Re-Harakhti, saying, "Everything you yourself have accomplished is extraordinarily good, you who made the Ennead as your foremost task, even though justice was not prevented from sinking down into the Abyss. But please

---

* Xois was a city in Lower Egypt, in the Delta region, and a center of the Amen-Re worship; this would be its heavenly counterpart.
† Osiris was a god of rebirth and the annual cycle of planting and harvesting.

consider the situation from where you stand, for I live in a land which is filled with demon-faced couriers who have no fear of any god or goddess. And I have only to tell them to go forth and they will collect the heart of anyone who has performed evil deeds, so that they will then come to reside within my realm. But consider what significance there is in my being stationed here in the west while every one of you remains over there? Who that is among you might claim that he has more power than I do? But realize that you have made injustice your work. For when Great Ptah furnished the heavens is it not so that he likewise said to the stars which are there, 'It is in the direction of the west, where sits King Osiris, that you must set each night?' And he said to me, 'Following the gods, so too will the nobility and commoner both find their ultimate rest in the realm wherein you reside."

Then the letter of Osiris came to where Almighty God was gathered with the Ennead, and Thoth took the letter and read it aloud in the presence of Re-Harakhti and the Ennead. And they declared, "Him of abounding prosperity and ruler of all matter (Osiris) is quite right in everything which he has conveyed."

Then Set spoke, saying, "We should go off to Central Island that I might engage in combat with him."

So they journeyed to Central Island, upon which Horus was judged correct, and thus Atum sent a message to Isis, stating, "Bring Set with you bound in chains!" Thus Isis brought Set as a captive, bound in chains, and Atum spoke to him, saying, "Why do you refuse to accept our settlement but rather wish to take for yourself the position deserved by Horus?"

Set answered him, "Not at all, my gracious lord. Have Horus, the son of Isis, be brought here, for all I care, and given the position of Osiris, his father."

Thus Horus, the son of Isis, was summoned. And the White Crown was placed upon his head and he was inaugurated, to take for himself the position of Osiris, his father. And such was spoken to him, "You are now the good King of Egypt, you are the lord of excellence in all lands for all time."

After this Isis let out a loud shriek for her son Horus, and said, "You indeed are the good king, and my heart is full. And your divine countenance has bathed the earth with light."

Then Great Ptah spoke, saying, "Then what shall be Set's fate, for Horus that has been inaugurated into the position of Osiris, his father."

And Re-Harakhti said, "Have Set, the son of Nut, be given into my custody that he might reside with me, and be as a son to me, that he will make the heavens thunder and thus be greatly feared."

Then someone went and told of this to Re-Harakhti, saying, "Horus, the son of Isis, has emerged as Pharaoh."

And Re-Harakhti was overcome with joy and declared to the Ennead, "You will declare a festive celebration across every land for Horus, the son of Isis!"

Then Isis said, "Horus has emerged as Pharaoh, the Ennead is engaged in festive celebrations, and all the heavens are awash with jubilation. They put wreaths upon their heads when they heard that Horus, the son of Isis, had emerged as the great Pharaoh of Egypt."

And concerning the Ennead, they were now contented, and the whole land enjoyed peaceful celebrations, when they heard that Horus, the son of Isis, had gained the position left by Osiris, his father, the lord of Busiris.[72*]

Soleos: Well done, Phaedo.

Thaeo: Yes, but one thing I am curious about is whether or not the contendings of Horus and Set is in some way tied to that of Gawain and the Green Knight; just as we find where the king goes out hunting while his brother remains at home with the king's wife. But that he refuses his wife on the first day but for the kiss he receives from her, and thus is forced to give the Knight a kiss on his return. And as we find with Gawain that he gains another kiss on the second day, which he must then impart himself to the king. But rather than what transpires here, we might guess that upon the third day his wife would have sex with his brother, which in turn would force his brother to sodomize him on his return. And this appears to equate well with the situation between Horus and Set spoken of by Phaedo.

---

[*] Where the body of Osiris lies and the place of his birth (Plutarch, '*Isis and Osiris*' 21)

Epitheus: And recall too before, when we considered that David and Jonathan were brothers who fought, each being unable to overcome the other, that this likewise had something to do with the establishment of a covenant between them. But that if David had confronted his sibling Jonathan then, as with the rest, the daughter of Saul he is said to have married (Michal) would likewise have been his own sister.[*] And thus we could suggest the confrontation arising from the very same motive, which was a battle of the two brothers for their sister.

Thaeo: Yes. But we also compared Jonathan with Cu Chulainn, and it was Cu Chulainn who went to woo Blathnat and beheaded her husband Cu Roi Mac Dari.

Epitheus: This then makes the connection between Cu Chulainn and Jonathan make perfect sense, if we presume that it was David who was beheaded by Jonathan, in the battle of the brothers for their sister Michal ('brook'), who may have represented the earth.

Phaedo: And this too is like other episodes wherein the wife of a man conspires with her lover to slay her husband, as in the Egyptian tale of the two brothers, Anpu and Bata. For after the god Re had given orders that a wife be made for Bata, she was made by Khnum to be exceedingly beautiful and came to live with him in his house. But he warned her to not leave the house in case the flood waters might sweep her away. And likewise he foolishly confided in her that his heart was kept secure in the highest flower of a nearby cedar tree.

> Now it was several days later that Bata went out hunting as was his usual daily routine, so his wife decided to go outside and loiter beneath the cedar tree, which was not far from the house. But in doing so the sea caught a glimpse of her and so pursued her with a surge, so she dashed back for the house to escape it. But the sea called to the cedar tree to grab her for him, but it was left holding only a lock of her hair. This was then carried away

---

[*] See *The Death of King David: A Dialogue*, and Eupolemus 'fragment 2' of Alexander Polyhistor's 'On the Jews' in Eusebius '*Praeparatio Evangelica*' 30.1-3 (see Charlesworth 2009, Vol. 2: 865-866).

by the flood and borne upon its currents all the way to the kingdom of Egypt, coming to rest at a place near which the washermen of Pharaoh were situated. And the scent of that lock did linger upon the clothes of Pharaoh, so that there emerged a good deal of consternation among Pharaoh's washermen because the king had made mention to them concerning this scent which lingered upon his clothes. So they were left in great anxiety every day, because they did not know what could have caused it.

Each day the overseer of Pharaoh's washermen went down to the riverbank, suffering from a heavy heart because of the anxiety which surrounded him day after day. Once he stood upon the riverbank, placing himself directly opposite from where the lock was sitting in the water, and he ordered a man to descend and fetch it for him. Then he recognized that it produced an extremely pleasant scent and so delivered the lock to Pharaoh.

The wise men and magicians of Pharaoh were summoned and told him, "This lock of hair belongs to the daughter of Re, who bears the substance of every god within her. We will make of her a gift to you from a foreign land. So send messengers into every foreign land so as to locate her, and let the messenger who travels into the Valley of the Cedar take with him many men, so that they might bring her back."

So Pharaoh said, "That which you have spoken seems best to me." So the messengers were dispatched immediately.

Several days later those messengers who had travelled into every foreign lands had returned to report back to Pharaoh, but the men who had gone off to the Valley of the Cedar had not yet returned. And this was because Bata had killed them all, only allowing one to escape, that he might convey his story to Pharaoh. Then Pharaoh dispatched a contingent of soldiers and charioteers to fetch her, and accompanying them was a woman who was laden with all manner of rich clothes and jewelry fit to entice her. So the girl went back with her to Egypt and at her coming there was a great deal of celebration throughout all the land of Egypt. And Pharaoh loved her highly and bestowed upon her the title of High Queen.

So Pharaoh spoke to her to obtain information concerning her dealings with her husband, and she replied unto Pharaoh, "Please go and cut down the cedar tree, since thereby you will bring about his death." Thus Pharaoh ordered his men to venture out with solders equipped with axes to cut down the cedar tree. And arriving at the place where the cedar tree grew, they struck off the flower from it, wherein resided Bata's heart, and at that same moment Bata collapsed down dead.[73]

Epitheus: And recall too the story of David's sons Absalom and Amnon with their sister Tamar;[*] and this too could be compared to the violation of Dinah by Shechem, the son of Hamor. But whereas Simon and Levi are condemned for their acts in slaying the men of Shechem for his rape of their sister,[†] this likewise could have truly arisen from the two sons fighting over their own sister, if we equate Dinah with Tamar. But this would be made even more obvious by equating Amnon with Abraham, who caused his own sister to become his wife, so that Tamar could then be compared to Sarah.[74]

And it is possible here that the story was that Shechem himself was circumcised, which might hearken to an original punishment by castration, where he subsequently is banished to live as lord of the Abyss, while the other two brothers become the sun and the moon, similar to that which we find with the sons of Noah.[‡] As we find here the slaying of Amnon by Absalom, this too might not be so different from the slaying of Abel by Cain, for Absalom too flees after his crime. So too Cain and Abel represent the moon and sun fighting over their sister; and we could associate Amnon with the (Egyptian) moon god Ammon, with Tamar as his sister, but she is said to be the sister of Absalom but also his daughter.[§] So thus too if Amnon is equated with Abraham then Absalom would be equivalent to Abimelech.[**]

Thaeo: And this would indicate that they are all distantly related versions of a similar story, in the sense that Abraham is equivalent with Gawain, and Abimelech ('father king') with King Bertilak de Hautdesert. But this would also fit the idea of him going out and fighting someone in the woods, in this case Gawain with the Green

---

[*] 2 Samuel 13
[†] Genesis 34
[‡] See *The Zodiac Mysteries*
[§] 2 Samuel 13:1, 14:27
[**] Melchizedek, the king of Salem

Knight, and giving him an injury, but only later realizing that it was his own brother, which is presumably what we find between Jacob and Esau.

Epitheus: Truly.

Thaeo: And the kissing of brothers between Jacob and Esau might well reflect the same exchange found with Gawain.[*] So we would have to presume the situation of the hermaphrodite king giving birth to a son and daughter, where the son returns to slay the father and take his sister as his own wife, which is similar to that of both Oedipus and Abraham; or the situation where there are two sons and a daughter, where one son takes his sister as his wife and then flees, only to be caught and sodomized in return by the other son, who likewise castrates him.

Epitheus: And we could compare this to the brothers Set and Horus, where Set is the one who slays Osiris, and where Horus returns then to punish Set, who might have taken Osiris's wife as his own.

Thaeo: So thus it might be summarized that Set had thrown his brother Osiris into a pit, but where Osiris had already given rise to a son through Isis. When grown his son Horus then travels to the kingdom of Set and there makes a bargain with Set to give to him anything he received himself. Horus is then enticed by Set's wife and the act of sodomy allows him to cut off Set's phallus; and he thus reclaims the kingdom of his father, but that afterwards the two are reconciled. Then Horus becomes king as Osiris reborn and gains his wife back again, being at the same time his own mother.

Epitheus: This is fascinating, and it too could be related to the story of Joseph, who himself refuses the wife of Potiphar, Pharaoh's captain of the guard, but who later acquires Asenath, the daughter of Potiphera, priest of Anu, as his wife;[†] which makes a closer connection if we presume that Potiphar and Potiphera are, in fact, the very same.

---

[*] Genesis 33:4
[†] Genesis 39:1, 41:45

But likewise we find that Joseph is compared to a goat, at least in that his death is simulated with goat's blood, just as Jacob imitates a goat when he receives the blessing from his father.[*] And in this case too Esau is said to have gone out hunting, as Bertilak does.[†]

Thaeo: Yes. So too, just as with Gawain and Bertilak, the meeting of Joseph with his brothers involves a kiss, as the meeting of Jacob and his brother Esau involves a kiss.[‡]

Epitheus: And likewise this is true of David and Jonathan,[§] of whom he says,

> Anguished I am for you Jonathan, my brother,
> You create so very much satisfaction within me
> And the love you had for me was unsurpassed,
> Even being more than the love felt for women[75]

---

[*] Genesis 37:31, 27:16; Joseph is referred to as the 'Lamb of God' by Jacob in 'The Testaments of the Twelve Patriarchs' ('Testament of Benjamin' 3:8; see Charlesworth 2009, Vol. 1: 826)
[†] Genesis 25:27
[‡] Genesis 45:15, 33:4
[§] 1 Samuel 20:41

CHAPTER 7

Phaedo: And the love which David has for Jonathan is precisely comparable to that between Gilgamesh and Enkidu, which is compared to a love like that for a wife. But further we too find a curious similarity between them and the descriptions of Jacob and Esau, where Esau is a man of the meadows and a hunter while Jacob is a civilized man who lives in tents.[76] But concerning how Gilgamesh and Enkidu came to battle with one another, this is told in the 'Gilgamesh Cycle', where first regarding Gilgamesh it says,

> He being one-third a mortal while the rest of him was divine
> Belet-ili,[*] it was who determined what form his body would take
> His facial features were rendered flawless by wise Nudimmud
> His countenance was confident, his looks firm and inflexible
> Given the radiance of Shamash, and the strong will of Adad,
> So too were his feet immense, his legs lofty, and his stride wide
> Towering in stature high above the heads of the common man
> His face was bearded like thatch; his hair burgeoned as barley
> Standing tall he made a fine display, exceptional for a mortal
> And as his body was lofty so too the haughtiness he displayed
> Within the walls of Uruk he would strut about with great show,
> Setting himself as the top dog, his head reared like a buffalo's
> None could claim to be his equal, and engaging in war games
> When he took his weapon, his fellows would have to take theirs
> And the young men of Uruk were beset even in their home-lives
> For Gilgamesh would not allow any young man to aid his father
> Rather, all through the day and night he lorded over the people
> He being, as he was, the shepherd of wide Uruk, the Sheep Pen,
> He being, as he was, their shepherd, yet still he was overbearing
> Gilgamesh would not allow any young girl to help her mother
> Their cry raised high so that even the gods were the recipients
> Above all the mightiest; more agile, clever, and indefatigable
> Gilgamesh could also not keep away from the braided heads
> Neither to spare the warrior's lasses, nor leave brides undefiled
> Their cry raised high so that even the gods were the recipients
> The gods in heaven heard all concerning Uruk's prideful king

---

[*] The mother goddess, also called Aruru below, and equivalent to Mami

"Is it Aruru who takes responsibility for this menacing bull?
Could there be one who is his equal; engaging in his war games
When he takes his weapon, his fellows must also take theirs
Gilgamesh will not permit any young man to go aid his father
He being, as he is, the shepherd of wide Uruk, the Sheep Pen,
He being, as he is, their shepherd, and yet still he is overbearing
Above all the mightiest; more agile, clever, and indefatigable
And Gilgamesh also cannot keep away from the braided heads
Neither to spare the warrior's lasses, nor leave brides undefiled."
Such does almighty Anu hear when he listens to their grievances
Then the cry went to the grand Aruru, "Aruru, you made man,
So produce a rival who can defy him, equal in temper and tone
That they may come to duel one another, and leave Uruk alone!"
Aruru listened to their pleas and she envisaged Anu's words
After cleaning both of her hands, Aruru drew off a piece of clay
And threw it forth so that it flew to the secluded countryside
Thus she made a man who was primal, the combatant Enkidu
He who was produced by a whisper, the lightning of Nimrod
The entirety of his body was covered by a coarse shaggy coat,
And from his head fell locks of hair the length of any woman's
They were tresses which were abundant as the growing wheat
With no knowledge of men nor of nation, dressed only in skins
He ate with gazelles and drank at the watering hole with cattle
Along with the other beasts he eagerly bent to drink at the pool

There a hunter and trapper saw him up close at the water's edge
And again recognized this very same man three days in a row
When this huntsman was perplexed, to see him with the herds,
He left in bewilderment, making his way back to his dwelling
But this made him uneasy, he kept to himself and spoke not
There was a sign of anguish in his face, uneasiness in his gaze
He harbored a kind of misery which imbued his deepest frame
The expression he took was like that of a world-worn traveler
This hunter spoke with his father so his voice might be heard,
"Father, I saw a young man who came down from the uplands,
When he strove on land he showed both strength and vitality
And he had an almighty power in him like the lightning of Anu
There I see him always wandering upon the mountainous range
Whenever I see him he's munching plants along with the beasts

When I see him he splashes in the water with the rest of them
But I remain far too fearful of him to attempt approaching him
Yet he is the one who keeps filling the pits I excavate to entrap
He is also the same one who removes all of the snares that I set
By doing so he aids the grazers, and other untamed creatures
So that they are able to evade all my attempts to capture them
That I might accomplish naught in those uncultivated places."
The father of the hunter listened, and gave him a ready reply,
"Go to the King of Uruk, Gilgamesh, for that land is his territory
His strength is also an almighty power, like Anu's lightning
So go now and set forth on your way to the kingdom of Uruk
For there you will find such women who sap the vitality of men
There you will find Shamhat the prostitute, take her with you,
You must remain hidden until the coming of this burly man,
Until he makes his way to the watering hole with the buffalo
She must take off her clothing before him, make herself naked
So when he sets his eyes upon her he will move in closer to her
Then wild beasts, his former kin, will be as strangers to him."
The youth listened to every word of advice his father gave him
Then the hunter set forth to seek his regal majesty, Gilgamesh
He made his way on the road, to the city of Uruk, the Sheep Pen
There he came into the court of Gilgamesh, conveying to him,
"I saw a young man who descended down from the uplands,
When he strove on land he showed both strength and vitality
And he had an almighty power in him like the lightning of Anu
But I remain far too fearful of him to attempt approaching him
Yet he is the one who keeps filling the pits I excavate to entrap
He is also the one who removes all of the snares that I have set
By doing so he aids the grazers, and other untamed creatures
So that they are able to evade all my attempts to capture them
That I might accomplish naught in those uncultivated places."
So after listening Gilgamesh spoke to this man, to the hunter,
"Proceed huntsman, and take with you Shamhat the prostitute,
So that when he makes his way to the watering hole with buffalo,
She must remove her clothing before him, making herself naked
And when he sets his eyes upon her he will move in closer to her
Then wild beasts, his former kin, will be as strangers to him."

So the hunter proceeded, taking with him Shamhat the harlot

Together they walked the road and traversed the entire span
So that in three day's time they had arrived at their destination
The hunter and the harlot concealed themselves and waited
They were there for a day, then two, sitting near the water hole
Until buffalo came down to the pool's edge and began to drink
Likewise, wild animals came to the water to alleviate their thirst
So too the one who lived in the uplands, the wild man Enkidu,
Him who ate with gazelles and drank at the water with cattle
With the other beasts he bent low to drink for his sustenance
And Shamhat first set her eyes upon this primeval cave man
A savage young man from the vast stretches of the wilderness,
"That's him, Shamhat, so now is the time to bare your breasts
Angling your thighs enough that he might see you splendidly
But refrain from retreating before him, show interest instead,
For when he sees you he will approach you from sheer instinct
Then shed your clothing entirely, allow him to mount your hill
And treat this wild man in just the way women favorably do
That the wild beasts, his former kin, will be as strangers to him
He won't refrain from unleashing his lustful desires upon you."
She undid her garment, angling her thighs; he spied her naked
And she did not retreat before him, but rather showed interest
Then shed her clothing entirely, allowing him to mount her hill
She treated this wild man in just the way women favorably do
He didn't refrain from unleashing his lustful desires upon her
For six days and intervening nights was he enflamed with lust
Repeatedly forcing his vigorous ejaculations within Shamhat
By which time he had been thoroughly fulfilled of her allure
Then he made his way to return to the wild ways of the beasts
But when the gazelles saw Enkidu approach, they scampered
And no longer did the buffalo of the wilderness approach him
Now his body was no longer hirsute, his skin now far too bright,
While his legs, by which he ran with buffalo before, were slowed
Enkidu could sense he had lost his vitality, unable to run apace
Still he found his thoughts more profound, his mind more wise
Realizing this he returned, sitting near to where the harlot stood
The prostitute noticed the expression which lay upon his face
And when she spoke to him he listened closely to what she said,
"Now you have grown wise Enkidu, and are similar to the gods
So why would you now still wander the wilderness with beasts?

107

Rather instead, I'll take you to the city of Uruk, the Sheep Pen
There you will be in civilization, where Anu and Ishtar reside
There you will find King Gilgamesh, a man foremost in strength
Who is himself like a buffalo, of supreme power among men."
Thus she spoke to him, and he found her words were agreeable
Knowing how he had changed, he now thought to make friends
So Enkidu raised his own voice, and spoke to the prostitute,
"Then let us go together, Shamhat, take me wherever you go
Let us go to civilization, where the gods Anu and Ishtar reside
Let us go to find King Gilgamesh, a man foremost in strength
Who is himself like a buffalo, of supreme power among men
And there I will confront him, so let it be a contest of strength
So thereby making it plain in Uruk that I be proven supreme
There I will go, and thereby I will change the course of destiny
And it will be that the one born in the wilderness will prevail!"
Then Shamhat said to him in reply, "Then come, let us travel,
Let me show you happiness and of all other diversions I know
Then let us travel, Enkidu, to the city of Uruk, the Sheep Pen
Where you will find the young men wearing splendid sashes
Where each day is a festival, and drums resound throughout
There the young women will display their fine bodies to entice
Bursting with elevated spirits of mirth, all are imbued with joy
Where at night the men of valor sleep in peace and serenity
You, dearest Enkidu, have never known of such a life as this
Let me lead you to Gilgamesh, the one of gladness and sadness
Then you might see him yourself, and look upon his own face
He is to me of such a handsome appearance, and distinguished
So too I consider that his entire body is imbued with seduction
But I say to you that he is much stronger of arm than you are
You will not find him to be sleeping either by day or by night
So, my dear Enkidu, change your mind from challenging him
Gilgamesh is one favored by the sun god Shamash himself,
On top of this Anu, Ellil, and Ea bestowed him with wisdom

"Even before you descended from the high mountainous tracts
Gilgamesh had already had a dream concerning you in Uruk
After he awoke he provided all the details of it to his mother,
'O Mother, there was a dream which I witnessed last night
There was an array of heavenly stars gathered around me

And what was like the lightning from Anu falling above me
But when I attempted to lift it up, it proved to be too weighty
So I attempted to shift it, but even then it would not budge
Around it I could see standing there all the citizens of Uruk,
The population amassed over it, the men, and the youth too,
And all of them were kissing its feet as though it were a baby
But this thing too did I possess a dear affection for, like a wife,
Then I took it up and brought it to you, setting it at your feet
Thereupon you deemed it to be my equal, by how you favored it.'
So the wise mother of Gilgamesh, who knew all, now spoke,
The untamed heifer Ninsun, who knew all, said to Gilgamesh,
'My son, when you saw an array of stars gathered around you
And what was like the lightning from Anu falling above you
When you attempted to lift it up, it proved to be too weighty
When you attempted to shift it, even then it did not budge
Then you took it up and brought it to me, setting it at my feet
Thereupon I deemed it to be your equal, by how I favored it
But this thing did you have a dear affection for, like a wife
All this means is that a mighty companion will seek you out
One who holds the ability to preserve the lives of his friends
And who will prove supreme in the use of his arms anywhere
That his might could be compared to the lightning of Anu
And truly you will have a dear affection for him, like a wife,
But he will also be a companion who acts as your savior.'
When he had had a second dream he went to the goddess,
Then Gilgamesh raised his voice to be heard, to his mother,
'But Mother, I also had a second dream during the night
In this one a copper axe fell down into the streets of Uruk
It landed in the middle of the city and the folks gathered
The people of the entire land stood over it, amassed above it
Then I took it up and brought it to you, setting it at your feet
But this thing too did I possess a dear affection for, like a wife,
Thereupon you deemed it to be my equal, by how you favored it.'
So the wise mother of Gilgamesh, who knew all, now spoke,
The untamed heifer Ninsun, who knew all, said to Gilgamesh,
'The copper axe you saw in actuality represents a fellow man
And truly you will have a dear affection for him, like a wife,
And I will deem him to be your equal, by how I favor him
One who holds the ability to preserve the lives of his friends

109

And who will prove supreme in the use of his arms anywhere
That his might could be compared to the lightning of Anu.'
Then Gilgamesh raised his voice, speaking to his mother,
'Then so be it, by the word of Ellil, the supreme authority
By this will I come to have a friend to give me good counsel.'
And as such Ninsun recounted each of these dreams to me."
So Shamhat knew Gilgamesh's dreams and told it to Enkidu,
"The significance of these dreams is that you'll be dear friends."[77]

Shamhat took Enkidu to where he could gaze down upon Uruk
Then she spoke so that her voice might be heard, to Enkidu,
"Gilgamesh caused the walls of Uruk, the Sheep Pen, to be built
And too the walls of the holy house Eanna, an unmatched jewel
You can see its side there, which spans it like a copper stripe
Evaluate its fortifications, for there are none others like them
And there too is the stepping stone, which has stood forever
Then make your way to Eanna, the sanctified shrine of Ishtar,
For there will arise no man nor monarch who could surpass it
Climb upon the great wall of Uruk and walk the entire circuit
Take a look for yourself at the foundation stones and the bricks
You will see for yourself that these are the best of bricks, baked!
The Seven Sages being the only ones who could have set its base
Within is one square mile of housing, one square mile of orchard,
Another square mile of clay pits, not to mention the courtyard
This being the square in the temple of Ishtar, Queen of Heaven
The temple grounds and the three square miles make up Uruk."
Enkidu thought in his heart that this place was not suitable
Not knowing how he could live here rather than in the uplands
Shamhat told him that he ought to ask such a thing of Ninlil
Now Enkidu was in Tirannu,* he was kneeling and facing her
As he looked up at the goddess he was overwhelmed with tears
He felt an odd divine power and thus he put his trust in Mulliltu†
Enkidu spoke his words so that they might be heard by her alone
How he had been born and grew up in the mountainous tracts
How he had lived his life with the beasts and ran with the buffalo
And why he must then leave this life he knew to now live in cities

---

* A name for the kingdom of Uruk
† The goddess Ninlil

They jointly discussed the matter, and spoke together for a time
And after coming to a decision he rose and then turned away
Now knowing deep within his heart that he could not go back
After this Shamhat then removed the two robes that draped her
One piece of clothing she gave to Enkidu that he might dress
And the second piece of clothing Shamhat took to dress herself
Then took him by the hand and, like a goddess, led him away
To the dwelling of the shepherds, with a sheep's pen at hand
And there the shepherds were all gathered round about him
Who came from their own interest, saying among themselves,
"How this burly young man is so much like Gilgamesh of form."
"And so too of sturdy stature, with the fortitude of fortifications."
"Surely he is one of those born in the mountainous uplands."
"The strength of his arms is as great as the lightning of Anu."
So then they placed food before him, but he did not reach for it
So then they placed drink before him, but he did not touch it
Enkidu showed no interest in it, but rather looked inquisitively
He had never known anything of drinking beer nor eating bread
This is something which he had never been taught when a boy
He had rather known only the eating of raw meat for his hunger
He had rather known only to drink the milk of cows for his thirst
So the harlot then spoke that she might be heard, to Enkidu,
"This is food you must eat, Enkidu, for it means your existence
Likewise you must consume the beer, for it is the land's fortune."
So then Enkidu took up the bread and ate it until he was full
And took to drinking beer, until he had finished seven whole jars
Then he fell back and was quite content, his heart was cheered,
So now his face took on the look of a man who was rejuvenated,
Covered his hairy body with unguent, anointed himself with oil,
So from then on he became just like other men, dressing himself
He took up the use of the war weapon and became like a hero
Now allied with the society of men, he contended with the lions
So the shepherds could sleep without worry during the nights

With his arms he took on wolves and frightened off predators
So that when the old herdsmen lay to sleep, Enkidu kept watch
And he was approached by a young herder, who spoke to him,
"You would rest content if you stayed here at home amongst us
There's much going on in Uruk, the Sheep Pen, you do not know."

Enkidu heard from him about the manner of Gilgamesh the king
He learned of both his splendor and arrogance, and his pastimes
Shamhat told him that she knew something of the bed of Ishhara[*]
But that they must learn more from someone who was let within
One who was allowed to enter the homes of the fathers-in-law
So with her Enkidu went and waited, on the night she suggested
Then while they were waiting she saw the young man appear
Enkidu was glad and looked with his eyes and perceived him
So he spoke to the prostitute, and made his voice heard, saying,
"Shamhat, call the man over here, I would like to speak with him
So I might find out what he might be doing and why he is here."
She said she would call him by his name and shouted to him
Then Enkidu went to where he was standing and spoke to him,
"Young man, I merely wished to ask you where you were going
And why you are expending yourself and in such a great hurry?"
The young man replied to Enkidu, so his voice might be heard,
"I do so because I've been invited to the father-in-law's house
It is the fate of the people, where daughters-in-law are selected
There I have the duty of keeping the ceremonial table supplied
With all kinds of dishes and delicacies of the father-in-law's city
And also for the king of wide and broad Uruk, the Sheep Pen
So too I say, 'Open the way among the people for bridegrooms!
Do this for the king of spacious Uruk, Gilgamesh is his name
Open the way among the people for grooms, Gilgamesh comes!'
And he will be the first to impregnate the future wife, the bride
He shall be first to have her, the husband will only be second
This arose from the decree which came from the word of Anu
This was his birthright, his destiny, from the origin of his navel."
Upon hearing this from the young man, Enkidu's face went red
He was now resolute to make his way through the gate of the city
Making himself ready for a confrontation with the bull of Uruk
Asking the harlot to go with him, who knew the place very well
As they went Enkidu took the lead and Shamhat followed him
So he entered the wide and broad city of Uruk, the Sheep Pen
When he walked through, all the population stood on every side
As he was standing there in the street of Uruk they talked of him
"Is he not just the same shape as Gilgamesh, if even a bit shorter

---

[*] Goddess of marriage

But he also has bones which are thick, being from the mountains
He has thus known only the eating of raw meat for his hunger
He has thus known only to drink the milk of cows for his thirst
Know that in Uruk, the Sheep Pen, there is no end to sacrifices
Know that here in the city the young men are clean and purified
Hear the lusanum-instrument play for the man who is honest!
At last one has appeared who can challenge divine Gilgamesh!"
So there he remained within the street of Uruk, by the entrance
He waited at the threshold until the arrival of the mighty bull
To block the entry so that Gilgamesh would be unable to go by
And the entire citizenry of Uruk was there gathered about him
The population amassed around him, the men and youth too,
And all of them were kissing his feet as though he were a baby,
When that young man made his appearance at the threshold
Then was the bed made ready for an evening to honor Ishhara
The king came there every night to engage with the young girls
Yet there remained a man of equal strength for divine Gilgamesh
Enkidu stood in front of the door of the father-in-law's dwelling
Set on making sure that Gilgamesh had no way to get through
So there by the door of the father-in-law's home they wrestled
They came to grips within the street, there in the central square
The fracas caused every wall and door-frame to shift and shake
Confronting one another like two bulls, hunkered and brawled
Until Gilgamesh was forced down, his knee set upon the dirt
Then his fury shriveled, he backed away, and then he withdrew,
Enkidu spoke so that his voice might be heard, to Gilgamesh,
"When your mother gave you birth, you were to be matchless
The untamed heifer Ninsun, of the cow shed, assured you alone
Would rise in supremacy, praised above all the fighting men
The god Ellil declared that you would be the people's sovereign
And who was meant to be a king among kings, outshining all
But now a rival has arisen who has come up to challenge him
So no longer might he boast of rising above and defeating any."
And as Enkidu spoke a new realization arose within the king
The pride of Gilgamesh now reduced to rubble, his eyes flooded
When he finished speaking, they now kissed and were friends
Those gathered there grew emotional and overcome with tears

Then the mother of Gilgamesh arrived, and he himself spoke,

"This burly young man who descended down from the uplands,
He strove on the land and showed both his strength and vitality
Who has proven himself supreme in use of his arms anywhere
So that his might could be compared to the lightning of Anu
And so too his sturdy stature, with the fortitude of fortifications."
So the wise mother of Gilgamesh, who knew all, spoke to her son,
The untamed heifer Ninsun, who knew all, said to Gilgamesh,
"My son, within your gates you have been honored as the king
But you must accept that your fate is just the same as any man
You might cry in grief now, but he will save the life of a friend
He knows how to fight and can provide you good battle advice
While you hold the staff of rule, with your servants and subjects,
You are prideful within your gates, having forsaken all humility."
Overcome with heartfelt tears of woe, deeply troubled he spoke,
"Enkidu had no other home but the wilderness in the uplands
And from his head fell locks of hair the length of any woman's
This man born out in the wilderness, how could any beat him?"
And Enkidu was standing there, listening to every word he said
He pondered to himself, seated himself, and also began to weep
As his eyes too became greatly bleary from the rivulets of tears,
The muscles of his arms no longer rigid, his strength abating,
They then fell into embracing, and shook hands with each other
Then Gilgamesh spoke that his voice might be heard, to Enkidu,
"Please tell me why your eyes overflow with such tears of woe
You too appear to be upset and are suffering a harsh anguish?"
Enkidu spoke so that his voice might be heard, to Gilgamesh,
"It is due to the wailing from your own grievance, my brother,
What has caused my neck to strain, my arms to become weak,
It is because of what I see that my strength has abandoned me."[78]

So they are reconciled and become adoptive brothers. Then the story goes on to tell of their battle with the beast Humbaba, then the Bull of Heaven, before Enkidu faces a reprisal brought by the gods. But we find that he too, like Balder, experiences a dream which leaves him deeply distraught prior to this.

CHAPTER 8

Thaeo: Here too what is intriguing is that we find quite similar episodes in the poem concerning Beowulf, for there he engages in hand-to-hand combat with the demon Grendel, and then later in life goes on to fight against the dragon. And we found too that the body of Grendel appeared upon the moon, or rather a headless bear.[*]

Epitheus: Yes.

Thaeo: So perhaps Humbaba could be considered the same monster as Grendel, for the form of his name is similar enough to that meaning 'mead-wolf', or more specifically the '*haoma*-wolf' (*haumavarga*), which we could associate both with *soma* and the sacred mead. And if we were to proceed one step further and presume the name 'Haoma' meant the moon god, then it would be related too to Hama or Heimdall.[†]

Epitheus: Thus it might be possible to recognize the dual aspects of a god, alternating between the demon who is stricken down and the youthful god who takes his place; in other words, it is not so different from Jacob's contest with God before the sunrise and the appearance of Esau following.[‡]

Thaeo: No, indeed. And likewise, the one who travels with Beowulf when he fights with the dragon is his loyal companion Wiglaf; and him we considered comparable to Thor's squire Thialfi.[§] And in the earliest (Sumerian) version of the story, Gilgamesh's trusted-companion is not his adoptive brother but his servant. Though what we might have here is the confusion between two situations; for Hercules also has a companion in Hylas, though he does not accompany Hercules upon his first labor in confronting the Nemean Lion.

---

[*] See *Roar of the Tempests: A Dialogue*
[†] It is not unreasonable to presume that the *haoma* was drunk so as to give one the character of the wolf to be seen upon the moon's surface, and thus likewise had some connection to the gaining of immortality.
[‡] Osiris and Set likewise battled every dawn upon the banks of the Nile.
[§] See *Roar of the Tempests: A Dialogue*

Epitheus: Yes, and when we spoke of this before we thought that this lion too, who is born upon and then fell from the moon, might well be comparable to the beasts Grendel or Humbaba.

Thaeo: Truly, and we noted that the confrontation of Jacob at the ford equates with the confrontation of Cu Chulainn with Fer Baeth, his foster brother, where Cu is speared in the thigh with a holly spear; just as Jacob is injured in his thigh in his contest with God. And this we found corresponded with the constellations of *Perseus*.[*] And I think too that this could be seen to duplicate the death of Achilles through a wound to his vulnerable heel by the arrow fired by Paris and guided by Apollo.

Epitheus: Just so.

Thaeo: But likewise there might be further reason to link Cu Chulainn with Jacob and Achilles, for in his contest with Etarconol they meet at a ford, and Etarconol said that he would either take Cu's head or that he would take his. But in their mismatched contest Cu Chulainn strikes him with his sword down to his navel and then Fergus runs a cord through his heels and pulls him to their camp, dragging him behind his chariot.[79] And I am struck by how this not only resembles how Hektor is pulled behind the chariot of Achilles, but more so how the very name of 'Etarconol' is similar to that of 'Hektor'.

Soleos: Yes, what you say is intriguing; while it might even have something to do with the constellation of *Orion*, for the storm god Thiassi has the star *Rigel* as his heel.[†]

Thaeo: And, as you recall, the death of Orion is brought about too through the involvement of Apollo, for when he was set to marry his sister Artemis, Apollo was not approving of it and so sought to do the hunter harm. As it is said, he challenged his sister to a test of her skill, and given as she was to prove her superlative ability as an archeress, at once took up the challenge. So when he took her out to

---

[*] See *The Death of King David: A Dialogue*
[†] See *The Eden Enigma: A Dialogue*

a spot where they had a wide view of the sea, and pointed out to her something which bobbed distantly upon the waves, she readily took aim and fired, ably striking it with her first arrow. But her satisfaction was short-lived when she soon discovered that this far-off speck, the one she had so keenly struck with such deadly aim, was her husband-to-be, Orion. Thus in return for this she honored him by setting him amongst the constellations.

Soleos: Good. And the left foot of *Orion* is likewise the source for the constellation *Eridanus*.[80] And in the story of Orion and the scorpion, he is to have received scorpion's poison through his heel, which was mitigated through the antidote given him by the giant Ophiuchus.[81]

Thaeo: Quite. And it would not be out of place to compare the heel of Achilles with the heel of *Orion*, which is the star *Rigel* which means 'foot' (in Arabic).[82]

Soleos: Yes. And we would most certainly be remiss not to acknowledge this particular point in the heavens. For the giantesses Fenia and Menia say of Thiassi that he is the greatest of all, when they chant,

> Frodi, you did not display the furthermost acumen,
> Wise judge of men, when you procured the slave girls
> You selected them only for their physiques and looks,
> Though you failed to seek knowledge of their ancestry:
> Hrungnir was powerful indeed, likewise was his father,
> But Thiassi far surpassed them both in his mightiness
> Idi and Aurnir are represented in our line of descent,
> These brothers of mountain giants are our ancestors[83]

And this likewise matches the epithet of the constellation *Orion*, which is known as the 'Great One'.

Thaeo: That is quite clever, Soleos.

Soleos: But there is something else which might be of some interest, for the stars here are likewise known by astrologers as the whirlpool, which in Greek is 'zalos',[84] and this is also identified as the source of the river constellation *Eridanus*.* And what makes this particularly interesting is that in 'zalos' the 'z' can be pronounced '*th*';† which means that 'zalos' could also be pronounced 'thalos'. And recall too that it was the bronze man Talos who was to have had a vulnerability in his ankle which was exploited by the Argonauts, if you recall what transpired here, Thaeo.

Thaeo: Indeed I do, for it says,

> After this they sailed from Anaphe to Crete, but were hindered from going ashore by the giant Talos. Some say that he was from the Race of Bronze, but others say that he had been given as a gift by Hephaistos to King Minos. But he was, in any case, a man made of bronze, though others say he had the form of a bull. But he had one singular vascule which went all the way from his neck down to his ankle, where there was a bronze nail fixed at its end. This Talos remained on guard by sprinting about the island three times a day. So at that time too, when he spied the Argo coming towards the coast, he chucked stones at it. However, Medea devised a trap for him and brought about his end. Some say this was accomplished when he was driven mad from her drugs; while others say that she promised to give him immortality through removal of the nail, bringing death to him when all his ichor spilled out. But yet others even claim that he was killed by Poias, who shot him in his ankle with an arrow.[85]

But I likewise recollect what is said by Lycophron:

> For now Myrina moans as the wave-lapped shores await the arrival of grunting horses, the very moment the raging wolf (Achilles) leapt with an eager bound upon his Pelasgian foot the final strand, bringing forth an eruption of lucid water from that sand; releasing springs which had, until then, never been seen.

---

* The river Eridanus is also identified with the Nile River or the Ocean (Hyginus, *Astronomica* 2.32; see Condos 1997: 105)
† As, for instance, 'Zeus' could likewise be pronounced 'Theus'.

And this could mean something in relation to what you said, of the spring here arising from the foot of Achilles, which could be compared to the source of the River Eridanus.

Soleos: Superlative, Thaeo.   And this is leading us upon an interesting track, for it could well be that Talos is represented by the *Orion* constellation as well; for the giant Hayk is identified with the constellation of *Orion*, and Hayk is known to have killed the god Bel with an arrow, just as we find with Hod and Balder.[86]   And it is not surprising too to find that this itself is similar to the contests we spoke of before, being those between Cu Chulainn and Fer Baeth, and Jacob and God, where we find it is not his heel but his thigh which is injured.

Thaeo: Yes, and despite the celebrity of Achilles' heel, there is a similar story of a wound he received to his thigh, as it is recorded that,

> While the army was staying at Aulis a sacrifice was performed for the god Apollo, when suddenly a serpent went out from the altar to a nearby fig tree which had a nest in it. Once it had swallowed the eight baby sparrows in the nest and their mother too, the serpent then turned into stone. And Calchas deemed that this had been shown them as a divine sign by the will of Zeus, and concluded from it that Troy would fall after a ten-year siege. So they prepared themselves to set sail and conquer Troy. And while Agamemnon led the entire fleet, it was Achilles, then only fifteen-years-old, who was made commander of the armada. But not knowing the way to Troy they instead arrived in Mysia and attacked it, thinking it to be Troy. But when the king of the Mysians, named Telephos, who was a son of Hercules, saw his kingdom plundered he put together an armed force of Mysians and went out after the Greeks with a fleet of their own ships. They slew a great many of them, including Thersandros, the son of Polyneices, who refused to retreat. However, when Achilles charged in that assault, Telephos failed to hold his ground and ran

off. But while Achilles chased him he was entangled in vines and received a spear wound to his thigh.[87*]

Again here we recognize how a wound to the thigh is matched with a wound to the ankle, which is true too of the character Bran, called 'pierced thighs' but who is also wounded in his foot.[88] And likewise there is the (Welsh) character Echel, who is the very same as Achilles, and known as 'Echel pierced thigh'.[89]

Soleos: It should be mentioned here too that the Etruscan name for Achilles is Achle, which itself is our very word 'ankle', and thus the hero can never be truly separated from his legendary bane.[†] And if we were to associate these stars with a giant's ankle, they are also identified as an arrow;[‡] thus we can certainly come to recognize why the arrow and the heel were so closely identified with each other, as it is with Achilles, Talos, and indeed Krishna and Hercules.[§]

Thaeo: And there is the instance of the thigh of the Bull of Heaven torn off by Enkidu, which we might suppose becomes the 'Thigh' of *Ursa Major*; the constellation we considered to be precisely that of Grendel, who himself had a limb torn off and hung upon the rafters of Heorot.[**] But the 'Thigh' constellation in Egypt was that of Set, whose thigh was wounded by Horus, it is said, for having swallowed the crescent moon. And this too would make Set very like the Bull of Heaven.

---

[*] This has something to do with the vine god Dionysos.
[†] In a tale told by the Taulipang (in Brazil) 'Orion's Belt' was known to be the right ankle of the giant Zilikawai. (Staal 1988: 67)
[‡] 'Orion's Belt' is included in the 'North Arrow' asterism, so called because it always points north.
[§] Krishna was only vulnerable on sole of his foot. But when Krishna defeated Kalli Naga, a beast with a thousand heads, he is said to have been wounded there by the serpent, which is said to represent an arrow (Howey 1955: 45-46; Deane 2008: 173). Likewise, Hercules mangled two serpents in his infancy, and too is said to have suffered a wound to his thigh (Apollodorus ii 4.8; Pausanias viii 53.9; Hesiod, 'Shield of Hercules' 460).
[**] See *Roar of the Tempests: A Dialogue*

Phaedo: Likewise, the skin of the sacrificed bull (*Meskhent*) was utilized as a cover for the body of Osiris, as the 'Thigh' constellation (*Meskheitu*) was to have bestowed immortality.[90][*]

Soleos: And it is possible that this too makes sense of the circumstance concerning Enkidu, I mean as to why his confrontation with the Bull of Heaven made him vulnerable to death. What I am suggesting is that through his act of throwing the thigh of the Bull away in anger at the goddess Ishtar, presuming this thigh could be equated with the golden shoulder of immortality, then this act denied him and perhaps by extension, all humanity, of immortality.

Phaedo: And likewise we have the very same with Gilgamesh, if he is too equated with Achilles, though while not killed outright merely suffers the loss of immortality through his loss of the plant of eternal youth.[91]

Thaeo: Indeed, and recall too that when Gilgamesh gains the plant of youth that the thorn of the plant pricks him, just as we find that the thigh of Cu Chulainn is pierced by a holly shaft which he then throws to slay Fer Baeth; and which we might likewise compare with Achilles, who despite his mother Thetis washing him in the currents of the river Styx, failed to protect his ankle, by which she held him when dipping him into those phenomenal waters.

Epitheus: Well said.

Thaeo: But more so I cannot refrain from thinking of the parallel between the circumstance of Thetis and that of Metis, for in both of them we find a situation where a prophecy arose that each would give birth to a son who would overthrow his own father. This is what occurred in the birth of Achilles, which is why he had a mortal father rather than an immortal one. For it is said that Zeus and Poseidon fought over the virgin nymph Thetis, daughter of Nereus, when Themis prophesied that she would bear a son who would outstrip his father in deeds, and would thereby diminish the

---

[*] The Egyptian bull sacrifice was equated with Osiris's slaying of Set, while the sinews of the Bull of Heaven made the rungs of the Ladder of Heaven which led to the eternal stars. (see Budge 1999: 141, 240, 301)

121

reputation of his father. So Zeus refused her and instead encouraged his grandson Peleus, son of Aeacus, to have her; and so he went on an expedition to capture her. Upon the shrewd advice of the centaur Chiron he went to her while she lay sleeping and held her fast so that despite all of her efforts to escape his merciless grip, by transforming herself into many and various forms, he was yet able to subdue her and rape her within the sea-nymph's own grotto.[92]* But in the case of Metis, who likewise was swallowed by Zeus for the very same reason, she gave rise to the wise goddess Athena, who was influential in the birth of Erechthonios. And just as with Achilles so too did Erechthonios miss out on immortality.[†]

Epitheus: Yet this also puts me in mind of a similar episode, at least what remains of it, where Jonathan is shooting arrows towards a pile of stones behind which is hidden David, for we likewise know that Cu Chulainn, in his contest against Nad Crantail, stands atop a memorial stone to increase his own stature.[93] Likewise, there is the stone that Goronwy places before him when Lleu throws his spear, which pierces the stone but slays him just the same.[94]

Soleos: Good. And so too there is an instance of this in the felling of Hrungnir ('brawler'), being a tall giant formed out of clay. But when Thor defeats Hrungnir he is pinned down under the giant's great leg. And this might be due to some confusion with a wound received to his thigh.

Thaeo: But it seems then that there might have been some confusion too between the vulnerable claw of Grendel and the struck heel of *Orion*.[‡] And the vulnerability of Achilles' heel might likewise have been shared by Grendel, in the case of his single vulnerable claw being the only part of him which remained mortal.[§]

Epitheus: Yes. And likewise, as with Apollo and Hyacinth, when Perseus slays Acrisius by accident it is with a discus injury to his

---

* Thetis is referred to as a heifer, as a term meaning female (Lycophron, 'Alexandra' 855 f.)
[†] See *The Eden Enigma: A Dialogue*
[‡] Aurvandil's Toe (see de Santillana 1977: 261)
[§] See *Roar of the Tempests: A Dialogue*

foot. Thus Perseus here could be made equivalent to Esau and Jacob ('heel') to Acrisius or Achilles, who is said to have grabbed onto his brother's heel. And their contest is that between the sun and moon, which has two parts: where the sun overcomes the moon or where the moon defeats the sun; which is the contest wherein we are told that Jacob has been wounded in his thigh by his opponent.[*]

Soleos: Well done.

Thaeo: But then why not bring into this discussion Venus and Adonis, where a boar arrives to kill him with an injury to his thigh.[†] And Venus and Adonis are likewise the very same as Ishtar and Tammuz, where Tammuz is equated with the figure of *Orion*.[95] And the place where *Orion* is located is called the 'Hexagon' or 'Belt of the Zodiac';[96][‡] while Orion is known to be the one who according to Hebrew legend set himself against God and was thereby punished by being chained there in the heavens.[97] And we had already seen something very similar with the binding of the eagle, who was likewise identified with *Orion*.[§]

Epitheus: And recall too that it is Esau who is a bow hunter, as is Ishmael. And as such we might too regard both Esau and Enkidu to be *Orion* the Hunter.

Soleos: That is quite good, Epitheus. So too if Enkidu is comparable to *Orion* with his vulnerable heel, we might also contrast this with the constellation of *Hercules* the 'Kneeler', if we presume that the one is bitten in the heel by the serpent (*Eridanus*) while the other is crushing the head of the serpent (*Draco*).[**]

---

[*] Genesis 32
[†] Compare this with Apulius (xiii § 5) where a spear in the right thigh is deemed indistinguishable to a wound inflicted by a boar's tusk.
[‡] It might too be associated with the Hexad, the 'cosmic net' of the Gnostics (see Fideler 1993: 210-211)
[§] See *The Eden Enigma: A Dialogue*
[**] The god Krishna's life is divided between his being entwined by a big serpent that bites his heel and his victory in having freed himself from the serpent and stepping upon its head with his heel (see Howey 1955: 42-43). This is also attributable to *Scorpius* and *Ophiuchus* (see Olcott 2004: 326).

Epitheus: Yes, and as it says,

> Yahweh God then turned to the snake and said, "Because you
> have done this you will be cursed beyond all domestic animals
> and all beasts; so upon your belly you will slither and the dust of
> the ground you will taste for the rest of your life, and there shall
> be enmity between you and the woman, between her progeny and
> your progeny. He will kick your head and you will bite his heel,
> from this day forth."[98]

Soleos: Thus we might presume that originally it was the serpent
who bit the mortal heel of Gilgamesh, and it is for this reason that
like the others who are denied immortality, we find that he remained
one-third mortal. Thus we could assume that it was this bite, as with
Orion and the scorpion, which brought about his death.

Epitheus: Just so. But then haven't we now equated *Orion* with both
Gilgamesh and Enkidu?

Soleos: Indeed, you are quite right, and this is why it is more likely
that each one represents a constellation himself, one being that of
Orion and the other being that of the 'Phantom', or *Hercules*. And
this might be confirmed by the arrangement of the two
constellations, for *Hercules* is situated in the sky directly opposite
from *Orion*. And this suggests that a conflict arose when the winter
solstice was on the same radial axis as *Orion* (*Taurus*) and the
summer *solstice* was on the same radial axis as *Hercules* (*Scorpius*),
which would have been so when the spring *equinox* was entering the
constellation of *Leo* (about 8000 BC). And here the serpent
Eridanus rises up from the Underworld, while the other serpent
Draco lies at the apex of the sky and who is thus deemed to be
immortal.

Epitheus: I agree. But it would seem that the significance of the
'Kneeler' is that he was the one who was forced upon one knee by
his indomitable adversary; just as it is said that God could not prevail
against Jacob.

Soleos: Truly. And it is certainly like Beowulf who is said to stumble when fighting Grendel's mother. And we find just the same with Thor who is brought to his knee by Time (Elli); while so too we find the serpent *Draco*, *Ursa Minor*, *Ursa Major*, and the Egyptian jackal to all be emblems of Time.[99]

Epitheus: And the name Barak means both 'thunderbolt' and 'to bend at the knee'. But being on one knee is likewise the term for a gift ('berakah'). And we know that Jacob withstood God so as to attain from him a blessing, and so likewise it is the might of God which brings a man to his knees in prayer. But could we not see this too as part of the perpetual struggle: where the serpent's head is crushed but that he, in turn, bites the heel. And thus if we might regard the two brothers to be *Orion* and *Hercules* fighting over their sister, when the constellations become aligned with the *solstices* or the *equinoxes*, then it might be related to the yearly battle between the sun and moon. This would also mean that the sun and moon would not be absolutely related to either constellation, but that they would rather trade places.

Soleos: Quite perceptive, Epitheus.

Thaeo: And just as Hesiod tells us, Hercules was responsible for thrusting his spear into the thigh of Aries, who in turn he stabbed the thigh of Hercules.[100] Or in the case of Hercules against Achelous, in their battle over Dejanira, Achelous made himself a serpent and then a bull, which could likewise be *Scorpius* and *Taurus*.[101*]

Epitheus: Yes. And one can imagine too that since it is Minerva (Athena) who tosses this serpent up into the heavens to become *Draco*, that it could be that **EDEN** did likewise. Thus this would represent the eternal struggle of the mortal *Hercules* descending beneath the horizon with *Draco* being the immortal one.

Thaeo: This brings to mind again Erechthonios who is likewise said to be lame, since it could be that the serpent which Minerva fights and throws up into the heavens is actually the one that is found in the

---

* See *Roar of the Tempests: A Dialogue*

basket of Erechthonios. And that this is the eternal half, and then there would likewise be is a lame, or mortal, half.[*]

Soleos: Thus we could well see the cycle between *Hercules* where he is smiting the head of the serpent *Draco*, and *Orion* who is being bitten in the heel by the serpent *Eridanus* combined into a myth of the god who slays the dragon but at the same time is injured in his heel.[102]   As likewise in the story of the Aztecs where we find Hunupu's foot bitten off by the Earth Monster while she was deprived of her lower jaw, and Krishna who is likewise injured on his foot by the serpent Kalli Naga.[103]   And Horus, after defeating Set, places his foot upon his head while he secures him with a chain.[104]

Epitheus: Thus we are seeing again the eternal confrontation with the serpent.

Thaeo: Truly it seems so, and this struggle too being symbolic of mortality and immortality.   Thus Jacob is likewise equivalent to Achilles and to Gilgamesh, who suffers the loss of immortality; while each of them too has an adversary (Esau, Hektor, and Enkidu).[†]

Soleos: And thus they could well be represented by the constellations of *Hercules* and *Orion*.   Though, depending upon how we might view the figure of *Orion*, *Rigel* could be either seen upon his thigh or upon his heel, since, as we have seen, there is little distinction between the wound to either.[‡]

Epitheus: Yes.   But should we then consider that *Orion* the bowman corresponds with Enkidu and Esau, or rather that the hunter who first spots Enkidu was Gilgamesh himself?

---

[*] In Egypt the 'lameness' of the dead was associated with the baleful influences of Set. ('Book of the Dead' plate xviii, chapter lxxiv; Budge 1999: 292)
[†] Jacob too could be said to have been denied immortality, as Achilles and Gilgamesh, as depicted through his lameness.
[‡] Orion is illustrated with *Rigel* shown either on his foot or his thigh.

Soleos: As you are leading us in that direction, Epitheus, we might well consider this matter more fully, if that would be to your liking.

Epitheus: Certainly, it would.

Soleos: Then if we were to identify every episode within the 'Gilgamesh Cycle' and then attempt to associate each one with a specific constellation–thus forming a sequence about the entire *ecliptic*–what do you think would be the best choice among the connections we could make to provide us with a starting point?[*]

Epitheus: We could perhaps start by linking the Bull of Heaven with the constellation of *Taurus*.

Soleos: Yes. So let us test this out to see if this might be accurate. And in doing so we must then identify episodes which correspond with constellations to either side of *Taurus*, which are those of *Aries* and *Gemini*, or perhaps anything within their vicinity.

Epitheus: Yes.

Soleos: And what do we find occurring prior and subsequent to the slaying of the Bull of Heaven?

Epitheus: Prior to the slaying of the Bull of Heaven is the killing of the demon Humbaba, while afterwards comes the death of Enkidu, although I am not entirely certain of this.

Soleos: Indeed you are, but then do these constitute a match, either with *Aries* or *Gemini*.

Epitheus: I do not recognize here a match.

Soleos: So it might be that *Taurus* does not represent the Bull of Heaven, or that we have launched ourselves into a wild goose chase. But let us not give up just yet, but rather begin again by attempting to identify something else we might utilize as a starting point.

---

[*] See *The Gilgamesh Cycle*

Epitheus: Well, the scorpion men he encounters at the mountains could have something to do with *Scorpius*.

Soleos: Good. Then let us consider this one, and as this it follows immediately after the death of Enkidu, we would likewise have to imagine it to be associated with *Libra*, which lies on the other side of it. Thus, in this case, the episode with Ishtar and the Bull of Heaven would have to be matched with *Virgo*, which makes perfect sense, given that this is a representation of the Goddess.

Epitheus: Yes. So in tracing our way backwards from this we could identify *Taurus* not as the Bull of Heaven but rather as Gilgamesh, when he is referred to as a 'wild bull'.

Soleos: And this would appear at once to satisfy all of our requirements, as we might then identify *Orion* with the hunter, who is the first man who spots Enkidu after he comes down from the uplands; while *Auriga* is associated with the goat star *Capella*, and thus could be the shepherds Shamhat then leads him to.

Epitheus: I would have to agree with what you say, Soleos, for following this would be the contest between Enkidu and Gilgamesh, after Enkidu has come into the gates of Uruk. And then after they battle, Enkidu becomes Gilgamesh's adoptive brother. And it would make sense to me that this would be *Gemini*, and then so too the lions which they meet upon the mountain passes must be the constellation *Leo*.

Soleos: This, again, would make perfect sense, given that in ancient Mesopotamia the constellation of *Cancer* was associated with the Tigris and Euphrates rivers; and it is the river Euphrates which is the one said to guide them west to the Pine Forest.[105]

Epitheus: And what follows then is their contest with the demon Humbaba, and this would have to be placed between *Leo* and the slaying of the Bull of Heaven which we thought was *Virgo*; but there remain no constellations here apart from *Corvus*.

Soleos: Then we might have to devise something else for Humbaba, for we might consider Humbaba to be represented by *Ursa Major*, which could be positioned here, although it is more often aligned with *Cancer*. Though I cannot help but imagine that he could also be associated with the 'Sphinx' constellation we were speaking of before.[*] And this figure appears in the form of a cherub, being a combination of the lion, maiden, and bird (*Leo*, *Virgo*, and *Corvus*).[†]

Epitheus: Yes. And this would make some sense, given that in the following episode with the Bull of Heaven, that Enkidu rips out the bull's leg and throws it at Ishtar. Thus this might be represented by *Ursa Major*, which would then follow the 'Sphinx'.

Soleos: Well said. Then, as we said before, *Virgo* would be the Goddess of Heaven; and it now makes sense to find that *Taurus* lies directly opposite *Virgo* through the sky's pole, while taking on here the identity of the Bull of Heaven.

Epitheus: Perfectly.

Soleos: Then *Libra* would have to be the location corresponding with Enkidu's death, and this fits too with things we said previously, in relation to this particular constellation.[‡]

---

[*] It might be presumed that the 'Sphinx' constellation was deemed significant when it was aligned with the vernal *equinox*, however in Egypt it might well have been aligned with the Egyptian New Year, which occurred about the time of the summer solstice. Thus, if the former, the construction of the Great Sphinx then would be around 12,960 years ago or about 11,000 BC. If the latter then it would be around 6,480 years ago or c. 4500 BC, thus predating the Giza Pyramids by about 2,000 years–which is far more reasonable. (The Egyptian First Dynasty arose c. 3100 BC.) The Great Sphinx faces east, which is perhaps how the sphinx form in later times acquired its moniker, 'Living Image of Atum'. This also means that during Egypt's most prosperous time the sun would have been in *Leo* at the Egyptian New Year, and *Sirius* would have heralded the sunrise at this time.
[†] It is possible that all animals in the heavens were given wings merely as a matter of course, apart from those constellations adjacent to *Aquarius* which were viewed as being finned. Thus too for the same reason are angels represented with wings, to indicate their heavenly origin.
[‡] See *The Zodiac Mysteries*

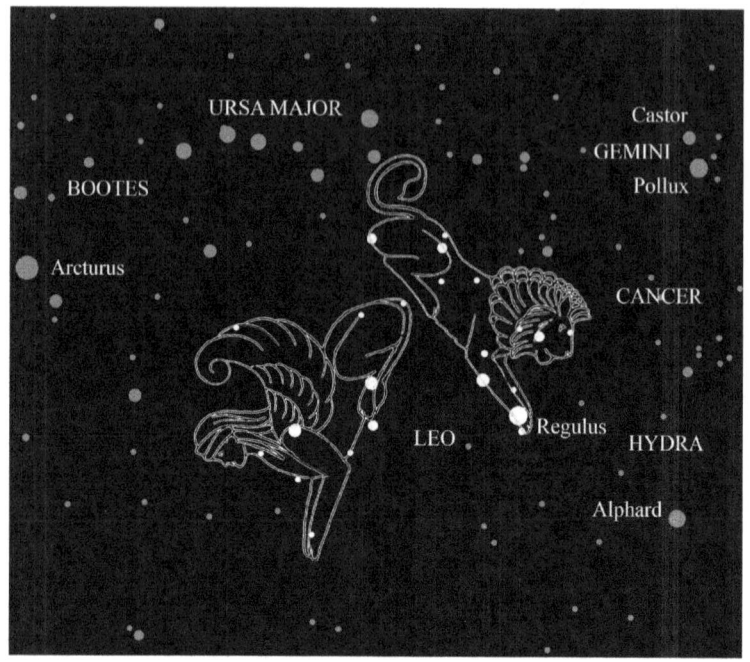

Two ancient asterisms within *Leo*?: the Lion and the Sphinx.

Epitheus: Truly.

Soleos: Then we arrive at the scorpion, who in Mesopotamia is shown holding the scales of *Libra* within its claws, but which is likewise associated with death and mourning, and as such represents a fitting location for Enkidu's funeral.[*]

Epitheus: Indeed.

Soleos: So then, as you mentioned earlier, the scorpion men must appear at *Scorpius*, and *Sagittarius* would then correspond with the beer-maid Siduri. And this too would make sense given that we

---

[*] *Libra* was associated in ancient Mesopotamia with death and the underworld. (White 2008: 34)

could link Siduri and her garden with the warrioress Athena and the tree of the Hesperides.

Phaedo: And likewise we thought that Athena could be readily identified with Ishtar,[*] and Siduri was known as the 'Ishtar of wisdom'.

Soleos: Yes. Then the constellations which follow are *Aquila* and *Capricornus* before we reach *Aquarius*.

Epitheus: And it would seem to me that this latter must surely correspond to the Great Flood story recounted by Utnapishtim; and likewise this constellation is to have been the very source of that deluge.[†] So the remaining span must correspond to the crossing of the sea and the Waters of Doom.

Soleos: And this could well mean we would have to include *Corona Australis*, which was known in ancient Mesopotamia as the 'Cargo Boat'; being the ship by which Gilgamesh and Urshanabi made their way across the sea and Waters of Doom.

Epitheus: So then we might too surmise that the constellation of *Capricornus*, which before we found could be identified with a marsh associated with the underworld abyss, could be the Waters of Doom which they cross prior to reaching Utnapishtim.

Soleos: Well done. Then following the recollection of the Great Flood by Utnapishtim, we then arrive at the constellations of *Pisces* and *Pegasus*. And as before we recognized, the 'Great Square' of *Pegasus* to be the 'Field of the Blessed' and the source of the rivers, which we likewise found was linked with the god Shiva as source of the Ganges.[‡]

Epitheus: Yes, we did.

---

[*] See *The Eden Enigma: A Dialogue*
[†] *Aquarius* is linked to Deucalion and the Great Flood. (Krupp 1991: 138)
[‡] See *The Zodiac Mysteries* and *The Eden Enigma: A Dialogue*

CHAPTER 9

Soleos: This is also where Utnapishtim himself is said to have been located, which is likewise described as the location at the 'source of the rivers'.[*] And so too it is the place where there is located the 'fountain of life' and source of the sacred brew of immortality, thus it is fitting that this too is where Gilgamesh finds the plant which would bring him eternal youth.

Epitheus: Entirely.

Soleos: And here is where Gilgamesh descends down into the Apsu, or the world Abyss, so as to gain this plant of immortality. Travelling down the pipe (*'ratu'*), this would match what we were saying before, which is that the circlet of the 'western fish' of *Pisces* is likewise in communication with the Abyss, and that this was the conduit through which it could be reached. This likewise would be similar to the breach made by Odin when he used a drill (*'rati'*) to gain access to the cave of Gunnlod so as to acquire the Mead of Poetry.

Epitheus: Truly astounding.

Soleos: Then after acquiring the plant it comes to be stolen out of his grasp by the earthly predator, the serpent; and this too occurs by the side of a pool which must then be found between *Pisces* and *Taurus*, and thus in the neighborhood of *Aries*, which could well prove to be the constellation of the sea-dragon *Cetus*.

Epitheus: That would certainly make sense, which before we identified as a baleful constellation.

Soleos: Though I cannot help but think that the serpent who gains eternal life by eating the plant, and thus shedding its skin to regain its youth, has something in common with the polar constellation *Draco*. For this, along with the other constellations immediately around the

---

[*] The Tigris and Euphrates rivers

pole were thought to represent eternal life because they never set below the horizon.

Epitheus: One might think.

Soleos: And it is interesting too that the only part of the 'Kneeler' which does not pass below the horizon is his left knee and foot. As Aratus says,

> When the Lion (*Leo*) makes his appearance then these constellations (around *Aquarius*) pass from view, which had been on the decline when the Crab (*Cancer*) ascended; and along with them passes the Eagle (*Aquila*) from view. And the 'Phantom' (*Hercules*), set upon his knees, himself but for his left knee and foot descends below the turbid sea.[106]

Or in other words, the only part of the 'Kneeler', being the foot with which he crushes the serpent's head, is the only part of him which retains its immortality. And this is precisely contrary to the vulnerable left heel we find on *Orion*.

Epitheus: As you say.

Soleos: And thus by coming to *Cetus* this would conclude things by bringing us around again to the constellation of *Taurus*, but also too the *Pleiades*. And this certainly appears to be no accident, for this constellation was identified with the commencement of spring by the ancient Egyptians, and likewise marked the start of the Mayan and Aztec New Year.[*]

Epitheus: What you have done is entirely edifying, Soleos, but there is one thing arising from it which still confuses me.

Soleos: What is that?

Epitheus: It does not appear to me that Gilgamesh must be the constellation of *Hercules*, as we surmised, for from our assessment

---

[*] Including the Maori of New Zealand who call them the Matariki

Gilgamesh was linked with the bull *Taurus*, and we found the hunter and the shepherds who first encounter Enkidu were represented by *Orion* and *Auriga*. But then where is Enkidu himself?

Soleos: An intelligent observation, Epitheus. I can only answer this by suggesting that Enkidu may have appeared originally as *Orion*, whereas Gilgamesh, going on his quest after his friend Enkidu's death, would yet be aligned with *Hercules*. Or we must suppose that Enkidu would have made his appearance somewhere between *Orion* and *Taurus*, figuring that he came after the bullish display of Gilgamesh but prior to when he is spotted by the hunter.

    Enkidu then would make his appearance around the star of *Aldebaran*, which is precisely opposite the constellation of *Libra*. And as we considered before, that *Libra* was associated with death; and thus we find at this point that Gilgamesh dons a lion skin to wander in his journey which takes him from *Scorpius* through *Cetus*, which is half of the entire cycle. Thus, likewise, the former half would have begun at *Taurus* and concluded with the death of Enkidu at *Libra*.

Epitheus: I understand, and with Enkidu being dominant for half the cycle and Gilgamesh in the other, it could mean we are seeing precisely what we have previously been speaking of already; that the two could be the same two brothers of sun and moon, where Enkidu represents the sun and Gilgamesh the moon, with each ruling over half of the year.

Soleos: That is a very promising conclusion; and thus likewise we must presume that if the *Pleiades* and *Taurus* were aligned with the winter *solstice*, when the sun starts to predominate, this would place the spring *equinox* at *Leo*, the summer *solstice* at *Libra*, and the autumnal *equinox* at *Capricornus*.

Epitheus: And if we began at the *Pleiades* and continued at 12 equal intervals around the ecliptic, the constellations we find would be: *Taurus*, *Orion*, *Gemini*, *Leo*, the 'Sphinx', *Virgo*, *Libra*, *Scorpius*, *Sagittarius*, *Capricornus*, *Aquarius*, and *Pisces*. Or, if we included too an interval at the close of the year, representing 5 *intercalated* days between *Pisces* and *Taurus*, this could be represented by the sea monster *Cetus*.

Soleos: Nicely done.

Epitheus: Thank you. But might this not also permit us to date the origin of the cycle itself, presuming all of our assumptions are correct?

Soleos: It might well. But it would appear we are left with only two possible alternatives: the first being that the appearance of the sun corresponds to the spring *equinox*, or otherwise with the winter *solstice*. So in the first case, when the sun is at the *Pleiades* at the time of the spring *equinox*, which would be the Age of Taurus–two ages back from where we are now–assuming each age is one Great Month or 2,160 years in duration, this would place its origin at around 2300 BC. Whereas if we were to presume that it was at the winter *solstice*, which would be in the Age of Leo, this then would span five ages back or 10,800 years, which would place it at about 8800 BC. And although this could cause us to conclude that the story of Gilgamesh must first have been composed shortly before being written down, around 2000 BC, there is something which causes me to consider that an earlier date might well be justified.

Epitheus: What makes you think so?

Soleos: Knowing that the 'Gilgamesh Cycle' was being written down around 2000 BC, then it goes without saying that the story must already have developed prior to this.

Epitheus: Yes.

Soleos: But it seems to me that if we consider Gilgamesh to be the moon and Enkidu to be the sun, we before recognized the similarity in how this pair is described in comparison to Jacob and Esau, who are likewise representative of the moon and sun, as well as the others we have considered.

Epitheus: Truly.

Soleos: But further we might even consider their names, for we find that Gilgamesh, who is known in Greek as Gilgamos,[107] has the root form of 'Gilgam'; so that his name would truly be Gilgam-esh or 'Lord Gilgam'. And we might likewise pronounce this as 'Jilcam' which sounds a great deal like 'Jacob'; and thus too we have associated both of them with the moon.

Epitheus: That is quite masterful.

Soleos: And as for the name of Jacob, being 'Jacob-El' or 'Jacob-Hur', this means precisely the same, 'Lord Jacob'.[*]

Epitheus: Yes.

Soleos: But so too if we take the resemblance of 'Gilgam' with Achilles, in the root form 'Agill', likewise his great adversary Hektor has a name easily comparable with Enkidu. And in this sense we might then presume that the battle between these two great heroes is no different than that fought between Gilgamesh and Enkidu; or likewise, that of the moon against the sun for dominance over the earth.[†]

And as we said Achilles is the son of King Peleus and the goddess Thetis, as Gilgamesh likewise had a mortal father and a divine mother; while both too are denied eternal life. So then we might consider that these three: Jacob, Gilgamesh, and Achilles are entirely similar, as likewise we must Esau, Enkidu, and Hektor. But there is a problem which arises when comparing the name of Enkidu with Esau, though we might well pursue this question from a different avenue.

Epitheus: In what manner?

Soleos: As Phaedo mentioned before, Achilles' name could well arise from the word 'ankle'. And thus could we not suppose that the other figure, of Hektor or Enkidu, was related rather to the 'neck', by

---

[*] Considering the Biblical names Abihu and Abiyah, and Elihu and Elijah, the suffixes can be considered the same, and thus 'hu' and 'yah' mean equally the divine name.
[†] Likewise if Achilles' name is compared with Cu Chulainn's

136

which he met his own end? For we find in relation to Achilles and Jacob that they are both associated with the heel: one through grabbing his brother's heel, the other because it remained his vulnerable part.

Epitheus: Just so.

Soleos: But, as we said, Jacob killed Esau by letting loose an arrow, which is rather more like the death of Achilles. Unless this arrow was to have stuck him in the neck, which would make him more like Hektor, who was killed by a spear thrust to his neck when he fought Achilles at the Scamander River.

Epitheus: Truly.

Soleos: On top of this it would seem as though one of the two twins was born by an unnatural manner. And this would make sense if it were deemed that a natural birth is what brought about mortality, while an unnatural birth bestowed immortality. So we could assume that it was because Jacob grabbed Esau's heel, as he made his way out of his mother's side, as do Indra and Set, that this remained his only mortal part. Thus it makes sense that Jacob would have hit him with an arrow to his heel, or rather that initially he himself was thus wounded. So we might well consider whether the true reason that Jacob was named after the heel was because he was precisely like Achilles.

Epitheus: That is true.

Soleos: And so here we would have Gilgamesh, Achilles, and Jacob as the moon and Enkidu, Hektor, and Esau as the sun.[*]

Epitheus: Yes.

---

[*] Achilles is known as the 'swift runner' while Hektor is known for his shining bronze helmet. (See also *The Iliad* xviii, 390; Fagles 1990: 478.)

Soleos: And thus the adversary of the moon might either be known as 'Sol' (Saul, Esau) or as 'Neck' (Enkidu, Hektor), being the place where he received his wound.

Epitheus: Incredible!   But we also noticed that there existed a correspondence between Jacob and Esau on the one hand and the contest between David and Saul on the other; and likewise with that between Set and Horus.[*]   And this also had something to do with the calibration of the calendar. So could we not consider this in terms of the relationship between David and Saul, for we do have a contest between the two of them, yet we also found that David rather corresponded with Set?

Thaeo: Indeed. And this raises the question of whether there were in fact two contests: one where Jacob slew Esau and another where Jacob confronted his own father. This then would be more like the contest between David and Saul, but also suggests that in addition there would be a contest between David and Jonathan, being the two sons of Saul. So we would have to believe that in one case Jacob beheaded his own father, but was himself lamed in the thigh, and then in the next contest slew his brother with an arrow. And recall that both from Isaac and from God did Jacob receive a blessing.

Epitheus: Yes.

Thaeo: Likewise, we discovered that something quite unusual lies behind the story of David, Saul, and Jonathan; and that there is truly more to Jonathan than meets the eye, when we considered him to be equivalent to the god Dionysos.

Epitheus: And further there is the presence of the son of Saul called Ishbosheth and the son of Jonathan named Mephibosheth. But 'bosheth' ('shame') was merely added to prevent the actual speaking of the abominable name of 'Baal'. Thus their real names would be Eshbaal and Meribbaal, which mean 'son of Baal' and 'destroyer of Baal'; and this makes perfect sense given that Baal is equivalent to Balder, the sun.

---

[*] See *The Death of King David: A Dialogue*

And thus we might have this very situation, if we equate Saul with Baal, that Jonathan is said to have eaten the honeycomb after which Saul slays him,[*] if he carried this act out rather than refraining. Then we find that Jonathan had a son named 'destroyer of Baal', and this Meribbaal then emerges himself at a later time to slay Saul ("Baal"), who likewise had given birth to a son named 'son of Baal'. Then we must presume that Eshbaal eventually becomes Baal himself, while Meribbaal matures into Jonathan. And we could presume that these contests likewise indicate the presence of a name change, from Eshbaal to Saul and from Meribbaal to Jonathan, just as we find Jacob's name becoming Israel in his contest. And this is not unlike what occurs between Set and Osiris, for Osiris too gives birth to a son Horus who then eventually matures, himself, into Osiris.

As such too my brother Protheus suggested just such a transformation, so that the one who defeats the other finds himself lamed; so that Jacob slays his brother Esau, and at this moment Esau gives birth to a son who escapes. And we can recognize here an even greater equivalence, when we suggest that Saul was beheaded by David in the cave but himself suffered emasculation in return, and likewise that Jacob beheaded Esau but himself was wounded in his thigh and left lame.[†]

And so too we find that Meribbal is himself said to be lame, which would match precisely the fate of Jacob, while Eshbaal is said to have met his death through beheading, which would match what we presume to be the fate of Esau and Saul.[‡] And notice here that Meribbal is introduced just prior to the mention of Eshbaal being slain, though it is David who, in turn, is the destroyer of the killers of Ishbosheth. As it says,

> The sons of Rimmon the Be-erothite, Rachab the Baanah, travelled until about noon when they had reached the house of Ish-bosheth while he was taking his mid-day nap. And they found that the doorkeeper of his house had been cleaning wheat but she had become tired and fallen asleep, such that Rechab and his brother Baanah were able to steal themselves inside. And

---

[*] 1 Samuel 14:43-45
[†] See *The Death of King David: A Dialogue*
[‡] 2 Samuel 4:7, 1 Samuel 31:9

when they had gotten into his house, while he was lying upon his bed in his bedroom, they struck him, killing him, and then beheaded him. Then they took his head and went by way of the Arabah through the night, bringing the head of Ish-bosheth to David in Hebron. And they declared to the king, "We bring you the head of Ish-bosheth, Saul's son, your foe who sought to kill you. Yahweh has been my master, the king's avenger today, upon Saul and his children."

However, David replied to Rechab and his brother Baanah, the sons of Rimmon the Be-erothite, "As Yahweh lives, who has brought me safely out of every danger, when one reported to me, 'Know that Saul is dead,' thinking that he was declaring good news, I took him and had him killed at Ziklag, being his reward for passing along this report. But how much more when vile men have murdered a good man within his own house and upon his own bed, would I not seek recompense for his blood from you and wipe you off the face of the earth?" So David gave the order to his young men and they slew them, cutting off their hands and feet, and then hung them beside the basin at Hebron. But they took up the head of Ish-bosheth and set it within the tomb of Abner in Hebron.[108]

As for the fate of Mephibosheth it says,

There was a famine in the days of David that lasted for three consecutive years, and so David went before the face of Yahweh, and Yahweh said, "There is a bloodguilt upon Saul and upon his house, because he killed the Gibeonites."

Thus the king summoned the Gibeonites, who were not a people of Israel but were a remnant of the Amorites. And although the people of Israel had sworn an oath to spare them, Saul had wished to destroy them in his fanaticism for the people of Israel and Judah.

David said to the Gibeonites, "What might I do for you, and what reparations could I make that you will come to revere the traditions of Yahweh?"

And the Gibeonites answered him, "The matter between us and Saul or his house is not one of silver and gold, nor do we wish the death of any man in Israel."

So he asked, "Then name yourselves what I should do for you?"

And they said to the king, "For the man who gave us no peace and wished to bring about our demise, such that we should enjoy no land within the entire territory of Israel, would have seven of his sons be brought to us that we might hang them before Yahweh at Gibeon, upon the mountain of Yahweh."

The king replied, "I will hand them over."

But the king did not hand over Mephibosheth, the son of Saul's son Jonathan, because of the oath which was sworn by Yahweh between them: between David and Jonathan, the son of Saul.[109]

So this would have us believe that David has spared Mephibosheth, yet it goes on to say,

The king gathered the two sons of Rizpah, daughter of Aiah, whom she had borne to Saul, named Armoni and Mephibosheth; along with the five sons of Merab, daughter of Saul, whom she had borne to Adri-el, son of Barzillai the Meholathite. And he gave them over to the Gibeonites, and they hanged them upon the mountain in front of Yahweh, and thus the seven of them died at once. And they were put to death upon the first day of reaping, at the start of the barley harvest.[110]

So this amounts to a strange tale of the hanging of a son of Saul, also named Mephibosheth. And here we find that David is responsible for the slaying, indirectly, of this Mephibosheth, while sparing the son of Jonathan of the same name. So what precisely must be going on here; might we rather presume that these two sons named Mephibosheth are, in fact, the very same?

Thaeo: Such a thing is difficult to answer, but it does indicate that the hanging of the seven was a rite associated with the barley harvest, where they are taken up the mountain of Yahweh and are there sacrificed before God.

Epitheus: So then let us proceed to see what happens following this:

Rizpah, daughter of Aiah took some sackcloth and spread it out upon the rock as a bed for herself, and from the start of the harvest until the rains showered down from the sky she did not permit the birds of the air to approach them by day, nor the beasts of the country by night. And when David had been told what Rizpah, daughter of Aiah, the concubine of Saul, had done, he went forth and brought the bones of Saul and those of his son Jonathan from the men of Jabesh-gilead—who had themselves taken them from the public square at Beth-shan where the Philistnies had hanged them the day that the Philistines had killed Saul on Gilboa. And he took from there the bones of Saul and the bones of Jonathan his son, and also collected the bones of those who had been hanged, then buried the bones of Saul and Jonathan his son in Zela, in the land of Benjamin, within the tomb of his father Kish. And they did everything that the king commanded them to do. And following this God paid heed to their prayers for the sake of the land.[111]

Thaeo: So we find here that God had seemingly refused to hear the prayers of the people concerning their land, until David collected the bones of Saul's house and dealt with them properly; though it is certainly odd that God here extends his wrath so as to include assurance that the rains will not fall. For it says that Rizpah guarded the bodies from the start of the harvest until the time when the rains fell, and this would indicate from the end of one growing season to the start of the next, at which time the bodies were properly buried and God then restored the bounty of the land.

Epitheus: Yes, I am at a loss to explain it.

Thaeo: We could conclude that this associates these deaths with the solar year; and specifically, if we were to divide the year between Jonathan and Saul, that we likewise find the appearance of David to slay King Saul, which we before identified with the commencement of King David's reign.

Epitheus: We did.

Thaeo: And here we find that the calendar is principally that of the sun, wherein Saul rules for a period of years until it becomes out of step, at which point David enters and rules for a time so as to bring the nominal calendar back into line with the solar calendar.[*]

Epitheus: Truly, that is what we found.

Thaeo: Thus we have David slaying Saul rather than Meribbaal slaying him, but that after the termination of his reign Jonathan would have to return, and thus this could explain the presence of the son of Meribbaal, who is Micah ('who's afraid?').[†] For then this would mean that when David slays Saul that he gives birth to Micah, who in turn would have to re-establish the yearly balance between Jonathan and Saul; since we figured that David confronts Saul in the cave. But he rules then for his duration of time before the arrival not of Saul's son Eshbaal but of his son Micah.[‡] So we find then a contest between Jonathan and David rather than between Jonathan and Saul, where afterwards there arises an agreement between the two of them which permits David to rule for a duration of time. Until in the end there arrives the grandson of Saul who restores Saul's kingdom, and who himself must then become King Saul.

Epitheus: Such a thing could well be, and certainly makes sense to me.

Thaeo: Then each of these contests occurs with the defeat of one and the arising of his replacement in the form of a son; where Meribbaal is the slayer of Saul who himself gives rise to a son Eshbaal, who then grows over six months to become the avenger of Saul's

---

[*] See *The Death of King David: A Dialogue*

[†] 2 Samuel 9:12. Nothing else is said of him, but the name Mica is the old Persian form of Mitra. (see Kent, Ronald G. (1953), Old Persian: Grammar, Lexicon, Texts (2nd ed.), New Haven: American Oriental Society, §78/p. 31b; Ware, James R. and. Roland G. Kent (1924), 'The Old Persian Cuneiform Inscriptions of Artaxerxes II and Artaxerxes III', Transactions and Proceedings of the American Philological Association. The Johns Hopkins University Press, 55: 52–61.)

[‡] Assuming Micah is the son of Saul's son rather than Jonathan's son Meribbaal.

("Baal's") death through the slaying of Jonathan, who himself gives rise to a son named Meribbaal and so the cycle continues. But that every 8th year it is David who must defeat Saul, for the duration of the entire solar year, before he is then defeated with the restoration of Saul's reign and of the regular sequence.

Epitheus: So this would cause us to associate Jonathan with the moon and Saul with the sun, but what would David then be?

Thaeo: As you said, it is similar to the situation of Osiris, wherein he gives birth to a son Horus after he is slain by Set. And then Horus arises to claim his father's former kingdom by conquering Set, while he himself matures to become Osiris, and thus the cycle repeats. And in the case of the (Egyptian) gods Re and Set, the calendar of Re is 360 days long, but after 72 years it would be off by an entire year. Thus there was then inserted an entire year or a 'year of Set'. But then there was also a situation where 13 months comprised the solar year, constituting the entire Zodiac of 13 signs, or the 13 body parts of Osiris; where each year is instead 364 days long, so that every 28 years one entire month must be added.

Epitheus: Yes.

Thaeo: So we ought to consider that in the first case we have substituted Re for Osiris, for the contest as it is recorded by Plutarch is said to be between Osiris and Set.[112]

Epitheus: True.

Thaeo: Thus we could well consider that the original rivalry was with Re, given that the calendar comprises a 360-day solar year.

Epitheus: That makes perfect sense.

Thaeo: Then instead of the contest being between Re and Set it could likewise have been between Re and Osiris, where each rules over half of the solar year. But as we know, there emerges a discrepancy as the calendar is thrown off each year by 5 days.

Epitheus: Indeed.

Thaeo: So then when this year goes out of balance we would have to imagine that a third figure emerges, and this one would then be Set, known as the 'scarlet ass', and according to Plutarch the one who engenders maladies.[113] And for this reason too we must associate him again with David who is described as being 'ruddy', and who we before identified with Set.[*]

Epitheus: Yes.

Thaeo: Thus we have the situation between Osiris and Re, where Osiris gives rise to Horus and where Set is responsible for the slaying of Osiris, but so too that his phallus is lost which we considered to be equivalent to the castration of David.[†]

Epitheus: Indeed.

Thaeo: And before we compared the dismemberment of Osiris with that of Dionysos, but in each case too of their subsequent rebirths. And in the case of Osiris he is said to be both castrated and dismembered, but likewise the one who performs this act is Set, the uncle of Harpocrates, who is the son of Osiris.

Epitheus: Yes. And here too, just as in the case where the paternal uncle of Harpocrates is Set, the 'scarlet ass', we likewise find the paternal uncle of Jacob to be Ishmael, who is described as a 'wild ass of a man'.[114]

Thaeo: Just so. But likewise we find that the slayers of Ishbosheth, the son of Saul, themselves have their hands and feet cut off on the orders of King David. And this would make sense given that when Ishbosheth was slain by Mephibosheth that he in turn would be dismembered, which we considered was a possibility for Jonathan. And we also find Set castrated by Horus; so too that Jacob is lamed

---

[*] See *The Death of King David: A Dialogue*
[†] See *The Death of King David: A Dialogue*

in the thigh by his opponent; and likewise that David was castrated in the cave when Saul was beheaded.

Epitheus: Indeed. So too we find that Mephibosheth, the son of Jonathan, is made lame in his legs, although we are told that this was due to an accident.[*]

Thaeo: But if we recall too that Dionysos was prematurely born but grew quickly before being dismembered by the Titans, that he was born prematurely in the seventh month; from a mortal mother and a divine father, who are named as either Semele and Zeus or Amaltheia and Ammon.[115] And Amaltheia bore the visage of a goat which is also true of the God (Dionysos), and Dionysos was taken to a cave upon mount Nysa, on an island of the river Triton. And again I think the period of seven months must signify the duration between the *solstices*.

Epitheus: Truly.

Thaeo: So consider what the Phrygians thought of Dionysos: that he was imprisoned and slept during the winter but was freed and awake during the summer.[116] Likewise that he made his appearance at the time of the winter *solstice*, where Apollo was likewise representative of the summer.[117]

Epitheus: Yes.

---

[*] 2 Samuel 4:4. It is difficult to reconcile, however, being born lame with becoming lame. If this is the same figure, we could assume that he is born lame, but like children who are born with a shorter leg which grows out. Thus being born lame was judged to be the inheritance of his lamed father.

CHAPTER 10

Thaeo: We might further consider this relationship between Dionysos and Apollo by recognizing that both were considered to be aspects of Helios (the sun).[118]

Epitheus: That is interesting.

Thaeo: Likewise, we know that Achilles slew Hektor but was in turn slain by Paris, whom we before thought was comparable with Perseus, and so too Perseus was responsible for defeating Dionysos.[*]

Epitheus: Yes.

Thaeo: And, Perseus fought Dionysos and his army of sea-maidens at Argos, throwing the God into lake Lerna while his army was pursued and slain.[119] And Dionysos is associated too with the *Hyades* through his name Hyes,[120] and so we should not be surprised to find that the *Hyades* are located in the constellation of *Taurus*, for the God was called both the bull and the 'son of a bull'.

Epitheus: Not at all.

Thaeo: Yet again from the implications of this we cannot presume there are here only two figures, but that there must have been three. When we have the sequence of Hektor being slain by Achilles and himself being slain by Paris; and thus so too we have a similar circumstance with Apollo, Dionysos, and Perseus.

Epitheus: But Osiris is a reborn god just as Dionysos is a reborn god; and the episode of Jonathan also leads to him being reborn in the form of Meribbaal, who is Baal's slayer.

Thaeo: Yes. But then too we identified Perseus with *Ursa Major*, which is placed along the ecliptic at the location of *Cancer*.[†] And although this is often deemed to be a bear, it is likewise identified as

---

[*] See *Roar of the Tempests: A Dialogue*
[†] See *Roar of the Tempests: A Dialogue*

a boar. So thus too the boar which attacks Adonis certainly makes more sense.

Epitheus: In what way?

Thaeo: In the sense that we could then compare the two we were speaking of before, which were *Orion* and *Hercules*. And we can identify which constellation culminates (reaches its peak) when *Orion* sinks, and this constellation is none other than *Ursa Major*, which likewise corresponds to Perseus or Paris; while we also know that *Orion* represents Tammuz or Dumuzi, who is the very same as Adonis.

Epitheus: Yes.

Thaeo: But we also find that Dionysos is involved with another heroic figure, Theseus, the son of Poseidon and Aethra. For it is Ariadne who gave him aid in his confrontation with the dreaded Minotaur, when Dionysos took her for himself, as Hesiod says,

> Golden-haired Dionysos grabbed flaxen-haired Ariadne,
> The fair daughter of Minos, to have as his bosomy bride,
> While Zeus, son of Cronos, made her eternal and timeless[121]

Epitheus: But could you not please tell us the entire story?

Thaeo: If you would like to hear it, Epitheus, certainly. I believe I have enough of the pieces at my disposal to attempt a fair reconstruction of events. And it might be relevant here, as before I spoke to you of the line of Inachos as far as Hercules,[*] that I now speak of the descendants of Agenor; for Poseidon with Libya are said to have had two sons named Belos and Agenor. The first of these became king of Egypt and himself had twin sons (Aigyptos and Danaos), while Agenor went to Phoenicia where he married Telephassa and had three sons named Cadmos, Phoenix, and Cilix; and also a daughter named Europa. And once she had grown into her teens Zeus became desirous of Europa and went to her in the

---

[*] See *Roar of the Tempests: A Dialogue*

form of a tame white bull with rosy breath, and took her across the sea to Crete upon his back where they made love. From this she gave birth to three sons named Minos, Sarpedon, and Rhadamanthys.

Meanwhile Europa's father had sent out his sons to find her whereabouts, giving them orders to not even think of returning until they had located her. They were joined in this endeavor by her mother Telephassa and also Thasos, a son of Poseidon. Their extensive search failed to discover her whereabouts, but knowing they could not return home they each instead colonized their own land: Phoenix somewhere in Phoenicia, which took their name from him; Cilix nearby in the land of Cilicia which is upon the Pyramos River; while Cadmos and Telephassa went to Thrace with Thasos, who was the founder of the city of that name. And this is all that need be said concerning the sons of Agenor.

Europa, however, soon thereafter became wife to Asterios, king of Crete, and there her children grew. And by the time they were fully grown Sarpedon was at war with Minos over Miletos who then fled to Caria, which he renamed Miletos; some of which was given to Cilix to make them his allies. Thereafter Sarpedon became king of Lycia after fighting against them with Cilix, who had hitherto been at war with them. So Rhadmanthys made his way to Boetia while Minos remained in Crete. Minos established laws upon the island, as had Rhadmanthys once done before him–and thus when these two died they were made judges in Hades. But as Minos continued to live in Crete he married Pasiphae, who was the daughter of Helios (sun) and Perseis (moon).[122]

When King Asterios died he had no heir, thus Minos sought the throne of Crete for himself; but there were others who opposed his being crowned king. So he devised a ploy, claiming that the kingship was his according to the will of the gods. Then, so as to substantiate this claim, he declared that anything he prayed for would at once be granted him. Thus upon a given sacrificial day to Poseidon he beseeched the god to deliver him an oceanic bull, and in return for this he would make of it an offering to the god. But when Poseidon graciously granted the king's request, sending to him a fine bull forth from the sea, Minos took another to sacrifice and caused the sea-bull to instead be sent amongst his prized herds. Thereby did Minos gain the kingdom, but his treachery had made Poseidon wrathful, from him not having sacrificed the bull as he had pledged.

Thus he caused Minos' wife Pasiphae to become lustful at the very sight of this bull. And driven mad as she was by desire she sought out the aid of the engineer Daedalos who then created for her a cow out of wood. This was set upon wheels and was entirely hollow inside, for he skinned a cow to attain the hide which he then stitched over the entire construction. It was taken out into the field where that particular bull was known to graze, and he had Pasiphae climb inside. The bull did come and seeing the cow was inclined to cavort with it and mounted it as if it were a true heifer.

But from this foul union came a most abominable creature, which was at first named Asterios after his father, but who became known universally as the Minotaur, because he had the body of a human but the head of a bull. And this is the origin of the Minotaur as given by Apollodorus.[123] But this is what is said of him by the poet Ovid,

So now this horrible abomination, a shame to Minos, matured
The monster-child of Minos' queen, half-man and half-beast,
Its being yet bore testimony of her shameful detestable deed
And the king decreed that this disgrace to his name be sent far
Concealed within the encircling convolutions of a labyrinth
It was renowned Daedalus who conceived and built the maze
Made to deceive the senses, with paths which wound around,
So that one quickly becomes confused, and loses his bearings,
Just as in Phrygian pastures Meander winds forward and back
Choosing direction without surety, so it turns upon itself again
The waters go first towards the source or then back to the sea
So too did Daedalus, by constructing his fathomless maze, do
Designed to befuddle, so that he himself almost didn't make it
Finding the path leading out, so complex was the web he made[124]

Now I must tell you the origin of Theseus, and will begin with Pandion, who had four sons named Aigeus, Nisos, Pallas, and Lycos. And after their father's death they went against Athens and divided it up into four kingdoms, although Aigeus was the real power amongst them. His first wife was Meta, the daughter of Hoples, but he also married Chalciope, the daughter of Rhexenor. Yet he had no children, and as such grew fearful of his brothers taking power away from him. So he thus travelled to the oracle at Pytho (Delphic oracle) to find the manner by which he might have a son, and the god gave him this answer: "The gaping mouth of the wineskin, valiant man, should not be undone 'til you are upon Athens' height."

Not knowing what this meant, however, he commenced his return journey to his kingdom in Athens, stopping along the way at Troezen. There he lodged with Pittheus, the son of Pelops, and having learned the oracle from him and gathering its meaning, thus caused Aigeus to become drunk and then had him go into the bed of his virgin daughter Aithra. But it is documented that upon that same night the god Poseidon also had sex with the lithesome girl in her bed. Then he told her that if she were to give birth to a boy that she must rear him without his finding out who his father might be; and he left a sword and sandals beneath a certain rock, telling her that when her son was strong enough to push this rock over, so as to reveal them, that she should then have him travel to him bearing these articles.[125]

So in due time Aithra gave birth to a son she named Theseus, and when he had grown up, being now fifteen years old, he went and pushed over the rock which was over the sword and sandals. With these in hand he made his journey to Athens and vanquished every manner of road robber and highwayman along the way.[126]

Now when Minos sought to invade Athens, but lacking the capability to do so, he appealed to Father Zeus, who sent upon them both famine and plague. But an oracle providing the means by which to end the famine and plague that beset the Athenians caused them to offer Minos any manner of penalty he might seek from them. So Minos proclaimed that they must offer regularly seven boys and seven virgins, bearing no arms, to act as food for the voracious Minotaur.[127] And it was upon the third of these tributes that Theseus offered himself up to accompany the sacrificial victims to this indulgence at Knossos; as it is told by Ovid,

> In this Cretan labyrinth the bizarre biform Minotaur was caged
> And twice did he send in Athenians to provide for his meals
> Every nine years were they selected as provender for the ogre
> But at the time when the third passage of nine came around
> The monster met his end at the hand of Theseus, Aegeus' son,
> Aided by Ariadne, Minos' daughter, did he find his way out
> For she had given him string to gather to reach the gate again

Then he went sailing away with Ariadne from there to Naxos,
But he showed her no care after he raped her upon the sands
When he abandoned that devoted girl on the seashore of Dia
There poor Ariadne cried until the arrival of loving Bacchus,
Giving her a place among the stars as the Crown of Heaven,
As the circlet she wore on her head was hurled into the sky,
Going through the stratosphere, on its way gems became fire
Yet it still had the shape of the crown, called *Corona Borealis*
Ariadne's circlet lies between two hands clenching a serpent,[*]
As well as those which show the kneeling figure of Hercules[128]

But contrarily to this it is said that when Theseus was on his return journey and came to port at Naxos that night that there Dionysos was smitten with love for her and stole her away to Lemnos where they made love, and in the course of time she bore him four sons: Thoas, Peparethos, Staphylos, and Oinopion. But further, it is said that when Theseus had set sail his father Aegeus had told him to take down his black sails and to raise white sails in their place so that he would know that he had not been slain. But his miserable state after having lost Ariadne had caused him to forget to replace the black sails with white; thus when Aegeus spied the ships approaching, as he beheld them from atop the Acropolis, he thought that Theseus had been slain and at once flung himself from his high vista to his abysmal doom. Thus when Theseus arrived and learned of his father's death he was made king of Athens in his place.[129]

Soleos: Masterful, Thaeo. And I might add to this that just as Theseus had to lift a stone so as to gain the weapons left for him by his father, such too is also said of Bodvar. For it is said of him,

After King Hring died his son Bodvar then became ruler of the realm, however it was not long after this before he grew restless. So he called together a gathering of the men of the kingdom and there proclaimed that he was determined to go upon a journey, but would first marry off his widowed mother to Valsleyt, a jarl of the kingdom. Then after partaking in the wedding feast Bodvar rode forth alone, but took not much in the way of silver or

---

[*] The constellation *Ophiuchus*

gold or other riches. Still he had for himself good weapons and garments and rode upon the finest of steeds.[130]

Now there lay a certain cave wherein Bodvar's father Bjorn had once lived, and there was there the treasure gathered as a share for each of his sons. Likewise were there three weapons left protruding from a rock: a sword, an axe, and a dagger, each expertly made.[131]

According to the advice of his mother he made his way first to the cave. And there the sword came loose as soon as he took the hilt in his hand. The sword was such a true one that whenever it was drawn it would bring about a man's death, but also it might never be placed beneath a man's head nor set upon its hilt. Likewise, it could only be called upon but three times during the life of its master, for then it could not be drawn out by the same man, so stubborn was its character. Any of the brothers would've wished to have had such a peerless treasure. He made a sheath for this sword out of birch wood.

Then Bodvar went on to locate his brother Elk-Frodi, but there is nothing worth telling of his journey before he came late in the evening to the spacious hall from where Elk-Frodi reigned. Bodvar guided his horse to the stables, as though he was owner of the place. Frodi only arrived back late in the day and eyed the stranger with suspicion. Bodvar did not, however, appear to pay him any mind and didn't utter a word to him. But the two horses, on the other hand, had begun to strive with one another, so as to kick the other out of the stall.

Then Frodi spoke, saying, "Surely only an arrogant man would dare seat himself inside without first seeking my permission." But Bodvar simply shielded his face with his hood and gave no reply. Then Elk-Frodi rose, pulling out his own short sword and forcing it down, so that all but its hilt lay buried. Then he repeated this gesture again, yet Bodvar did not flinch. So lifting aloft his sword thrice Elk-Frodi turned his malicious gaze towards Bodvar, for he thought that this stranger had no conception of fear and was intent on getting the better of him.

Bodvar figured that he knew what Frodi was up to and thus he ought to refrain no longer. So jumping onto his two feet he moved in beneath the other's arms. But Elk-Frodi had a strong grip himself, and they were soon contestants in a vicious scuffle, that is, before Bodvar's hood fell. For when Frodi recognized that it was his own brother he said, "Welcome, brother, for we have battled far too long."

"But as yet no one has been harmed by it," replied Bodvar.

And Elk-Frodi replied, "Yet you would find it better for yourself, brother, if you ceased contending with me; for should we begin to fight in earnest, and not hold back, you would soon notice how greatly our strength differs."

So Frodi invited him to stay, and even to take half of everything he owned, however Bodvar refused. He believed it wrong to slay someone else for his wealth, and was determined then to be on his way. Frodi accompanied Bodvar as he went, saying to him that he had given hospitality to several men, but most often men who were of no great strength or stature. And Bodvar was gladdened by his brother's comment, thanking him and saying, "Then it is well, for people should be allowed to go freely, even if you find them deficient."

Elk-Frodi replied, "I have gained all I have through ill-practice, but your destiny is plain enough. Travel to the kingdom of King Hrolf, for all of the best men desire to be his man. He is not only generous, but has unsurpassed nobility and bravery, far beyond that of any other king." Then Frodi reached out and gave Bodvar a shove, saying, "But brother, you are not quite as strong as you yet could be." And then Frodi caused blood to flow from his own calf, saying to Bodvar that he must drink it, which he did.

Then Frodi reached out and pushed Bodvar again, but this time Bodvar was firm upon his feet. "Now you have renewed strength, my brother," Frodi said, "So I think this drink has been to your benefit. So henceforth you will surpass most men with your strength and dexterity, as well as in nobility and bravery. And this is something which makes me exceedingly glad."

So Frodi next stamped his foot upon a nearby stone, so that it made an impression into the rock above his elk-hoof to the nub on the back of his leg. Then he said, "I will observe this hoof-print every day to see what lies within it; for earth will be there if you have died from disease, water will be there if you have drowned, and blood will be there if you are slain by a weapon. But if this last is so then be sure that I will act as your avenger, because I am fond of you above all other men."

So with that they went their separate ways, and Bodvar continued upon his journey. He went on to Gautland, but King Thorir Hound's Foot was not at home. Yet Bodvar and Thorir were so much alike in appearance that one could hardly distinguish one from the other, so the folks there thought that it was Thorir who had returned home again. So Bodvar was set upon the high seat and served in every manner as though he were the king. And likewise, as Thorir was married, Bodvar lay to sleep at night in bed with his queen.

Yet Bodvar refused to lie beneath the bed covers beside her, which she considered to be odd behavior, since she thoroughly believed that he was her husband. But Bodvar let her know everything and she agreed to keep it a secret. So things went on like this for a time, with them sleeping each night with a quilt placed between them, until Thorir returned home. So the people then knew who Bodvar truly was, and the brothers experienced a heart-felt reunion. Thorir declared that there was no man upon the earth he would have trusted to lie in bed with his queen but Bodvar. Thorir then invited him to remain with them there, offering him half of all his property, but Bodvar replied that he had no intention of accepting it. So Thorir rather asked Bodvar to select anything he might wish to take for himself, even to give him a company of his own men, but Bodvar declined just the same.

Then Bodvar rode forth on his way, and Thorir went with him for a time; and the brothers parted in closeness, but also shared inexpressible fears. Though there is nothing noteworthy to report concerning Bodvar's journey until he came to Denmark and was but a short distance from Hleidargard.[132]

Interestingly enough this transformation of Bodvar is precisely what we find in instances where a man of timid character grows strong, while too acquiring a new name; significantly, within this same story, when Hott drinks the blood of the Yule beast and he is renamed Hialti.[*] And we find that after this name change he is then

---

[*] See *Roar of the Tempests: A Dialogue*

capable of fighting on equal terms with Bodvar, which is just as we find with Jacob.

Epitheus: Truly. And in these stories likewise we find that the two combatants, unable to gain a full victory over the other, then emerge as great friends.

Soleos: Precisely. So we have two situations here where after the drinking of blood the man is able to stand up against the other; though in one case he drinks the blood of the beast before the contest, as with Hialti, while in the other the calf is cut so that he may drink the blood, as with Bodvar. But I think there is something here too of further interest.

Epitheus: What would that be?

Soleos: We know that Jacob speaks of receiving a blessing from God,[*] but the word 'blessing' also has its origin in the word 'blood'. Thus the blessing received by Jacob from God could be the very same sort of activity as the drinking of his blood to give him strength.

Epitheus: Astonishing. But this would bring us back to the name of 'Barak' which holds the meaning both 'gift' and 'to be upon one's knee'.

Soleos: Yes. But Barak likewise means 'thunderbolt', and thus we might consider whether there is some meaning here given the unique strength of the storm god.[†]

---

[*] Genesis 32

[†] Similarly to Hercules, Theseus is known to have engaged in a number of contests and labors in his travels, and even to have carried with him an oaken club. Further Hyginus mentions that the figure of Theseus lifting the stone at Troezen was represented by the constellation of *Hercules* (Hyginus, *Astronomica* 2.6; see Condos 1997: 116). And his association with the lyre (*Lyra*), but only in this sense, makes him like Apollo.

Epitheus: We had considered just such a thing, Soleos, concerning the bear-hero who was rewarded for his service by being made the thunder god.[*]

Soleos: And so here it is Bodvar, who is called Biarki ('little bear'), who is the very same character as Beowulf, as the one gaining strength from his brother's calf; while Hialti ('hilt') gains it from a creature akin to Grendel. And too we should not find it strange that Jacob is associated with the moon just as Thor is associated with thunderstorms, where we already know that there exists a close association between the moon and weather.

Epitheus: Indeed, there are few stronger.

Thaeo: Continuing on this line, as with Bodvar and Theseus who each take a sword from a stone, we have Arthorius, who of course is better known the world over as King Arthur. And his name having the meaning (in Welsh) of 'bear' associates him with Biarki and likewise Perseus, who also have names meaning 'bear'.[†] And it says of Arthur,

> Once the archbishop had sung the mass up to the gospel, then at daybreak, just after they had performed the offering, there appeared a large square slab of stone like an anvil, and trapped within this anvil lay a sword. And they who saw this miracle then went rapidly to the church to relate it to everyone. The archbishop exited carrying holy water and some treasured relics, and seeing the stone he poured the holy water upon it. Then he perceived the writing upon the sword, to the effect that whoever might draw the sword from out of the stone would be Christ's choice as king. And once the archbishop had read all the words he then spoke them aloud to all. Then they placed a guard there on the stone and went back into the church singing '*Te Deum Laudamus.*'[133]

---

[*] See *Roar of the Tempests: A Dialogue*
[†] See *Roar of the Tempests: A Dialogue*

And then who is the one able to withdraw the sword but young Arthur, when it says,

> Kneeling down Arthur gripped the sword with both hands and lifted it free from the anvil, as though nothing were hindering it, and brought it back holding it aloft. And they escorted him to the altar and he placed the sword upon it. After he had done this they blessed and anointed him, performing every one of the rituals of coronation. When Arthur had thus been crowned and after the singing of mass, the company of barons then exited the church. But looking forth there was no trace of the stone and they had no idea where it had gone. Thus it was that Arthur was chosen to be king, and the lands and the kingdom of Logres enjoyed his peaceful rule for a long time.[134]

But I cannot help but think that it may be similarly of interest to find that Arthur's name not only means 'bear' but that he was associated with the constellation of *Ursa Major*, which is known (in Cornwall) as 'Arthur's Wagon'.[*] And we find at his impending death, it says,

> King Arthur was fatally wounded from having had a lance driven through his chest. They collected around Arthur and were given to pronounced lamentation, but he spoke to them, saying, "Do not grieve so, for I am not fated to die. Rather I will be taken to Avalon where my wounds will be healed by my sister Morgan." Thus Arthur was carried to Avalon, and declared to his people that he would one day return and that they should be prepared for his coming.[135]

And this same constellation also bears the name of 'Irmin's Wagon', which is the one which rides along the Milky Way, known as the 'pathway of the gods'.[136] And thus not only could Arthur be associated with eternity but likewise shares at least one similar distinction with Perseus, in that he was known to have slain an old hag just as Perseus had killed the Gorgon Medusa, when it says,

---

[*] It has been pointed out that the Aztec god Quetzalcoatl bears some resemblance to Arthur. And there are similarities with other figures from the episode of Quetzalcoatl bleeding his calf and incest with his sister. (see Markman 1992: 291, 354, 374)

Arthur then leapt through the cave mouth and propelled his knife Carnwennan directly at the hag, in such a way that it cleaved her down the middle making of her two vats. Caw of Scotland took this blood and kept it.[137]

And it was believed that the blood of the Gorgon too held within itself peculiar restorative powers, even over death; while its head was of especial importance as a symbol of protection and healing; and it is represented by the star *Algol*, which likewise does not fall beneath the horizon.

Soleos: You appear to be on the right track, Thaeo.

CHAPTER 11

Thaeo: And, as we spoke of before, it is Perseus who defeats Dionysos, although the usual contest is between Dionysos and Apollo. But whereas it says that in defeating Dionysos that he then leapt into the lake and into the arms of Thetis, this might also have something to do with this.

Epitheus: But what do you mean, Thaeo.

Thaeo: I mean concerning the story in which Dionysos is known to have ridden across a swamp upon an ass, which is associated with the constellation of *Cancer*. The story goes that Hera had maddened Dionysos so that he was forced to wander the earth, and when making his way through Thesprotia to the Dodonian oracle he approached a river but could not find a way to cross. But there he found two donkeys and one of them took him over on his back so that he did not have to touch the water. And coming to Dodona and being cured of his madness, the God put both of them into the sky as stars, which are in this very constellation.[138]

Epitheus: I see.

Thaeo: Likewise, I believe this makes sense of the contest among the trio Dionysos, Apollo, and Perseus. And my reason for saying so builds precisely upon what we had been speaking of before in relation to Jonathan, Saul, and David.[*] Because we have already considered Jonathan to be similar to Dionysos, and likewise that Saul was the sun as is Apollo. And thus we could likewise equate Perseus with David, and here again this makes sense through the association of Perseus with *Ursa Major*, which is likewise aligned with the constellation of *Cancer*.

Epitheus: Yes.

Thaeo: So too that very same region of the heavens is meaningful to the nature of King David's reign, which also explains the

---

[*] See *The Death of King David: A Dialogue*, also *supra*.

confrontation between Dionysos and Perseus, and I will attempt to explain precisely what I mean by this. For we have proposed that the reign of King David was necessary to restore the calendar with the seasons after seven years had passed under the reign of King Saul. We spoke before of both Saul and Jonathan ruling half of the year, or 180 days each; while King David's reign was to have lasted a full 400 days. Thus this requires both Saul and Jonathan to remain absent for the time-being, and as such we must recognize the defeat of Saul by David, and likewise the ability of David to forgo his own replacement by Jonathan, requiring that they form a covenant, as we have said.

Epitheus: Certainly.

Thaeo: Then I am suggesting precisely the same arrangement in relation to Dionysos, Apollo, and Perseus, where instead the year would be divided between Dionysos and Apollo; where Perseus symbolizes the intervening period, represented by the constellation of *Cancer*, and thus the 'Bear'. And thereby, through this, the calendar might similarly be brought into alignment. This then makes perfect sense of the journey of Dionysos across the lake upon the donkey, because this crossing must represent the restoration of the sun from its appearance in *Taurus* back to *Cancer* at the time of the summer *solstice*. And this path would take him back across the 'river', which is the Milky Way.

Epitheus: I see what you mean.

Thaeo: But having done so, Dionysos would then be reborn and the sun would continue its movement, year by year, from *Cancer* again into *Taurus*. Thus we can comprehend why Dionysos would be associated not only with both the donkey (*Cancer*) and the bull (*Taurus*), but also with the serpent (*Scorpius*) and the goat (*Capricornus*), which lie opposite these. As such it makes sense of the journey of Dionysos, representing the path of the sun which is thereby returned to its original location in the calendar, through the addition of a certain number of days. Thus *Cancer* would be represented by the gods Dionysos, Ishmael, David, and Set; although we might also presume that they were at one point meant to be the donkey themselves.

Epitheus: That is quite a good assessment, Thaeo. And from this we could consider likewise Jacob and Esau, being the sons of Isaac with their uncle Ishmael. So that at the solstice Jacob gains supremacy over Esau but is lamed and that Esau gives birth to a son who in turn defeats him, and as such would play the same role of Set in relation to his nephew Harpocrates. But when Jacob is castrated this permits him to be killed but be restored back to life again, while the sun on the other hand is reborn through the act of beheading; the new sun being born out of the neck of the old sun.

Thaeo: Indeed, I could not have said it better. And for this reason we might well presume that Jacob took the form of a boar, and as such that his brother was identified to be a goat, thus appearing as *Cancer* and *Capricornus*, being the two halves of the year.

Epitheus: Such a thing would make sense, given that Esau lives in the hilly country of Mount Seir, and Seir means 'goat'. And this would likewise explain why Jacob dons the skin of a goat so as to mimic the hairy coat of his brother.[*]

Thaeo: Yes, and gaining the upper hand over his brother by disguising himself as a goat, which would have occurred when the sun was in *Capricornus* (winter *solstice*). Thus too we can well recognize the source of the blessing received from Isaac, and that the poor eyesight of the god along with Jacob's disguise grants him the blessing of supremacy over his elder brother; or as we might say, rule over half the year in place of his brother.[†]

Epitheus: Just so.

---

[*] Genesis 36:6-8, Genesis 27:16
[†] Thus they probably represent the two brothers engaged in eternal conflict as mentioned by Celsus. (see Hoffman 1987: 105)

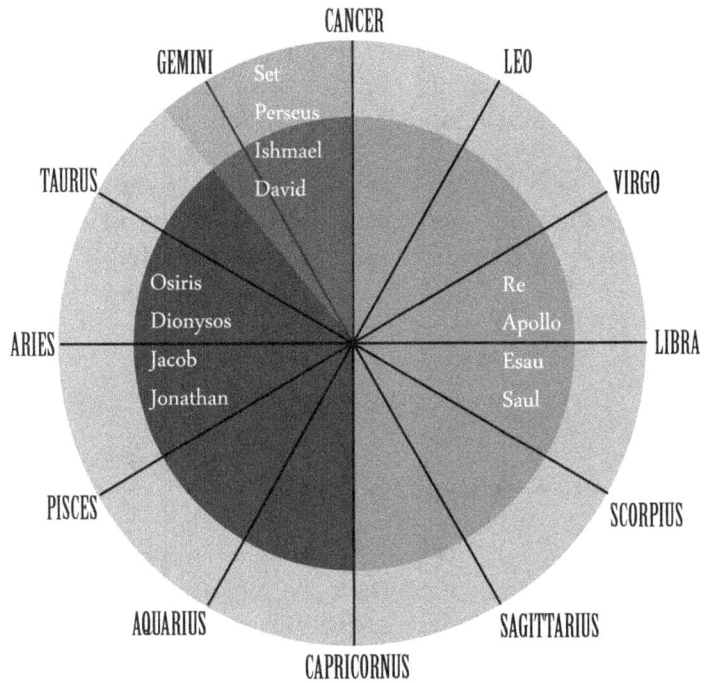

Mythical characters represent the conflict between summer and winter and the recalibration of the 360-day calendar.

Thaeo: Thus if we were to call attention again to Egyptian matters, the sun god Re battles with Osiris, who is both associated with the moon and is dismembered. And we must remember that Set with his 72 cohorts were responsible for the slaying of Osiris, which makes sense only given a 360-day year of Re. Thus we have this episode of the killing of Re and additionally the dismemberment of Osiris by Set as two distinct episodes. So then in this one Set as an ass would represent the year added due to the accumulation of days from the five-day calendrical shortfall.[*] Then too we have the birth of the son of Osiris, Harpocrates ('Horus the Child'), who is himself

---

[*] *Cancer* is associated with the ass and thus presumably with Set. But the constellation of *Ursa Major*, which is aligned with *Cancer*, was called the 'soul of Set'. (Plutarch, '*Isis and Osiris*' 21)

emblematic of the sun. Thus it could be that originally the situation might have been that Horus was initially the son of the god Re, which makes sense; while there might have been another son of Osiris, who might be Anubis. As it is, the rising importance of the cult of Osiris would no doubt provide the reason for his appropriating of the position of Re, and thus also the story of him floating down the Nile in a sarcophagus and having Horus as his son. But at the same time the initial story of Osiris, of him being dismembered by Set, was likewise retained; and thus these were then at some point woven together, which is the situation which must have existed when they were recorded by Plutarch.

Epitheus: Most likely.

Thaeo: Then too we are aware of the interesting situation arising from the story of King David, and this we might summarize simply as Saul ruling for half the year and Jonathan ruling for half the year, split along the *solstices*. This continues for seven years, until the 8th year when David comes and takes over from Saul for the period of one extended year of 400 days, after which he relinquishes it back to Saul. But we might add to this from the story of Jacob and Esau; wherein the primary adversaries are brothers rather than father and son, and comparable to David and Jonathan being treated as adoptive brothers; in the figure of Jacob being lamed. And this is equivalent to Jonathan too, who himself was to have fathered the lame child named Meribbaal. While we also find that when Jacob struggles with God he also acquires a new name. So then we might add into this Osiris who fathers his own lame child Harpocrates, who then goes on to defeat Set, who had dismembered his father. But then in each of these cases we find Israel is truly Jacob, Meribbaal is truly Jonathan, and Harpocrates is truly Osiris. And of these three, every single one of them, is said to be lame.

Epitheus: Yes, it is quite amazing. And I am sure my brother would wish to hear about this.

Thaeo: Thus too we find that the temporary rule of Osiris over Re and David over Saul is ended when the former is castrated, thus representing not only his loss of potency, but the restoration of the corrective interval; or, as we might say, 'thus drops the cleaver of subtraction', so that the accumulated days again are reduced to nothing.

Epitheus: Splendidly put. But mightn't we too think that Jacob must have met with his uncle Ishmael, which we could compare to that between Bodvar and Elk-Frodi; if we were to equate them not with a bear and an elk but instead with a boar and a donkey? And that from his uncle he acquired his greater strength to aid him in his struggle against Esau at the time of the winter *solstice*, just as Bodvar is so aided in his fight against the dreaded Yule beast. And this too might indicate that the wrestling match of Jacob initially had two parts, the struggle with God being not that with his brother Esau but that with his uncle Ishmael, whereby he gains the blessing from him, which is his blood. Then afterwards it is in his struggle with his brother Esau that he beheads him but is himself castrated and rendered both impotent and ready for rebirth.

Thaeo: Well done, Epitheus. And it puts me in mind of one further episode, which is told of the very same ass which carried Dionysos across the river. And it has to do with the god Priapus, who is the son of Dionysos and Aphrodite.[139] For he is said to have gotten into a disagreement with the ass that had carried Dionysos across, and this we are told had something to do with the argument he had with the mule concerning his own erect organ. And this became such a dispute among the two of them that Priapus then killed the donkey; and it was because of this that Dionysos then gave it honor by placing it in the heavens, as we were speaking of before. And I cannot help but think that this disagreement was one over the matter of size, but nonetheless likewise there is no reason to think that it could not also be equated with the castration episode of Osiris or David. In any case, it is for this reason that donkeys were the animals sacrificed to the god Priapus.[140]

Phaedo: And such a connection is even more pronounced when considering the Egyptian Ass and the great serpent known as the 'Eater of the Ass' (Apep),[141] for it is said that Horus spears a serpent which is riding upon the back of the Ass. And that this Ass so too represents the intercalary month, which traverses the gap left at the end of the calendar to bring it back into alignment with the seasons. When this has been done the serpent is then speared by Horus, or the Ass is then consumed by a serpent. Thus the discrepancy really depends upon how the Ass is taken: whether he is an animal temporarily commandeered by the influence of Set for just this one month, or whether the Ass itself represents Set and the additional 14th month. For then the serpent upon the Ass's back represents Set's rule over him for this duration, in which case he is the sun. And it is likewise the ass who carried the sarcophagus in the processions of the god Osiris, which box contained the phallic representation of the god.[142]

Thaeo: Tremendous! And we ought not forget too Achilles and Hektor, for each of them also gives rise to a son: Hektor to Astyanax and Achilles to Neoptolemos, also known as Pyrrhos ('russet'). And here too we find Pyrrhus is named after the color of his hair, which is ruddy like Set. And the story of Achilles slaying Hektor and then being struck upon his vulnerable heel by an arrow fired by Paris, and guided by the god Apollo, is hardly different from the mistletoe dart fired by Hod at his brother Balder, and guided by the god Loki; while at the same time we might conclude that the dart struck him in the thigh, not only because this is where Cu Chulainn was wounded by the holly shaft, but likewise because Adonis himself was gored in the thigh by a boar.

Then again, If we look at the situation where Adonis is attacked by a boar, which was apparently sent by Aries. And we likewise take the story of Hephaistos trapping Aries in bed with his wife Aphrodite, we would have to presume this amounts to two halves of the year divided between Hephaistos and Helios, with the boar representing Aries. Thus for this to follow Hephaistos must be equated with Adonis; and we know too that Hephaistos is the 'lame god'.[*]

Epitheus: Yes.

---

[*] This is not entirely clear, and in one version of the story it is Hephaistos who is to have killed Adonis when he was out hunting wild boars. (see Frazer 1998: 486)

Thaeo: Then the interval where Aries lies in bed with his wife would be the same as we find where the boar rules over the year until the calendar is brought back into alignment with the seasons again, and Hephaistos gains back his wife; while we already are aware of the close association between Adonis and Aphrodite.

Epitheus: Truly.

Thaeo: This too would be similar to the situation concerning Hercules and Aries that we mentioned before. By which I mean that there must have been two circumstances where each spears the other. This we find likewise in that Jacob is said to have received a dislocated thigh while Esau is said to have been shot with an arrow by Jacob.

Epitheus: Yes.

Thaeo: And so too, considering Apollo and Dionysos, it was Dionysos who was revered at the Delphic festival during the three winter months;[143] and where too we might consider that the god does not merely represent the moon, but likewise could even represent the winter sun. Thus we might see them as two gods in partnership, especially in relation to the Delphic oracle, but the identification of both Apollo and Dionysos with the sun is mentioned by Orpheus, who states that Bacchus is also the bright-haired sun (Apollo).* But

---

* Bacchus fanatic, much-named, blest, divine,
Bull-faced Lenaean, bearer of the vine;
From fire descended, raging, Nysian king,
From whom initial ceremonies spring:
Liknitan Bacchus, pure and fiery bright,
Prudent, crown-bearer, wandering in the night;
Pupil of Proserpine, mysterious power,
Triple, ineffable, Jove's secret flower:
Ericapaeus, first-begotten named,
Of gods the father, and the offspring famed:
Bearing a scepter, leader of the choir,
Whose dancing feet, fanatic Furies fire,
When the triennial band thou dost inspire
Loud-sounding, Tages, of a fiery light,
Born of two mothers, Amphietus bright:

likewise we might associate this intrusion of Dionysos as resulting from the very same recognition we mentioned before, since the *Dionysia* was largely a festival of phallic emphasis.

And for this a further connection might be drawn between Dionysos and the character of Hyacinthus. And like Dionysos' sea-maidens, Hyacinthus had his own troupe of female companions called the Hyacinthides, who are the daughters of Erechtheus, and who were worshipped alongside Dionysos, all of whom were slain.[144] But more importantly is that Hyacinthus was killed from an errant discus throw made by Apollo. But the god, having been fond of him, caused him to rise again, and this is likewise the fate of Dionysos. So we could identify them in opposite terms, for Apollo is deemed to be contrary to Hades, while Dionysos is associated closely with Persephone.[145]

Thus in this case it could not be said that their relationship is one of confrontation, and indeed Apollo and Dionysos are shown displaying friendship towards one another;[*] though this could well indicate a sign of their reconciliation as we have seen before. But it is possible that the Apollo who kills Hyacinthus went by the name of Apollyon, which means 'destroyer', or this could rather be a reference to Dionysos.[†] And this could be identified in the slaying of Orpheus by Dionysos, which was not only perpetrated from his envy that Orpheus held favor for the god Apollo over himself, but because Orpheus himself was as an embodiment of Apollo.[‡] And this we can see for ourselves when we identify both with the playing of the lyre and the pronouncement of oracles.

Wandering on mountains, clothed with skins of deer,
Apollo, golden-rayed, whom all revere
God of the grape with leaves of ivy crowned,
Bassarian, lovely, virgin-like, renowned
Come blessed power, regard thy mystics voice,
Propitious come, and in these rites rejoice
(Hymns of Orpheus, li 'To Trietericus', revised by author; Taylor 2007: 114)
Also, a fragment of Euripides (see, Guthrie 1993: 43)
[*] A vase painting about 400 BC shows them holding out their hands to each other. (see Otto 1965: 203)
[†] Dionysos was often called the 'destroyer'.
[‡] Variously vaguely identified as having been sent by Apollo (Pindar, 'Pythian Ode 4') or being Apollo's companion (see Guthrie 1993: 42).

168

Epitheus: Truly.

Thaeo: And curiously enough Apollo himself is identified as Apollo Hyacinthus.* Thus we could recognize this as the passing of the year between two representatives of the sun, who are both identified with Hyacinthus; who exist in harmony until Perseus makes his appearance, after a certain interval, in his violent act to bring about the restoration of the calendar. And likewise we find that Perseus is associated with Apollo and thus has something to do with the cycle of the sun.[146]

Epitheus: Surely.

Thaeo: But I think this too would be like Theseus and Dionysos in their contest over Ariadne, for it is said that not only did Dionysos take Ariadne after Theseus had abandoned her, but that she had initially belonged to Dionysos before Theseus took her away from him. And this tie is even more complete when we consider that Ariadne is killed by Artemis at the command of Dionysos,† just as she (Coronis) is likewise put to death by Artemis at the command of Apollo, or turned to stone by Perseus.[147] And at the time Coronis (Ariadne) is slain she is pregnant with Dionysos' child, and it was Apollo's anger at her unfaithfulness which led him to condemn her so. Thus we can see here again a contest between adversaries over Ariadne, but where here she is not merely the passive object of their struggle.‡ And I cannot help but think that Theseus fulfills here precisely the same role as does Perseus, which is to make his appearance every so often for the sake of bringing the calendar back into alignment.

---

* The *Hyacinthia* was a festival of Apollo, and at Tarentum the god worshipped at the tomb of Hyacinthus was called Apollo Hyacinthus. (Polybius 8.38; see Otto 1965: 206)
† Odyssey xi, 321 f.
‡ Ariadne is also believed to have been one of the nurses of Dionysos, one of which is named as Ariagne, and who was amongst his other followers when they were slain by Perseus (Nonnus, *Dionysiaca* 47.664 ff.). Ariadne also shares some connection with the goddess Artemis (Otto 1965: 187).

169

location	sun	moon	sun's son	moon's son	extra month
Norse	Balder	Hod	Vali	Bo	Loki
Norse/Celtic	[Bel]	Bran (Odin)	Beli	Hermod	-
Cretan	Minos	Minotaur	-	-	Theseus
Greek	Apollo	Dionysos	Apollyon	-	Perseus
Greek	Helios	Adonis	-	-	Aries
Greek	Hektor	Achilles	Astyanax	Neoptolemus (Pyrrhus)[†]	Paris
Mesopotamian	Enkidu	Gilgamesh	-	-	-
Hebrew	Esau	Jacob	-	Israel[‡]	Ishmael
Hebrew	Saul	Jonathan	Eshbaal (Ishbosheth)	Meribbaal (Mephibosheth)	David
Egyptian	Re (Khepera)	Osiris	Horus[*] (Harpocrates)	[Anubis]	Set

**Gods and their sons who rule the year, and gods
which re-align the calendar.**

[*] Horus is identified more with the sun than the moon and was perhaps initially the son of Re.
[†] Called 'red' for his red hair
[‡] The name 'Israel', meaning 'divine son of Ra', seems misplaced here.

170

Soleos: Well done. We have been both transfixed and mesmerized by your exchange. And what you have been saying matches precisely the tale received from the north, in which Balder as the sun and Hod as the moon each give rise to a son. And though we find one emerging to act as Balder's avenger, named either Vali or Bo, these names might arise rather from a son of Balder being Vali, and the son of Hod being Bo. These, however, would be precisely the same if we could identify Hod with Odin, and Bo with Hermod, as we spoke of before.[*] And that these two are in perpetual conflict with one another over Nanna, who is at once the wife of Balder but likewise the wife of Hod.[148]

Epitheus: Undoubtedly.

Soleos: For in this conflict we find something quite similar to that of Cain and Abel, where one slays the other over their desire for Hother's (Hod's) own foster-sister. And although here Balder and Hother are not said to be brothers, we are aware from other references that they are. And in their battle first Hother wins the upper hand, then Balder, then Hother again when he slays Balder. And here we find it said that Hother is; like Apollo, Orpheus, and David; a man skilled in the art of music, and an accomplished player of all manner of instruments.[149] Likewise we find that Balder is beset by disease and left lame in his legs which causes him to take to driving a chariot.[150][†] And that after his defeat of Hother, Balder is said to refresh his troops by releasing water springs from the earth, and that Hother fled after his defeat and became a solitary wanderer over the countryside.[151] But this is followed by Balder's eventual defeat by Hother with Miming's sword, and that after Balder's death his burial mound gives rise to a great deluge, while the rest of the tale concerning the son of Rinda we have already told.[‡]

---

[*] See *The Zodiac Mysteries*
[†] The killing of one and laming of the killer is also the case when Hading slays Asmund with his spear, for Asmund lashes out with his last ounce of strength, wounding Hading's foot and making him lame for life. Hading later hangs himself after his king drowns in a vat of ale. (Grammaticus, *Gesta Danorum* i, 27, 34-35)
[‡] Concerning Balder's avenger see *The Zodiac Mysteries*

Epitheus: Yes.

Soleos: And recall too that Esau is also known as Edom ('red'), and we might suspect that Rebekah who gives them birth is equivalent to Gerd ('garden') and Frey to Isaac, who themselves we might parallel with Athena and Hephaistos.

And the conflict between Abel and Cain too was the matter over which one would gain the favor of their sister representing the unplowed (virgin) earth. And that the new husband (Cain) who takes her away from her former husband (Abel) from the time when the sun ("Bel") begins its descent into the underworld. Then presumably in the midwinter it would then be Abel who would return in the form of his own son, born from his sister, who would come to slay his brother.

So these gods, like Balder and Hod, or Gwythyr and Gwynn, also must claim the goddess as his own concubine during this time. In this it makes sense if Frey's adversary Beli represents the sun, since Gerd would then be the earth. And this could be just like the alternation between Apollo and Dionysos, where we would have Beli (Baal) being equivalent to Apollo, and Frey being equivalent to Dionysos, thus representing the two halves of the year. But as we are made aware of by the Norse poets there was at the end of the world, with the destruction of the old sun, a restoration with a new sun.[152]

Epitheus: Indeed so, and if we consider that it was Jonathan who exchanged rule during the year with his father Saul, then we would have to assume that Saul was rather like Tammuz,[*] who was viewed to be in decline during the hot season; so that Saul ruled from winter *solstice* to summer *solstice*, or during the growing season. This would mean that Jonathan would rule from summer *solstice* to winter *solstice*, but when he was killed, in turn, by Saul his body would then find restoration in the cauldron of *Capricornus*, which we likened to the swamp in which the renewal of the dismembered Osiris

---

[*] Thus Saul, through his identification with Tammuz and *Orion*, could then be equated with David's father Jesse, or the giant Thiassi, who is likewise *Orion*. (see *The Eden Enigma: A Dialogue* and *The Death of King David: A Dialogue*)

172

occurred.[*] Thus perhaps we yet find a remainder of this in the story of Saul and Jonathan being slain, for when Saul falls upon his own sword and is then beheaded, the young man who seized his bracelet and crown must have been Jonathan.[153†] And who is the one responsible for the slaying of this young man but King David himself.[‡]

And if we have here represented David by the donkey, then surely it must be Jonathan who is equivalent to Jacob. And it is thus possible to speculate that En-Gedi ('Goat Spring') was actually the location at which Jonathan confronted Saul, which would be entirely comparable to when Jacob confronted Esau at Jabbok ford, who himself was the lord of Seir ('goat').[§]

Soleos: Splendidly done. And through your inquiry we should be able now to perform a full assessment of the precise durations which were required to bring each calendar back into alignment.

Epitheus: Then please, let us do so.

---

[*] See *The Zodiac Mysteries*
[†] He is named Ebadus, the son of Agag, king of the Amalekites as given in Pseudo-Philo 65:4 (see Charlesworth 2009, Vol. 2: 377). Thus he is the son of a king, as Jonathan is the son of King Saul.
[‡] 2 Samuel 1:15
[§] Genesis 32, 33

CHAPTER 12

Soleos: Then first, consider that we are informed that Jacob lives at peace with Esau for the period of 18 years.[154] Taking this and assuming the same discrepancy of 5 days in the 360 day calendar accumulated over 18 years, would be 90 days, which is three months or one full season.*

Epitheus: Yes.

Soleos: And so too the giant from Gath slain by Jonathan was said to have 6 fingers on each hand and 6 toes on each foot, or 24 total digits,[155] where 24 multiplied by 5 days would produce 120 days, and this would be four months or one Egyptian season.

Thaeo: And we also might compare this with Cu Chulainn who has seven fingers on each hand and seven toes on each foot, or 28 total digits,[156] which adds up to the number of days in an Osirian month.[157]

Soleos: Good.

Phaedo: Recall too that there were known to be 42 judges of the dead in the Egyptian religion, and 5.25 multiplied by 8 gives us 42.† And concerning this number, regard too the story of Elisha and the boys, when it says,

> Then the men of the city spoke to Elisha, saying, "Know that the circumstances of this city are favorable, as my lord can see for himself, but the water here is foul and the land unproductive."
> So he said, "Bring to me a clean bowl with salt in it." And thus they brought it to him. And he walked to the spring and tossed the salt into it, saying, "Thus speaks Yahweh, the water has been made fresh, thus from this day forth neither deaths nor

---

* The Persians likewise used a 360-day calendar with the addition of an extra month every six years. (see Boyce 1990: 20)
† The number 42 appears 13 times in the Old Testament: Numbers 35:6; Judges 12:6; 1 Samuel 13:1; 2 Kings 2:24; 2 Kings 10:14; 2 Chronicles 22:2; Ezra 2:10, 2:24, and 2:64; Nehemiah 7:28, 7:62, 7:66, and 11:13.

174

miscarriages will result from it." And hence has the water remained good until today, just as was declared in the words spoken by Elisha.

He travelled from there to Bethel, and while he was on his way up several young boys emerged from the city to make fun of him, saying, "Go on up, baldhead! Go on up, baldhead!" So he turned and, looking at them, laid a curse upon them in Yahweh's name. And there came from out of the woods two she-bears who tore the forty-two boys to pieces.[158]

And likewise here the duration of time which is accounted for by the forty-two boys is managed through the appearance of two bears, which could be the bears *Ursa Major* and *Ursa Minor*.

Soleos: Stupendous!

Thaeo: And lest we forget, Soleos, the greatest of confrontations, the War at Troy, went on for 9 years before Achilles did battle with Hektor. For if we presume a calendar here of 364 days compared to a nominal year of 365.3 days (actual 365.242), then after 10 years an accumulation of 13 days would have amassed. This would be half a month, where each month is 26 days long.[*] Thus we could say that Achilles and Hektor battle for supremacy, but Achilles defeats Hektor in the 10th year only to himself be slain by Paris, representing the additional 13 days added to the year.

Soleos: And this number likewise corresponds with Quetzalcoatl who returns after 52 years.[159] For if we take the year to be 52 weeks, where weeks are 7 days long, then this equals 364 days. We might also divide this into 7 periods of 52 days each (being two 26-day months). So then after the passing of 52 years the calendar would require 52 days to be added, or thus eight periods instead of seven. This would mark the return of Quetzalcoatl from the spirit world into the land of the living.

We might include too the struggle between Beowulf and Grendel, where the contest occurs after Grendel haunts for a duration of 12

---

[*] A year of 364 days has the advantage of producing exactly 52 seven-day weeks. In this case every tenth year requiring the addition of 13 extra days, thus perhaps constituting the original 'unlucky 13'.

years, this time lacking 5 days per year, which would be 60 days or one full *tide*. And thus an extra *tide* must be added every 12 years. And so like Set, Grendel's haunting Heorot is responsible for the calendar to increasingly diverge from the seasons until he is finally slain by Beowulf, just as Achilles defeats Hektor. Thus Hrothgar we might presume to represent the beset sun, or the rightful ruler, as is Saul; with Grendel as the one who comes every Yule and Beowulf representing the extra *tide* which brings everything back into alignment.

Epitheus: Well done. And the reference to Yule fits in well with what we were saying before about Jacob being associated with the constellation of *Capricornus*.

Soleos: Indeed so, Epitheus. Likewise, Yule is associated with the goddess Berchta who is said to have roamed the days from Christmas to the Twelfth Night (Epiphany), representing the passing out of the old year as the ugly hag, and its transformation into the New Year, as the lovely maiden. Thus Yule Eve was known as 'Mother's Night', while the day of Yule (Christmas Day), with the birth of the 'divine child', was known as 'Child's Day'.[160] And so we might presume that Balder is the slain god who was reborn from the oaken Yule log.[161*]

Epitheus: That would be reasonable to assume.

Soleos: And this 'divine child' born at the time of the winter *solstice* was then merely a reincarnation of the universal deity, but born as his son. Having been slain he then arose again in renewed form to exact retribution upon his own murderers, just as does Horus against Set for the death of Osiris, or Vali in the case of Balder.

Epitheus: Indeed.

Soleos: And this universal deity was represented by a large branchless tree which was severed nearly to the very ground. But it

---

[*] The term 'Yule' acquired the meaning among the Chaldeans of 'infant'. (see Howey 1955: 93)

was from this tree too that a new shoot appeared, regenerating its universal powers through the device of the encoiled serpent. And this transition was represented by the burning of the Yule log on Christmas Eve, followed by the erecting of the Christmas tree the next morning as the bestower of divine bounty unto man.[162]

Thaeo: And we find too a circumstance when twelve young men dress in the costume of black sheepskins, just as Dionysos was known to do, who made his initial appearance at the winter *solstice*,[163] but whose full epiphany did not arise until the full blossoming of spring.*

Soleos: True. And as we find too Yule was a time of youthfulness,[164] associated with the constellation of *Capricornus*, but so too was the constellation of *Cancer* known as a manger or crib.[165] And thus we could well associate one with the birth of Dionysos and the other with the birth of Apollo; and for this reason the *sol invictus* ('unconquered sun') was born at the winter *solstice* and was thus represented by a goat.

Thaeo: Certainly nothing else would make much sense.

Soleos: And this could be represented in the confrontation of Thor with the Midgard Serpent, who is himself said to be a mere boy when he made this expedition; if we were to associate the Serpent with the "*inverse ecliptic*"† at the time of the winter *solstice*, which gains its greatest ascendancy at the very time when the sun is at its lowest point.‡

Phaedo: And likewise the serpent Apep was to have sunk back into the sea at the time of the Egyptian New Year, which occurred around the time of the summer *solstice*.

---

* This recalls a very interesting reference to the fact that Krishna and Thor defeat the serpent when a child, and that Grendel and other beasts are said to arrive and be destroyed at Yule. This suggests the myth represented the yearly cycle.
† An imaginary circle set perpendicular to the plain of the sun's *ecliptic*.
‡ See *The Zodiac Mysteries*

Soleos: Good. Thus the sun was at its hottest during the time after it began its decline, at which time the moon's reign would be on the ascendancy. Until the moon finally usurped his place; but in doing so we find that he himself was injured, so that he began his decline when the sun was reborn at the winter *solstice*. And likewise we must add to this that the figure of the moon was dismembered, corresponding to Dionysos, Osiris, and Jonathan, the first two of which we know to be identified with the bull.

Though how we assign one of the gods to a half of the year truly depends upon which season was deemed to be the more favorable, or specifically when the time of their growing season occurred. And we find that Tammuz in dying likewise leaves the land dead, thus Tammuz must rule from the winter *solstice* to the summer *solstice*. Although when the sun dominated the summer growing season, and deemed beneficial, then the sun rather ruled from the summer *solstice* to the winter *solstice*, when it was beheaded and gave rise to a son who would soon confront the moon at the winter's end.

Epitheus: Yes. What you say fits perfectly.

Thaeo: And it would make sense to think that Dionysos was born as a goat (*Capricornus*) and then grew into a bull (*Taurus*), before he was slaughtered and dismembered. Such that the duration from *Taurus* to *Cancer* was ruled in part by Perseus every eighth year; as Apollodorus says, the 'everlasting year' is equivalent to eight of our own years.[166] Thus we might regard it plain why we should see the sacrifice of kids and bulls remained part of the Dionysian rites.

Epitheus: But this eight-year cycle we likewise found valid for the reign of King David.

Soleos: That is intriguing, this recognition of a cycle of eight years used for the calibration of the calendar, since we find other known 8-year cycles in astral lore. And it is possible that any alteration in the calendar according to an 8-year schedule might have been tied to one of these others; and specifically I am thinking of the cycle of the planet *Venus*.[*]

Phaedo: Just so, Soleos, and there are special solemn rituals which are specifically linked to this duration, one of which I am aware of which is spoken of by Plutarch, who writes,

> "The construction which is set up near the threshing-floor every eighth year is not like the nest of a serpent's lair, but rather is made in imitation of the home of a chieftain or ruler. The assault upon it takes place without any noise, and along the approach called 'Dolon's Pass' through which, in a torch light procession, the Labyadae lead the boy—whose two parents must yet be alive—then set fire to the construction and toss over the table. They escape out the temple doors without ever glancing back again, which is followed by the peregrinations and indenturement of the boy, and his purifications which occurred at Tempe, which all give rise to suspicions of some profound yet perverted act of boldness."[167]

And this had something to do with the exile of Apollo after he had slain the beast Python at the Delphic oracle.[168]

Soleos: But such a duration was likewise known as the *octaeteris*, which was a period of eight years utilized to bring the solar and lunar calendars into agreement with one another. When these two calendars are reconciled then we witness the same phase of the moon upon the same day of the year. And this is based upon a cycle of 99 lunar months, which occur during 8 years.[†] And this too has something to do with the story of Atalante we spoke of before, Epitheus, for here we find the goddess Atalante represents the moon,

---

[*] This is the time it takes for Venus to appear at the same position in the sky on the same day of the year.
[†] 96 lunar months over an eight-year period (8 years × 12 months/year = 96 months) with three additional months. In this eight-year cycle called the *octaeteris*, one extra month was added to each of the third, fifth, and eighth years. (see Krupp 1991:150)

while Hippomenes is the sun.[*] And as there are 96 months in 8 years, the three golden apples then represent the three months which must then be added on so that the sum of the days of the months $((29.5 \times 96) + 90 = 2,922)$ equals the sum of the days of the years $(365.25 \times 8 = 2,922)$.[†] These apples which are thrown by Hippomenes as he races are what give him victory so that the moon must, in the end, be married to the sun.[169]

Epitheus: That is very clever.

Thaeo: And it occurs to me that these contests relating to the calendar are precisely what we find in stories concerning Poseidon. For Poseidon had a son named Eumolpus;[‡] and we find here Poseidon taking on the role of the avenger of his son, after he was slain by Erechtheus during the war between Athens and Eleusis. And Poseidon in vengeance struck Erechtheus into the ground with his trident.

Eumolpus, like King Lycurgus, was a king of Thrace, who while in Eleusis, it is said, founded the Eleusinian Mysteries. And he was known for his skills as a musician and played upon the lyre. Eumolpus led the Eleusinians and Thebans into battle against Athens, but an oracle declared to the Athenians that in order to save themselves from this plight that one of Erechtheus's three daughters would have to be sacrificed. This was duly performed so that the Athenians went on to defeat the Eleusinians; though afterwards, in an act of revenge, Erechtheus was pounded into the ground by Poseidon. As a result the crater which was produced filled with salt water and henceforth came to be known as the Erechthean Sea.

---

[*] Atalante is a huntress like Artemis who is a goddess of the moon. Atalante is also associated with *Sagittarius* as the 'Huntress' (see *The Zodiac Mysteries*).

[†] The 19-year cycle holds even greater accuracy and replaced this cruder method by the 5th century BC. (see Krupp 1991: 153)

[‡] Boreas ravaged Oreithuia who gave birth to Chione, who after maturing had intercourse with Poseidon and gave birth to Eumolpos. To conceal this from her father she threw the child into the ocean, but Poseidon took him to Ethiopia where he was reared by Benthesicyme, his daughter by Amphitrite. (Apollodorus iii 15 §§ 2-4)

Yet it appears to have been recognized that Poseidon and Erechtheus were likewise one and the same god, and this can perhaps be judged from the closing lines of the play 'Erechtheus', when Athena tells Erechtheus' wife Praxithea,

"In honor of your husband a shrine should be built in the heart of the city, and known for the one who murdered him, which is the name 'holy Poseidon'; but that amongst the populace, at the time when the cattle are sacrificed, he will be known as Erechtheus. And since you were the one who re-laid the foundations of the city, I name you as the one who will bring the city's first burnt-offerings; you shall become my priestess."[170]

Epitheus: Tremendous.

Thaeo: Not only this, but both Erechtheus and Erechthonios are married to a woman named Praxithea,[171] and thus they too could perhaps be identified with one another.

Epitheus: But what could this mean; that Poseidon, Erechtheus, and Erechthonios are all the same?

Soleos: It is perhaps so, Epitheus, but given one consideration, which is that they might be the very same being but not the same conscious will, and this I shall endeavor to explain. We find Erechthonios to be half-human and half-serpent, who could thus be the mortal ruler of earth; and who is matched by Erechtheus as the divine ruler, who is called the 'two-formed son of Earth' and dwelled upon Dragon Isle.[172] Yet he is equivalent to Poseidon, who is thus known as Poseidon Erechtheus.[173] And this could be of interest because it might imply that Poseidon was himself a composite being, of man and serpent, and that the serpentine component had a will of its own.

Thaeo: Likewise we know Erechthonios was lame and the son of Hephaistos, and thus he equates with other sons who have shared the same affliction. And from the name of Eumolpus ('good song'), who was a musician upon the lyre, we might compare him to Apollo–who attained this wondrous instrument from Hermes–Orpheus, or indeed Theseus.

181

Soleos: Well done. And we also know that the demon Grendel, who was the Yule beast, was enraged because his ears could not tolerate the joyous music being made in Heorot.[174] And this could set the demon's preference for discord in contrast with the universal harmony, which is likewise the jurisdiction of Apollo.[*]

Epitheus: Yes. And we recall too that David was a man of instruments and a player of the lyre.

Soleos: And such a thing would make sense if we were to contrast discord with harmony, as we might well do by contrasting the realm of Apollo with that of Hades, and the growing importunity of the calendar's deviation from the seasons.

---

[*] Abundant, blessed; and thy piercing sight,
Extends beneath the gloomy, silent night;
Beyond the darkness, starry-eyed, profound,
The stable roots, deep fixed by thee are found
The world's wide bounds, all-flourishing are thine,
Thyself all the source and end divine:
'Tis thine all Nature's music to inspire,
With various-sounding, harmonizing lyre;
Now the last string thou tunest to sweet accord,
Divinely warbling now the highest chord;
The immortal golden lyre, now touched by thee,
Responsive yields a Dorian melody.
All Nature's tribes to thee their difference owe,
And changing seasons from thy music flow
Hence, mixed by thee in equal parts, advance
Summer and Winter in alternate dance;
This claims the highest, that the lowest string,
The Dorian measure tunes the lovely spring
(Hymns of Orpheus, xxxiii 'To Apollo', revised by author; Taylor 2007: 94-95)

182

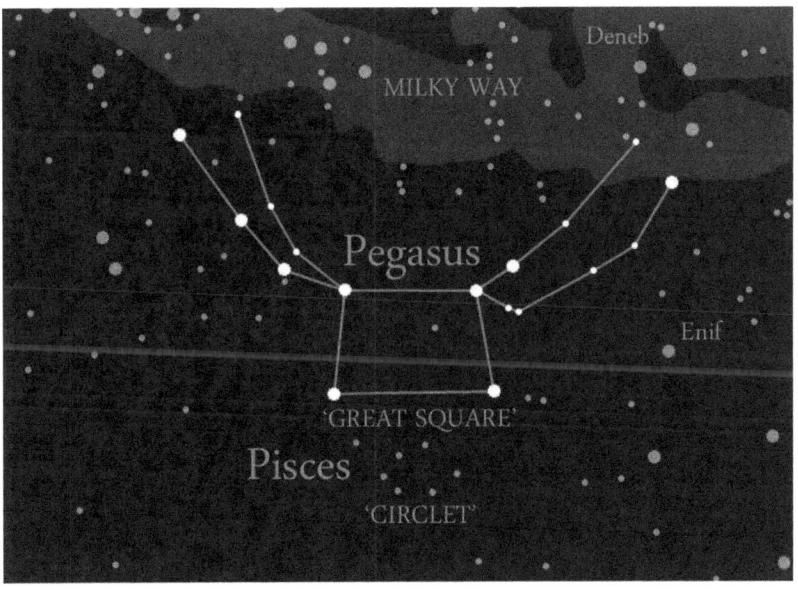

Illustration of the serpent-man from an Etruscan mirror[175] **compared to the constellation of *Pegasus*; Poseidon was Sea God and Lord of the Abyss.**

Thaeo: We have assumed that in the story of Adonis that it was Helios who was his adversary, which makes sense when comparing Adonis with Death and Helios with Baal, as these two (Death and Baal) were themselves in a perpetual competition. Whereas the third, who is Aries, is the one who sports with Aphrodite, the wife of Hephaistos; and it is said that it is Helios who spies them together. And here Helios would be the equivalent of Apollo and thus Hephaistos to Dionysos.

Soleos: And we likewise find in this case it is Poseidon who takes the role of mediator between Hephaistos and Aries.[176]

Thaeo: That is correct.

Phaedo: And in the Egyptian story of the two brothers we likewise find the sun god Re acting as a judge between them, appearing as a river which separates and flows between them to prevent mischief until his morning pronouncement.[177] And thus too is this so of Thoth in relation to Horus and Set, for if I recall rightly the Egyptian records say that this god acted as mediator, like a river between them, by means of which they were reconciled.[178]

Epitheus: Yes. So too in the case of David and Saul, the one who confers the kingship upon them is Samuel. And where his name we might recognize as being '*Sam-hu-el*', meaning essentially 'holy god Sam', or in other words, the sun ("Shem"). Yet before, as we had already identified Saul as the sun, what then would Samuel be?

Soleos: I think Epitheus, as with Mithras, we might regard that he was not merely the physical sun itself but would be a representation of the divine sun, or the true solar year; that is, rather than the 360-day year.

Epitheus: I see.

Soleos: Thus he is the one who acts as the supreme judge of the universe. So we might consider the relationship between Saul and Samuel as being like that between Apollo and Mithras: which are the perceivable sun but also the ultimate force of the universe. This in

Egypt would thus be the Atum, and in Israel it would be Isaac who confers his blessings. And in Greece, who judges the case between Venus and Adonis but Great Zeus himself.[179] And thus we might equate Samuel with Mithras, as the supreme judge.

Thaeo: And this time of year also heralds the birth of the *sol invictus*. So just as we must identify the judgement of Isaac to have occurred at the time of the winter *solstice*, in addition the festival known as *Haloa* was celebrated on December 26th, but curiously associated with the threshing-floor (*'halos'*) and dedicated to Dionysos and Demeter, though in the month dedicated to Poseidon.[180] And thus we now can understand the role which Poseidon takes as supreme judge.[*]

	sun (beheaded)	moon (injured/ dismembered)	*Cancer* (castrated)	supreme judge/*sol invictus*
Egyptian	Re / Horus	Osiris	Set	Thoth / Re[181]
Greek 'Persian'	Apollo	Dionysos	Perseus	Mithras
Greek 'Cretan'	Minos	Minotaur	Theseus	Poseidon
Greek 'Phoenician'	Helios	Adonis	Aries	Zeus
Greek 'Homeric'	Helios	Hephaistos	Aries	Poseidon
Iliad	Hektor	Achilles	Paris	Apollo
Israelite	Esau	Jacob	Ishmael	Isaac
Canaanite	Saul	Jonathan	David	Samuel

Gods factoring into the annual cycle, calendar, and acting as supreme judge of the universe.

---

[*] Poseidon was invoked in oath swearing (*Iliad* xxiii)

185

Phaedo: And it occurs to me that the seat of Samuel's power is located in Ramah. And this we might regard as being the seat of truth and judgement, as it bears the name of the ideal manifestation Rama.[*]

Soleos: Beyond this we might consider whether something very similar occurred in the struggle between Frey and Beli, where Frey is said to have stricken down the giant with a stag's antler. For if we are here equating Balder with Beli and so too with Abel, and Hod with Frey but so too with Cain, we find Cain was to have had antlers upon his head.[182] And we have already identified that the contest between Balder and Hod was over Nanna,[†] while too the contest between Beli and Frey was over Gerd. And we considered that Cain and Abel were originally making offerings not to Yahweh but to the goddess, who was their own sister, just as we found a similar instance in the case of Inanna and Dumuzi, if Phaedo, you would be willing to recount this for us.

Phaedo: I shall, indeed, Soleos.

> The brother was speaking to his little sister,
> Utu, the Sun God, said as he spoke to Inanna,
> "Young lady, all the ripe flax is enchanting
> Inanna, all the grain is resplendent in the fields
> So I will reap it for you, and carry it to you
> There is always need for linen, large or small
> So then Inanna, I will carry all of it to you."
> Inanna, the Queen of Heaven, spoke to Utu,

---

[*] Rama is the Babylonian god of the heavens, and the perfect avatar of the 'Supreme Protector' Vishnu, the foremost god of righteousness. Rama is the ideal judge of truth, rightness, and the ideal ruler.

[†] In only the *Eddas* is Loki made responsible for the deed, but even so it is still Hod who is put to death. In the other three versions found in Saxo's history, *Beowulf*, and *Hromundar-saga Greipssonar* there is no mention of Loki. Then there is Nanna, alternately Balder's wife in the *Eddas* or Hod's wife in *The History of the Danes* by Saxo Grammaticus, who provokes the contest between them. In the *Eddas* Nanna is the daughter of Nep and the devoted wife of Balder; and thus perhaps the daughter of Neptune, as is Aphrodite born from the sea.

"But brother when you bring me the flax,
Who will be the one who combs it for me?"
Utu, the Sun God, speaking to Inanna, said,
"Sister, I will be the one who will comb it."
Inanna, the Queen of Heaven, spoke to Utu,
"But Utu, after you have provided it combed,
Who will be the one who spins it for me?"
Utu, the Sun God, speaking to Inanna, said,
"Inanna, I will be the one who spins it for you."
Inanna, the Queen of Heaven, spoke to Utu,
"Brother, after you have provided spun flax,
Who will be the one who braids it for me?"
Utu, the Sun God, speaking to Inanna, said,
"Sister, I will be the one who braids it for you."
Inanna, the Queen of Heaven, spoke to Utu,
"But Utu, after you have provided it braded,
Who will be the one who warps it for me?"
Utu, the Sun God, speaking to Inanna, said,
Inanna, I will be the one who warps it for you."
Inanna, the Queen of Heaven, spoke to Utu,
"Brother, after you have provided it warped,
Who will be the one who weaves it for me?"
Utu, the Sun God, speaking to Inanna, said,
"Sister, I'll be the one who weaves it for you."
Inanna, the Queen of Heaven, spoke to Utu,
"But Utu, after you have provided it woven,
Who will be the one who bleaches it for me?"
Utu, the Sun God, speaking to Inanna, said,
"Inanna, I'll be the one who bleaches it for you."
Inanna, the Queen of Heaven, spoke to Utu,
"But Brother, once you've given a sheet to me,
Who will then come with me to my bridal bed?
Utu, who will lie beside me in the bridal bed?"
Utu, the Sun God, speaking to Inanna, said,
"Sister, you will enter your bed with the groom
It is he who emerged from the fruitful womb
He was conceived upon the holy marriage bed
The shepherd, Dumuzi, will come into your bed."
Inanna, the Queen of Heaven, spoke to Utu,

"He is not, brother, the man who stole my heart,
Rather it is the farmer, him who plies the hoe,
He is the gentleman who has stolen my heart!
For he collects together immense heaps of grain
And seasonally brings corn into my storerooms."
Utu, the Sun God, speaking to Inanna, said,
"Sister, take the shepherd, why would you not?
After all he has delicious cream, sweet milk,
And what he touches shines like the heavens
So Inanna, marry Dumuzi, why would you not?
Having bedecked yourself with rich necklaces
Dumuzi will deliver his richest cream to you
You who are allotted to be the king's guardian
So Inanna, marry Dumuzi, why would you not?"
Inanna, the Queen of Heaven, spoke to Utu,
"Why the shepherd? I refuse to marry him!
For he has only coarse fabrics, rough wool,
Rather, Utu, I would wish to marry the farmer,
For the farmer will grow flax fit for my robes
And the farmer will grow barley for my fare."
Then Dumuzi, the shepherd, spoke to Inanna,
"There is no reason for you to praise the farmer,
Why do you insist upon speaking about him?
For if he provides black flour, I will black wool
If he provides you white flour, I will white wool
If he provides you beer, I will give sweet milk
If he provides you bread, I'll give honey cheese
The farmer only receives my surplus of cream
The farmer only receives my surpluses of milk
So why do you go on talking about the farmer?
Are his possessions more abundant than mine?"
Inanna, Queen of Heaven, spoke to Dumuzi,
"Shepherd, but for Ningal you would be gone,
But for Ningikuga, you would live in the hills,
If not for Nanna, you'd have no roof over you,*
And if it were not to for my brother, Utu…"
Then Dumuzi, the shepherd, interrupted her,

---

* Ningal is Inanna's mother, Ningikuga her grandmother, Nanna her father

"Inanna, do not think to provoke a squabble,
For my father Enki is as noble as your father
And my mother Sirtur as noble as your mother
And my sister, Geshtinanna, as noble as yours
So rather, Queen of the Citadel, we should talk,
Rather Inanna, we ought to meet and converse
As I am noble as Utu; so too Enki is as Nanna,[*]
So rather, Queen of the Citadel, we should talk."
The words they spoke were filled with longing
Their clash, from the first, had brought on love
So the shepherd came to the palace with cream
Dumuzi came to the citadel carrying sweet milk
When standing before the door, he called to her,
"Open up your house, my dear, open the door!"
Inanna ran to her mother Ningal, who bore her,
Ningal gave advice to her daughter, and said,
"My child, the young man will be like a father
Daughter, to you he will also be like a mother
You will find him treating you as if your father
And find him caring for you as if your mother
Open up your house, my dear, open the door!"
So Inanna went, just as her mother directed her,
She washed herself, anointed herself with oil,
Draped her body with the finest of white robes
Set forth her dowry, lay beads about her neck
Taking up the royal emblem into her deft hand,[†]
While Dumuzi waited for her arrival impatiently,
Before Inanna opened wide the door for him
And within the house she was readily beaming
Holding the bewitching aura of the full moon
Dumuzi was overcome with delight as he gazed
Then moving even closer to her, he kissed her[183]

Soleos: Well done, Phaedo.

---

[*] Enki is a god of water identified with Sin, god of the moon, as is Nanna. This serves to disguise the fact that Dumuzi is the brother of Inanna.
[†] Probably the *shen*, representing the path of the sun and denoting the standard measure (cubit)

CHAPTER 13

Soleos: Thus a seasonal arrangement emerges here as with the roles taken by Cain and Abel.[*] For Cain could be related to Cernunnos ('horned one'), a Celtic fertility god, who like Pan is a god of abundance, regeneration, and is the lord of wild animals. And Cernunnos is depicted with the ears and antlers of a stag.[†] Abel then is likely linked to Belenus, who might be connected to the Celtic solar festival called Beltane (*bealtain*).[‡]

Epitheus: Yes.

Soleos: And in Frey's slaying of Beli ('bright'), he is in turn slain by a fire giant known as Surt, whose name means 'dark one', who is said to live in the realm of the south (Muspell).[184] Thus we might suppose that Surt represents what is opposed to the sun, as Hades is opposed to Apollo, and yet perhaps is still the sun.

---

[*] These gods are found often enough with the various gods taking on different but similar names. There are the Irish Beal or Beil, the Gaelic Beal, and the Welsh Beli ; the Celtic sun, healing, and horse god Belinus or Belenus ('bright') or Apollo Belenus and fertility god Cernunnos; the Celtic war god Belatucadrus ('fair-shining one'); the German pastoral god Beel; the Austrian pastoral god Belenos; the Russian god of light Bielbog (Byelobog) and of darkness Tschernobog (Chernobog); the Frank war god Hadu; the Etruscan conveyer of the dead Charun; the Greek Apollo or Phoebus ('bright') and ferryman Charon; the Greek Pollux and Castor; Ba'al or Bel or Belus, the Mesopotamian sun and sky god, and Sin the moon god; the Armenian god Baal-Shamin and Vahagn and Hayk; the Saxon god Baeldaeg or Beldegg ('bright day') and Siggi ('victor'); Herebeald and Haethcyn ; and Beal and Sighe. These gods too might be attested by Tacitus, who says that Castor and Pollux were worshipped as the Alcis, which could mean elk (*alsces*) (Simek 1993: 7). Another definition for alcis is 'gods', which could merely attest that the gods and elks were deeply wound together. The only other immediate reference comes from Saxo who says that Hother rode a chariot pulled by reindeer (Grammaticus 71; see Davidson 1979, Vol. 1: 70).

[†] He was associated with the shedding of antlers and thus growth and regeneration. (Adkins 2000: 45)

[‡] The words *bealtine* or *beiltine* mean 'beal fire'. (Grimm 2004: 612-613)

Epitheus: But what do you mean?

Soleos: What I mean to say is that the sun which rises at the summer *solstice* (Beli/Balder) is slain by Frey, and then it is the 'dark sun' (Surt) who returns to slay Frey at *Ragnarok* (winter *solstice*).

Thaeo: And this is just as we find when Fergus Mac Roich is killed in the water by Lugaid ('light'), but contrarily to this we find Lleu ('light') is killed in a river by Goronw Pebr ('fiery'). And likewise we find that Beli kills Bran ('raven'), and the character of Bran is wounded in his thigh and then beheaded.[185] And he is the same as the injured Fisher King (Bron), and holder of the Holy Grail who is sought out by Perceval for King Arthur, and healed of his affliction by him.[186]

Soleos: Then we might also consider Beli to be the same as Ellil, the god of fire and also the sun. But we find that Frey also acts here in the same role as Hod. And we might well wonder, if Gerd were to be found the sister of Beli, whether we could equate Gerd with Idunn, for Idunn is said to have slept with her brother's killer.[187] Thus we could conclude through comparison that Beli was the brother of Frey and that Gerd was likewise the sister of Frey and thus cognate with his own sister Freyia.

Thaeo: And Morgan Le Fay is both wife of the Green Knight and also the half-sister of Arthur. And it would make these far more alike if we considered the Green Knight himself to have a more peculiar connection with Arthur; and here regard the relationship between Gawain, the Green Knight, and Arthur to be the same as we have with Apollo, Dionysos, and Perseus; or Helios, Adonis, and Aries.[*]

Epitheus: Indeed.

Soleos: And the name Adonis is very like that of Addu, which is a name for Baal, while Beli meaning 'bellower' might imply that he

---

[*] Arthur himself is wounded in his thigh when he himself fights against King Floire, whom he decapitates.

191

was a bull; and this could be related to Bo, which likewise means 'bull'. Thus they appear to hold some connection with Baal, the bull, who is himself reborn from death. And I wonder, Phaedo, if you would be willing to provide yet another rendition for us, concerning the battle between Baal and Death.

Phaedo: I would be pleased to, Soleos, and will attempt to do so according to the best of my abilities. And I will begin after the construction of Baal's royal palace is completed, when it says,

Baal seated in his house, upon his high seat, said,
"No king or another will come to dominate the earth
I will send no tribute to Death, son of El,
And no obeisance to the Champion, El's Beloved,
So Death may be left whimpering all by himself
Let the Beloved One be bitter of heart
Only I will be the ruler among the gods
Only I bestow prosperity to gods and men
That only I bring bounty to earth's people"
Then Baal summoned together his boys, saying,
"Listen Gapn and Ugar, Galmat's sons,
You are going on an uncommon journey:
Go in the direction of Mount Targuziza,
Go in the direction of Mount Tharumagi,
To the mountains which hide the underworld conduit
Lift high the mount with both your hands,
Raise the mound aloft with your fingers,
Then descend into the kingdom of the underworld,
You will be deemed among those who fall into earth
Make your way to the realm's center, to the marsh,
The palace of mud, the kingdom of vile substance,
However, Holy Ones, never be unwary
Do not get too near to Death, son of El,
Lest he were to consume you like a lamb?
Lest he were to bite into you like a kid?
Just recall that the sun, the gods' light, gains its glow,
And the sky sparkles because of Death, El's Beloved
Go a thousand miles, ten-thousand acres at each step
Then at the foot of Death's throne, bow in reverence

And you will address yourselves to Death, son of El,
You will convey this to the Champion, the son of El,
The message given to you by the great warrior Baal,
The words given by the mighty conqueror of armies,
"Now I have made my silver house, my gold abode,
No king or another will come to dominate the earth
I will send no tribute to Death, son of El,
And no obeisance to the Champion, El's Beloved,
So Death may be left whimpering all by himself
Let the Beloved One be bitter of heart
Only I will be the ruler among the gods
Only I bestow prosperity to gods and men
And only I bring bounty to earth's people."

Upon hearing this Death refused to take it at all seriously, nor forgo
any of his power for the sake of Baal's arrogant desire for absolute
rule over every realm. So he sent his own message in reply to Baal,
answering that he would not relinquish any of his power, and that
Baal ought to beware of the reprisals that might be brought against
him, saying,

"Recall when Lotan, the snake in flight, was your kill,
When you put a final end to that meandering serpent,
The monstrous beast of seven heads,
The sky lost integrity and collapsed
Just like the loose folds of your garment did it droop
Alike, you will fall into the mouth of Death, son of El,
Into the sodden pit of the Champion, of El's beloved."
The gods went on their way, not straying right or left,
Proceeding all the way to Baal, on the peak of Zaphon
Then Gapn and Ugar reported to him, thus they spoke,
"This is the message we bring from Death, son of El,
The words spoken by the Champion, El's Beloved,
'I have an appetite like that of a ravening lioness,
I have a craving as deep as the dolphins of the sea
My pool ensnares wild oxen, my well entraps deer
When my appetite is big, like that of a ravenous ass,
Then I stuff my face at once with both of my hands
And when driven by an irresistible eagerness to eat,

One of my lips touches earth, one touches heaven,
And my tongue will reach all the way to lick the stars
Thus must Baal then be consumed,
And be swallowed down my gullet,
Just as an olive cake, earth's bounty, the trees' fruits."
The warrior Baal became terrified,
The Cloud Rider grew quite fearful,
"Depart and convey a message to Death, son of El,
Communicate this to the Champion, El's beloved,
'This is the message we bring from the warrior Baal,
The words given by the mighty conqueror of armies,
Praise be to Death, son of El!
Know I am your servant, and will serve you always.'"
The gods went on their way, not straying right or left,
So they proceeded all of the way to Death, son of El,
Making their way to the realm's center, to the marsh,
To the palace of mud, the kingdom of vile substance
They lifted up their voices to be heard, proclaiming,
"This is the message we bring from the warrior Baal,
The words given by the mighty conqueror of armies,
'Praise be to Death, son of El!
Know I am your servant, and will serve you always.'"
And Death, the son of El, was pleased with his reply,
He was more than willing to accept Baal as his vassal
Death called one of his servants to be his messenger,

Death conveyed his words and instructions to his servant, who then
went to deliver it to Baal upon Mount Zaphon and conveyed this
message out loud to him, saying,

"Hear the message of Death, son of El,
'Baal no longer will sit on his throne upon Zaphon,
He will be sent down into the pit of the earth gods'
But now as for you: with your clouds, your winds,
With your rain and thunderbolts,
Taking also your seven boys, your eight fine boars,
Take with you Pidray, maiden of day,
And also Tallay, maiden of the rainfall,
Go in the direction of Mount Kankaniya,

Lift high the mount with both your hands,
Raise the mound aloft with your fingers,
And then descend to the kingdom of the underworld
You will be deemed among those who fall into earth,
So the gods will be fully aware that you are dead."
And the warrior Baal did as he was told, and went,
At a sandy stretch of land, he was taken with a cow,
A young heifer in the pastures of Death's boundary,
And mounted her seventy-seven times,
Had sex with her eighty-eight times,
The cow was impregnated, giving birth to the Lord,[*]
And then when he came to the gate of Death's abode
There Baal was overcome, and slipped away from life

And Gapn and Ugar were going from place to place,
Making their way across every mountain within earth,
Going upon every mound in the depths of the lands,
They came to a pleasurable spot, to a sandy landscape,
There on the charming wayside at Death's boundary
And they found Baal, upon the ground where he died,
Where the great warrior had fallen,
They covered themselves with burlap,
And they covered him too with burlap
They cut into their skin with a blade,
Lesions upon themselves with a knife,
Making cuts on their cheeks and chin,
Scraping their arms with a cut reed,
Furrows on their bodies like a farm,
And scoring their backs like a field
They walked and went from the earth,
Then made their way toward El's tent,
At the meeting place of the two rivers,
Between the two basins of the ocean,
They raised the flap on El's tent and went inside
The sanctified hall of the sovereign Lord of Time
And then Gapn and Ugar said to him,

---

[*] Unfortunately the tablet has a gap at this point, and no more is to be found concerning this son of Baal named 'Lord' ('Bel').

"We were travelling from place to place,
Making our way across every mountain within earth,
Going upon every mound in the depths of the lands
We came to a pleasurable spot, to a sandy landscape,
There on the charming wayside at Death's boundary,
And we found Baal, upon the ground where he died,
Where the great warrior had fallen,
Where the Lord and Master of earth had met his end."
And benevolent El, the deeply feeling,
Stepped down from his throne, and sat upon a stool,
Then went from the stool to take a seat on the floor,
In an expression of grief he rained dirt upon his head
Dust wherein he convulsed tumbled down his crown
And he covered himself with burlap,
And he dug into his skin with a blade,
And lesions upon himself with a knife,
Making cuts upon his cheeks and chin,
Scraping his arms with a split reed,
Carving furrows on him like a farm,
Scoring his back like a plowed field
Then lifting his voice, he cried out,
"Now Baal has perished, what fate awaits mankind?
What will they do following the loss of Dagon's son?
Thus I will descend in Baal's place, into the earth."

At that time Anat was walking from place to place,
Making her way across every mountain within earth,
Going upon every mound in the depths of the lands,
She came to a pleasurable spot, to a sandy landscape,
There on the charming wayside at Death's boundary
And she found Baal, upon the ground where he died,
Where the great warrior had fallen,
And she covered herself with burlap
And she covered him too with burlap,
And she dug into her skin with a blade,
And lesions upon herself with a knife,
Making cuts upon her cheeks and chin,
Scraping her arms with a split reed,
Carving furrows on her like a farm,

Scoring her back like a plowed field
Then lifting her voice, she cried out,
"Now Baal has perished, what fate awaits mankind?
What will they do following the loss of Dagon's son?
Thus we shall descend in Baal's place, into the earth."
So the gods' light, the sun, journeyed down with her
After she wept profusely, and was drunk with tears,
Then she called upon the light of the gods, the sun,
"Take up the warrior Baal and place him upon me."
So the light of the gods, the sun, did as she asked,
She hoisted up the warrior Baal,
And set him over Anat's shoulders
She then carried him up to the summit of Zaphon,
And then she mourned over him, laying him to rest,
She sent him down into the pit of the earth gods
She butchered seventy buffalo,
An offering to the warrior Baal
She butchered seventy draft-oxen,
An offering to the warrior Baal
She butchered seventy sheep,
An offering to the warrior Baal
She butchered seventy hinds,
An offering to the warrior Baal
She butchered seventy wild goats,
An offering to the warrior Baal
She butchered seventy donkeys
An offering to the warrior Baal
Then she made her way to El,
At the meeting place of the two rivers,
Between the two basins of the ocean,
She raised the flap on El's tent and went inside
The sanctified hall of the sovereign Lord of Time
Coming to El's feet she knelt and paid obeisance,
She fell prostrate before him and gave him honor,
Then lifting her voice she cried out,
"Now Asherah and her sons ought to be pleased,
Let the goddess and her pride of lions celebrate,
For the warrior Baal is no more,
And the Lord and Master of earth has met his end."

El then summoned the Goddess Asherah-of-the-Sea,
"Hear me, Goddess Asherah-of-the-Sea,
Let me take one of your sons that he might be king"
And the Goddess Asherah-of-the-Sea said in reply,
"Why do you not rather make Yadi-Yalhan king?"
And benevolent El, the deeply feeling, answered her,
"I do not think he is suited to it, given his poor legs,
He would not be able to match Baal's javelin throw,
Or hope to challenge Dagon's son in a competition
And the Goddess, Asherah-of-the-Sea, said in reply,
"Why don't we instead crown Athtar the Great king?*
Have Athtar the Great be made king!"
So Athtar the Great climbed up to the top of Zaphon,
And seated himself upon the warrior Baal's throne
His feet did not reach the footstool,
His head did not touch the headrest
So Athtar the Great raised his voice,
"It is not possible for me to be the king atop Zaphon."
Thus Athtar the Great came down,
He went down from off of the warrior Baal's throne,
So he became Lord of the Underworld, ruling it all

Then Anat went on her way, travelling herself into the abode of
Death, to confront him for the bad work he had done, in claiming the
life of Baal.

And the sun, the gods' light, was bright
And the sky sparkled because of Death, El's Beloved,
First a day went by, then a further two days went by,
And Virgin Anat went up to him
With her feelings like those of a cow for her calf,
With her feelings like those of a sheep for her lamb,
In such manner was also the heart of Anat for Baal,
She went and took hold of Death by his robe's collar,
She grasped firmly upon the lapels of his clothing,
And lifted her voice to be heard, saying,
"Now you, Death, produce my brother!"

---

* Athtar the Great is the personified Morning Star

And Death, the son of El, replied to her,
"What is it you want from me, virgin Anat?
It was when I was travelling and had gone far
Wandering through every mountain in earth
Wandering through every hill in deep fields
Until I felt a desire to see the human world
Until I wanted to mingle among the many
Emerging upon my splendid desert paradise
My lovely span that laps the shores of Death
Then and there before me was Baal the champion
So what else to do but consume him like a lamb?
So what else to do but bite into him like a kid?"
And the sun, the gods' light, was bright
And the sky sparkled because of Death, El's Beloved,
First a day went by, then a further two days went by,
The days then grew into months,
And Virgin Anat went up to him
With her feelings like those of a cow for her calf,
With her feelings like those of a sheep for her lamb,
In such manner was also the heart of Anat for Baal,
She went and took severe hold of Death, son of El,
And with a sword she severed him,
And with a sifter, winnowed him,
And with a flame, she burned him,
And with a mill, she crushed him,
Then she spread him in the fields,
"Let the birds abstain from consuming what's left,
May the feathered fowl refrain from eating his bits,
Let his stuff beg to other stuff!"

In such manner did Anat deal with Death, then she returned to El
with the news. But the fate of Baal was, as yet, unknown. Thus El
identified the sign by which he would come to know if Baal had been
restored to the world of the living.

"But if the warrior Baal is yet alive,
If the Lord and Master of earth has been resurrected,
Then benevolent El, the deeply feeling, will dream,
The creator of the universe will experience a vision,

There the heavens will be raining balm,
The gullies will be awash with honey,
This will be a sign that the warrior Baal is yet alive,
And that the Lord and Master of earth is resurrected."
Thus the benevolent El, the deeply feeling, dreamt,
The creator of the universe did experience a vision,
And the heavens were raining balm,
The gullies were awash with honey,
So the benevolent El, the deeply feeling, was joyous,
He set his feet upon a footstool,
Threw back his head and laughed,
And lifted his voice to be heard, saying,
"Now am I able to ease back and rest,
Now the anxiety has left me entirely
For the warrior Baal is yet alive,
The Lord and Master of earth has been resurrected."
Then El summoned the Virgin Anat,
"Listen to my words, Virgin Anat,
Convey to the sun, the gods' light,
'O Sun, the fields' furrows lie in dire desiccation,
Baal has not been fructifying the cultivated lands,
Where then is the warrior Baal?
Where, then, is the Lord and Master of the earth?'"
Then the Virgin Anat departed,
And made her journey to the sun, the gods' light,
Then lifted her voice to be heard, saying to her,
"This is the message from El, the bull, your father,
The speech of the benevolent one, your guardian,
'O Sun, the fields' furrows lie in dire desiccation,
Baal has not been fructifying the cultivated lands,
Where then is the warrior Baal?
Where, then, is the Lord and Master of the earth?'"
To this the sun, the gods' light answered, saying,
"If you will pour out rich wine from the amphora,
Bring with you a wreath to offer to your forebears,
Then I will go forth and seek out the warrior Baal."
To this the Virgin Anat answered,
"O Sun, wherever you might go,
Wherever your journey takes you,

May the shield of El be with you."

Baal meanwhile had travelled down into the abode of Death, and there he was confronted by the astonished sons of Asherah.

> Baal gripped the sons of Asherah,
> He slapped the shoulder of Rabbim,
> He hit his mallet against the Waves,
> And he shoved pale Death down low,
> Then Baal went back to his throne,
> To his high place, the seat of royalty,
> The days grew into months,
> The months grew into years,
> Whereupon, in the seventh,
> Death, the son of El, spoke to the warrior Baal,
> Lifted his voice to be heard, saying,
> "Baal, I have been disgraced and all because of you,
> In your name I endured being severed with a sword,
> In your name I endured being burned in flames,
> In your name I endured being crushed in a mill,
> In your name I endured being winnowed in a sifter,
> In your name I endured being spread over the field,
> In your name I endured being scattered on the sea,
> Let me have one of your brothers,
> Then I might rest myself and eat until I am satisfied
> That there might be no cause for lingering bitterness
> Baal should give his younger brothers to me to eat,
> The sons of his mother for me to eat."
> And he went again to Baal upon the top of Zaphon,
> And he lifted his voice and called,
> "Baal should give his younger brothers to me to eat,
> The sons of his mother for me to eat."
> And they rammed into each other like camels do,
> Death was tough and Baal was tough,
> And they jabbed at each other like wild buffaloes,
> Death was tough and Baal was tough,
> And they bit into each other like noxious serpents,
> Death was tough and Baal was tough,
> They booted one another like rambunctious horses,

Death fell down and Baal fell down,
The sun called down from on high,
"Now hear me, Death, the son of El,
How do you intend to contend with the warrior Baal?
And how keep your father El, the bull, unaware of it?
He would assuredly ruin your throne's foundation
He would assuredly upset the balance of your chair,
He would assuredly crush your kingly rod of justice."
And Death, the son of El, grew afraid,
The Champion, El's beloved, worried,
Death felt menace from what she spoke
The sun confined Death to the lower realms, adding,
"However, you will consume the food of offerings,
And you will drink your fill of the wine offerings."
Then the sun pronounced judgment over the gods,
And sun spoke her ruling concerning the divinities,
"O gods, take Death for yourselves,
Take your ally, Kothar ('skillful'), for yourselves,
And Hasis ('wise'), who is well known to you,[*]
And in the oceans, among the Dragon and Heart,[†]
Kothar-wa-Hasis did ramble,
Kothar-wa-Hasis did wander[188]

---

[*] Kothar-wa-Hasis is another name for Death as is Hadad of Baal; likewise, El is equivalent to Dagon as is Anat to Astarte.
[†] The turbulence of the oceans was linked with a monstrous serpent and its rhythmic motion to a beating heart.

CHAPTER 14

Soleos: So here again we have the circumstance where it is the sun who acts as judge over the fate of Death in his contest with Baal.

Epitheus: Yes. And we find it is Anat with the sun who goes searching for Baal, like Demeter and Hekate searching for Persephone; and who mourns over Baal as when Isis and Nephthys seek out Osiris.[189]

Soleos: Just so. And we found before that the relation of Niord to Skadi is the same as that of Loki to Skadi, and of Thiassi to Idunn; and in fact of Odin to Gunnlod, Odin to Rind, and too Frey and Gerd: they are all an equivalent sequence used to describe a recurring cycle, being the contest between summer and winter.* The sun Demeter going down at winter would encourage the thinking that she went down to fetch her daughter and bring her back in the form of spring. And this is equivalent to the rest, even though Persephone (Kore) is female and Balder is male, and whereas in one case Hades steals her away, in the other he is slain by Hod.

Epitheus: But how might Baal and Death then relate to the others we have been speaking of?

Soleos: It is said that Death and Baal are in conflict every seven years.

Epitheus: Yes.

Soleos: And the god Kothar-wa-Hasis (Death) is the same as the Greek Hephaistos; and like Loki, Cronos, and Prometheus is described as having a very conniving mind.[190†] Baal is referred to as 'Lord of Earth', and in this case we find that Baal seeks absolute rule but is challenged by Death and that after this Baal remains alternately powerless and dominant for seven years at a time.[191]

---

* See *The Eden Enigma: A Dialogue* and *The Zodiac Mysteries*
† Anat and Hasis appear to be equivalent to Athena and Hephaistos. She is a weapons bearer, he a craftsman.

Epitheus: Truly. And after this period then Baal is reborn and gains back his standing again.[*]

Soleos: Precisely. And is not Death as a wanderer too like Dionysos, who is associated with the sea as Kothar was known as the son of the sea?[192]

Epitheus: Truly, it would seem to be.

Soleos: But if we consider Aqhat, who likewise brings about the first-fruits when killed, that this is followed by a seven-year period of mourning.[193] And this makes his death identical to that of Baal's.

Epitheus: One could hardly say otherwise.

Soleos: And just as we found with Athena desiring the weapons made by Hephaistos, so too Anat wished for the bow and arrows of Aqhat; and having rejected all her other offers for them she then offers him eternal life, which he likewise refuses.[194] But we may well imagine that certain details have been preserved although they might have become related differently. Yet we do find precisely the same arrangement, nonetheless, here where Baal gives rise to a son just prior to his own death, as we were speaking of before. And likewise the defeat of Death is brought about by him being burned, crushed, and scattered over field and sea by Anat.

Epitheus: Assuredly so. But then this makes me think, as we find Anat searching for Baal as Demeter searched for Persephone, what then might we make of the name of Persephone, other than that it means 'killer of Perseus'?

Soleos: Indeed so. And thus we find ourselves within very familiar territory, as this brings a solution to the issue of what became of

---

[*] Likewise, from the book of *Esther*, in the instance of Mordecai and Haman, where too we find them in confrontation, where Esther is the goddess Ishtar and Mordecai is the god Marduk (Frazer 1998: 658-665). And Marduk is equivalent to Baal, and thus is the sun while Haman (Hama) is the moon. And Haman's wife is named Zeresh (Esther 5:10), just as Abraham's wife is Sarah.

204

Perseus after his defeat of Dionysos. And as you have now declared, it could mean that he met his own end through the actions of Persephone, the Queen of the Underworld, who could likewise be compared with Ariadne.[195]

Thaeo: It is known that Dionysos lived and slept in the house of Persephone.[196] And just as here, where we find Baal impregnating the heifer before his own demise, so too the Dagda impregnates the cow Boand ('white cow'), thus leading to the birth of Oengus. And Oengus is also called Mac Occ ('young son') because he is conceived at dawn yet born before dusk,[197] which is just like what we have been saying all along: that the son of the sun was born at the time of his own father's slaying.

Epitheus: Truly.

Thaeo: And likewise if we recall that after David's appearance too, he eventually has to resign his throne back to Saul. Then, as we said before, Jesse the father of David, if equivalent to Thiassi, is likewise the constellation *Orion*.* And if we consider that David's mother too was the cow; which we saw in the case of Baal and the Dagda, with one giving rise to Bel ('Lord') and the other to Mac Occ; then if Jesse gives rise to one son every year, it is then only the eighth who is deemed suitable to rule; and who rises up to reign in Saul's place, as we believed, from *Taurus* and around one entire circuit of the ecliptic back to *Cancer*.†

Soleos: But would we be mistaken in suggesting that the very heifer encountered by Baal is not rather his own sister Anat (Astarte) being the goddess of the moon?[198] And while it is true that here the sun is a goddess, while Baal is made a god of the rains, we might associate him even more closely with the sun in his equivalence to the lord 'Bel'. And in this sense we could identify him with Shamash who is

---

* It also seems that the primal giant (birdman, *Orion/Gemini*) was associated with bulls due to his proximity to the Taurus group and that a cow (Gefion) was to have been his wife. The primal giant is also a keeper of oxen: Yima is said to have had good herds, and Hymir kept oxen, who is said to be Tyr's father.
† See *The Death of King David: A Dialogue*

known as the 'calf of the wild cow' where the cow represents the earth.[199] But in this case we need only associate the 'Bel' referred to with the coming of the spring *equinox*, when the sun was in *Taurus* at the time of the spring rains.[200]

Thaeo: Yes, we could well consider that this has something to do with Baal's eventual resurrection from the realm of Death.

Soleos: Then we could compare the seven-year period of mourning for Aqhat with the period of 9 days Frey must wait after his killing of Beli. And if this is deemed to represent the 9 months of winter, then it could represent the period of mourning of Gerd over her brother before the union with Frey can take place. Thus essentially, we might say, that the earth is upset with Frey for killing her brother (the sun) and thus withholds herself for these nine months before Frey eventually arrives. And one might imagine that Gerd likewise gives rise to a reincarnation of her brother who will in turn arise to kill Frey. Thus just as Frey goes to woo Gerd there might have been a similar episode of Beli going to woo Freyia, and who reacted in similar fashion. And this might be represented in the stories of giants arriving in Asgard to claim Freyia as his bride.[*] But each of these in their own way merely explains the sun's journey through the year.

Epitheus: Yes.

Soleos: While we might likewise say that in this particular version the cow (moon) and giant (*Gemini*) are the parents of Gerd. And she refuses to relent to the spring until after a period of 9 months.[†] And we know too that Baal made his appearance at the start of the rainy season, which was a sign of his abundant fertility.[201]

Epitheus: But could it be that this contest did not occur after seven years but rather every seven months? And my reason for thinking so

---

[*] Hrungnir (*'Skaldskaparmal'* 17), master builder (*'Gylfaginning'* 42), and Thrymn ('Thrymskvida')

[†] It was perhaps thought that the rituals of the harvest were to have, in effect, impregnated the earth so that in 9 months (assuming 3 months of summer) she would give birth with the coming of the spring rains.

is that in the story of Snow White she is said to have gained her supreme beauty when she was seven years old. But this might have something to do with her ruling the year for seven months, from winter to summer *solstice*. But when the Evil Queen (moon) ruled during the other half of the year then Snow White (sun) remained quiescent within her glass coffin.[*]

Soleos: That is very astute, Epitheus.

Thaeo: And the seven months could arise then from inclusive counting,[†] though it could likewise occur if the year were divided into fourteen months, or two seasons of seven months each. And, just as we considered with the 14 months implied within the duration of the siege of Troy, each month would then be 26 days and the year 364 days long. And ancient peoples might well have found good reason to adopt such a calendar.[‡]

Soleos: Yes, and again we might say so from the relative proximity of the reaches of northern Canaan to the lands of Asia Minor, so that it would not be surprising to find that they might possess similar calendars.

Thaeo: Indeed not.

---

[*] See *Roar of the Tempests: A Dialogue*
[†] The seven months are inclusive, thus December through June is counted as '7 months' and June through December as '7 months', which of course adds up to 14 months, although there are truly only 12.
[‡] Similar to the Osirian year, this is 364 days long but divisible by 2, while the Osirian year is 13 months of 28-days each and thus is not. The 364-day year is convenient for being precisely divisible by 52, producing this number of 7-day weeks in a year. But there must be a corrective introduced as the deviation here is far worse than the 'quarter-day' which requires a leap year every four years. Instead it would fall short by about 1.24 days per year.

**Bronze plate from Öland, Sweden from c. 600 AD.
One-eyed figure sporting goat-ears is held and about
to be attacked by Wolf figure.**

Epitheus: But beyond this, I think that this yearly exchange is not
only present in Nordic mythology in the circumstance of Balder and
Hod, or with Beli and Frey, but likewise with Odin and the Wolf.
And we are well aware of the goat-eared god being speared in the
foot by a man-wolf unsheathing his sword, perhaps to decapitate
him.[*]

So if we were to link up the Mead of Poetry story with that of the
Ragnarok story, where Odin is attacked by Fenrir but is avenged by

---

[*] This could be associated with the Celtic division of the year at May 1 and
November 1. Tammuz was killed by a boar on the summer solstice when
the sun gained in heat, in proximity to *Sirius*, and thus dried the land (see
Frazer 1998: 455). This could be related to the 'corn wolf' who was
associated with the harvest (see Frazer 1998: 457-459).

his son, it would seem that as in other instances of this sort, the god who is going to meet his end gives rise to a successor who in this case is Vidar, who arrives to tear the wolf in two.

Soleos: Indeed so. And if we compare this with the other instances, it would suggest that this contest between Odin and Fenrir is the equivalent of that between the sun and the moon, as we find Fenrir, Garm, and Moongarm all appear to be the same wolf seen upon the moon; whereas Odin would be in this sense equivalent to Tyr, who is himself associated with the bull.[*] And then we would have to believe that Odin, if identified with the Green Man,[†] could be matched with Grendel, while Fenrir could be matched with Beowulf.

Thaeo: Thus too Oedipus slaying his own father and thereby acquiring his own mother as a wife is likewise comparable with Odin, if we presume that the giant slain (Ymir) is his own father. At least we have considered that Odin might well have been similar to Noah, and likewise related to Niord.[‡] And it could be that Niord is comparable with Nereus, as lord of wealth and the sea, who is shown as a composite between a man and sea-dragon, just as we surmised to be true of Poseidon.[§]

---

[*] The bull god represented by Osiris, Baal, Dionysos and so on
[†] The Green Man is a common European representation of the vegetative god symbolizing rebirth and the return of spring.
[‡] See *The Zodiac Mysteries*
[§] O Thou, who doff the roots of Ocean keep
In seats cerulean, demon of the deep,
With fifty nymphs (attending in thy train,
Fair virgin artists) glorying through the main:
The dark foundation of the rolling sea
And Earth's wide bounds, belong much-famed to thee;
Great demon, source of all, whose power can make
The Earth's unmeasured, holy basis shake,
When blustering winds in secret caverns pent,
By thee excited, struggle hard for vent:
Come, blessed Nereus, listen to my prayer,
And cease to shake the earth with wrath severe;
Send on our sacred rites abundant health,
With peace divine and necessary wealth
('Hymns of Orpheus', xxii 'To Nereus', revised by author; Taylor 2007: 82)

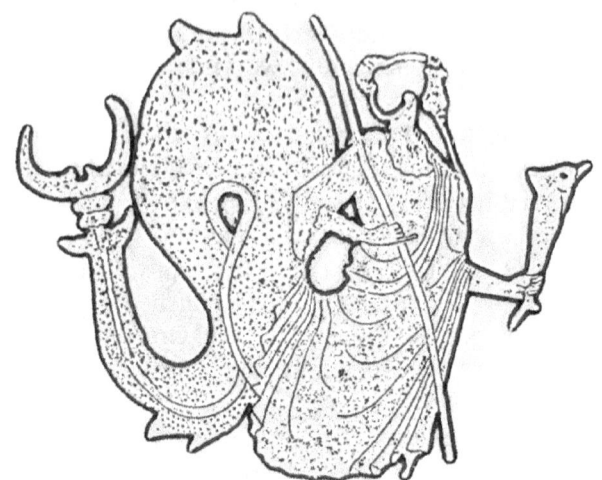

Illustration of Nereus from a Greek vase.

Phaedo: And such a depiction is likewise that of Dagon, who is the father of Baal.[*]

Soleos: And this slaying of Ymir might have something to do with the opposite event, if we were to associate the mead giant (Mimir) with the wolf. For it was Odin we presume to have struck off the head of the giant Mimir, when it says,

> Odin stood on the ridge gripping Brimir's sword in his hand, and wearing his helmet on his head. Mim's head then spoke the first wise words, conveying to him the sacred runes. Then every rune that had been fully engraved was stripped off and sent far, flowing every which way along with the sacred mead and came to be among the Aesir, the elves, and some to the wise Vanir; while others went all the way to the abode of men."[202†]

---

[*] Just as Odin was the father of Balder and Hod, so to is El (Dagon) the father of Baal and Death

[†] This is paralleled in the defeat of the satyr Miming by Hother, who then receives his sword and arm-ring. (Grammaticus 71; see Davidson 1979, Vol. 1: 70)

Thaeo: And this could well be true considering that *haumavarga* is the name for the mead wolf and this could well mean the wolf Moongarm.

Soleos: So we could associate this very wolf with Mimir, and this seems possible knowing that both Mimir and the wolf are to be found upon the moon.

Epitheus: Yes. And this would also make Odin similar to Achilles, for being speared in the foot by his adversary.

Thaeo: What you say is more true than you might think, Epitheus, when we consider that the god Dionysos was known to be a goat and that Apollo was known as 'Wolf Apollo'.[203] And we have already seen how these gods were associated with one another. It is not thus unexpected that Apollo is the god known to have guided the arrow of Paris to the heel of Achilles.

And if we were to consider Achilles to have been likewise associated as Jacob was, with the boar, it makes some sense that the boar was a sacrifice made to the god Apollo, wherein the thighs of the animal were burned for the god while the rest was consumed by the people.[204]

Epitheus: Spectacular!

Soleos: Thus too we might make sense of the laming of the goat as well as the dismemberment of the boar, if we were to conclude that winter came in as a goat and went out as a boar, and thus proceeding from *Capricornus* through *Cancer*. So there might have been some time when the boar was not yet marked by the arrival of a distinct third figure, but instead represented the god himself who was dismembered. As we suggested before, the boar may have been a manifestation of Osiris, and likewise the boar of Valhall was served up as food and then renewed within a magic cauldron.[205] And this cauldron we have also presumed to have been equivalent with the marsh represented by *Capricornus*.[*]

---

[*] See *The Zodiac Mysteries*

Epitheus: It is quite astonishing, given the striking similarity between the wounding of Adonis in the thigh by a boar and the wounding of Jacob in his thigh.

Soleos: And Adonis is wounded in the groin by the boar while hunting, though we might rather presume that Adonis himself took the form of a boar and that it is for this reason that the consumption of swine was prohibited amongst those of his cult.[206] And this taboo could arise precisely out of the notion that in sacrificing the animal that one was indeed sacrificing the embodiment of the god himself, and thus they would be restricted from eating swine flesh except upon his sacred feast days.[207]*

Epitheus: Truly. And thus likewise the very reason that the Children of Israel abstained from pork was because they were descended from Jacob, who was himself recognized to be a boar, similar to Adonis.[208] And this is interesting too because it would give meaning to the abstention of eating the thigh of the slaughtered animal, as it says in relation to Jacob's thigh.†

Thaeo: Yes, but according to Pausanias, in the temple of Aphrodite the thighs of all sacrificed animals except the pig were dedicated to the goddess within her shrine.[209] And this we might understand if we similarly thought as the pig of Aesop did, which is that the initial prohibition arose from the identification of the goddess with the pig, as in the case of Demeter.[210]

Epitheus: I am not aware of this fable.

Thaeo: Then I will tell it for you. It goes that,

---

* Thus the initial refusal to eat swine arises because it was deemed to be the flesh of the god, but then became an abomination which was explained by a boar having slain the god with a wound to the thigh. (Frazer 1998: 346-347, 486-487)
† The thigh was reserved for the god or priest. And the sacrifice of a goat lamb at the feast of Passover (vernal equinox) could well have been counterpointed by the sacrifice of a boar at the time of the Sukkot festival (autumnal equinox).

The pig and dog were attempting to surpass one another with their insulting, and the pig vowed that Aphrodite would rend the dog apart. But the dog replied sarcastically, "You might well vow by Aphrodite, since clearly she has an abiding affection for you, so steadfastly does she refuse to allow anyone into her temple who has partaken of your unclean meat."

To this the pig replied, "What more proof do you need that the goddess loves me, for does she not reject anyone who would slay me or mangle me in any way? But then consider how bad you smell, and even more so when living than when you are dead."[211]

Epitheus: That was very satisfying. But then did we not equate Jacob with Gilgamesh, who was distinctly a bull rather than a boar?

Soleos: Yes, and it could well be that at times that the bull and boar were variously used, as the bull is likewise found in a contest with the goat, as it says:

Capricorn smote the ankle of the young Taurus,
And Taurus deprived Capricorn of his day of return[212]

Epitheus: Yes.

Soleos: And it is interesting that the pair Adonis and Aphrodite are entirely equivalent to Dumuzi and Ishtar, and that this former (Adonis/Dumuzi) we know to have been identified with the constellation of *Orion*. Thus it is not out of keeping with what we were saying before, of *Orion* being fatally wounded in the thigh or the heel. So too we could consider that the shoulder of the Bull of Heaven came to be the 'Thigh of Heaven' (*Ursa Major*), as this was a bull led out by the goddess Ishtar, as well as a boar.

Epitheus: I see what you mean. And as *Ursa Major* is the constellation called the 'Thigh', from its position, where it never sinks below the sea, it thus represented everlastingness.

Soleos: And recall that it is said that Ishtar and the harlots established mourning for the thigh of the bull just as was done at the observance of Dumuzi's passing.[213]

Epitheus: Yes, I recall.

Soleos: And we find that Jacob imitates a goat and then is lamed; while we also have an instance where Thor's goat is found lamed. This occurs when the great cauldron is fetched form the giant Hymir for the sea giant Aegir, and it is after they attain the cauldron that the goat is found to be lame. And thus the boar would represent half and the goat half, involving a wound to the thigh or a wound to the heel.

Thaeo: And I cannot help but think that the very same meaning is to be found when it is said:

> The very same tusk, yet streaked with shining foam, after his defeated became the weapon of revenge upon his slayer, with a slash to the dancer's ankle from an unavoidable thrust.[214*]

Soleos: Truly. And the name of Aegir may also be related to the word for goat (*'aega'*). Thus we might presume here that the cauldron of Aegir is likewise the constellation of *Capricornus*, which is like the cornucopia of Hades.[215] And this is placed opposite to the constellation of *Cancer* which is known as the crib.[†]

Thaeo: And it should be mentioned that there exists a strong connection between Aegir and Poseidon, who is the father of Theseus. And likewise between Aphrodite and Ariadne, for the crown received by Ariadne is no doubt the one acquired by Theseus, which was made by Hephaistos and attained by him within the sea as a gift bestowed by Amphitrite or Aphrodite herself.[216‡]

While it should likewise be recalled that Hephaistos took up temporary residence with the goddess Thetis after being cast out of heaven; as Dionysos too fled into her arms at the coming of Perseus and his Argive army. And Ariadne is identified as the bride of Dionysos just as Aphrodite is made the bride of Hephaistos, and likewise with Persephone the bride of Hades.

---

[*] The dancer is Ankaios (Ancaeus) of Samos

[†] Thus representing the two passages of the otherworld, of ascent (*Capricornus*) and descent (*Cancer*)

[‡] Aphrodite wore her own golden crown (Homeric Hymns, v 'To Aphrodite' 6)

Soleos: And *Capricornus* symbolized the sun at its lowest point in the sky, the winter *solstice*, and thus the time at which the sun was thought to preferentially light the lower regions rather than the upper regions. And thus we have good reason to think that the symbol of the goat gained its greatest significance through its association with the goat constellation. And as we surmised this constellation to be the cauldron of regeneration, it makes perfect sense when it is associated with the winter *solstice* and thus the renewal of the sun.

Thaeo: Yes. And Pan, the god of abundance, is associated with the goat and the constellation of *Capricornus*. Just as we find that Dionysos is known for having been the recipient of a giant cauldron from Hephaistos which he then gave to the goddess Thetis.[217] But also we have associated this renewal of the sun with *Pegasus* and the Gorgon, who was likewise said to be of goat form,[*] and as such we might compare her to the awful Chimera ('she-goat'). Like the Gorgon too, the Chimera was a female being, and like the Aeon was a fire-breather, and like Aega, the goat of Amaltheia, who had the Gorgon's head in the center of her back.[218] The rest of the Chimera was a lioness, except for the tail which was a dragon's neck. And thus the creature possessed three heads.

Epitheus: So what is known concerning the Chimera?

Thaeo: The Chimera was the daughter of Typhon and Echidna. And it was the hero named Bellerophon ('killer of Belleros'), the son of Glaucos and grandson of Sisyphos, who was responsible for her slaying. Bellerophon was to have killed his own brother and thus was forced into exile, so he went to Argos, to the kingdom of Proteus, which is Tiryns. It was there that he was sought after by the Queen, Stheneboia, but when he rejected her forthrightly she then accused him of having attempted to ravish her. Naturally the words of spiteful and vain women are all too readily accepted as true and thus the king, revealing no apparent menace, caused Bellerophon to travel to Lycia, the kingdom of Iobates, carrying with him a sealed order from Proteus that the king ought to have him put to death. King Iobates had no wish to be responsible for the boy's murder, and

---

[*] See *Roar of the Tempests: A Dialogue*

thus instead charged him to destroy the dreaded and deadly Chimera, which had become such a bane to his land, thinking he had thereby sent him to his doom. To accomplish this task Bellerophon utilized his flying steed which he had captured when it came to drink in at spring of Peirene at Corinth, and accomplished this only with a golden bridle given to him by the goddess Athena.[*] This was the stallion Pegasus ('spring'), who was released from the neck of Medusa when she was beheaded by Perseus. So he went against and slew the beast by shooting it full of arrows, then piercing it with a lance, while he himself emerged without a scratch. But when he set his mind upon using his winged horse to take him into heaven, Zeus was enraged by his presumption and sent flies to pester the horse so that it lurched, sending Bellerophon falling down again to earth. But Pegasus went on up into the sky by himself and so exists there even today among the constellations, while his master remained a dejected and forsaken wanderer upon the earth.[219] And this very contest was shown side-by-side with that of Perseus confrontation with the Gorgon at Lessa in Corinth.[†]

Soleos: What is of great interest here is that Bellerophon is named after the man he killed, and it is likewise said that he was responsible for slaying his own brother. And thus it is not out of the question that this brother he killed had the name of Belleros.[‡]

Epitheus: And his fate mimics that of Cain, who himself was sentenced to be a wanderer upon the earth and loses his place in the garden of eternity, here equated with the heavens reached only by Pegasus.

Soleos: Yes. But we could identify this Belleros with the bull, or the constellation of *Taurus*. And then we find that the Chimera, who is composed partly of a lion, a dragon, and with a goat-head, rather represents the remaining constellations of *Capricornus*, *Leo*, and *Scorpius*; thus representing the *solstices* and *equinoxes*. But there is

---

[*] Or was given to him by Poseidon
[†] In the sacred grove of Aslepios the god is seated upon a throne which depicts the Argive heroes Bellerophon battling the Chimera and Perseus beheading Medusa. (Pausanias ii 27.2; see Levi 1979, Vol. 1: 194)
[‡] Apollodorus names them as Deliades, Peiren, or Alcimenes

little more we might say of Bellerophon, and thus there remains no sure way of knowing whether our conjecture might be true or not.

Thaeo: However, it could be that the Chimera represents the very same beast which was slain so as to give rise to the universe. And thus too slain by her own son, for if we have reconstructed things properly, this original being gives birth to a son and a daughter, being the fire god and moon goddess, and equivalent to Hephaistos and Athena. The moon goddess herself then gave birth to the sun, but her daughter outshines her and so in her envy she swallows her daughter. Although this daughter is again freed by the bear-hero (*Ursa Major*) who gains immortality for this act and takes his place as the god of thunder, the most powerful god of all.[*] This we have found not only relates to the story of the Gorgon but likewise to that of Andromeda, and it is also no doubt related to the story of Cronos swallowing his own children, the birth of Athena from the head of Zeus, and, it seems to me, this very story of Bellerophon and the Chimera.

Epitheus: And in the swallowing of the sun by the moon, which appears to be the situation in Snow White, we found that she might be equivalent to Athena while the Evil Queen would be the beautiful but vain Medusa;[†] so then Snow White's association with the sun makes her rather like the *sol invictus*.

And this seems not altogether different from the conception of the sun god being beheaded so as to release a new sun every winter; when once the new sun is born it is then reconciled with the one who beheaded his father, and thus this involves the slaying of the beast which is the very act which gives birth to the grateful son.

Thaeo: But it is not out of the question that the slain primordial god gave rise to twin sons, as does Isaac, for we likewise find this to be true of Osiris; for Horus is said to be the son of two sisters, who are Isis and Nephthys, and it is they who seek out the body of Osiris. And if we compare these two we find one giving birth to a son of light (Horus) and the other to a son of darkness (Anubis), where each

---

[*] See *Roar of the Tempests: A Dialogue*
[†] See *Roar of the Tempests: A Dialogue*

217

is born at a different season of the year: Horus at the time of the *vernal equinox* and Anubis at the time of the *autumnal equinox*.[220]*
But the correspondence becomes even clearer when regarding that Anubis (Anpu) has a confrontation with his younger brother (Bata) just as Esau does with Jacob. And recall too that Hercules was likewise born as the immortal twin with a mortal brother.[221] And we might also compare the wound to Jacob's thigh with Hercules, who is said to have suffered a wound from a stab in his thigh.[†] Then likewise we have the twin mortal and immortal pair of Castor and Pollux.

---

[*] Some west-central African tribes considered the Morning Star and Evening Star to both be wives of the Moon, and thus alike to the relationship of Isis and Nephthys with Osiris. (Krupp 1991: 187)
[†] This is done by Aries (Hesiod, 'Shield of Hercules' 460) or by Hippokoon's son (Pausanias viii 53.9), *supra*. Hercules' name is merely a Greek form of Har-akhti, which can also be spelled 'Heru-akhti', where 'Heru' is Horus. Thus there is some equivalence here, as Hercules is likewise identified with the sun.

218

CHAPTER 15

Epitheus: I am familiar with the birth of Hercules but not with that of the Dioscouri.

Thaeo: The story is very similar to that of Hercules, for Zeus had intercourse with their mother Leda, the queen of Sparta, in the shape of a swan, but then so did her husband King Tyndareus. As a consequence she gave birth to two pairs: one being Pollux (Polydeuces) and Helen and the other Castor and Clytemnestra.[222]

This is interesting because either Clytemnestra or Helen is also said to be the mother of Iphigenia, and it was she who was sacrificed upon the altar of Artemis because the winds were stilled so as to immobilize the ships of the Achaeans at Aulis. And this came about because Agamemnon had pridefully hunted down a deer within the sacred grove of Artemis, though it is sometimes said that a deer or bull calf was put in place of the girl by the goddess.[223]

Epitheus: Please, would you tell us more concerning this?

Thaeo: Indeed, it is said,

> After they had sailed from Argos and had come to Aulis, now for the second time, the armada was hindered by unfavorable winds. It was Calchas who determined through an oracle that they would be unable to proceed before Agamemnon's most beautiful daughter had been sacrificed as an offering to Artemis. And as soon as Agamemnon heard this he sent Odysseus and Talthybios to Clytemnestra to fetch Iphigeneia, telling her that he had pledged her in marriage to Achilles for his joining the expedition against Troy. Thus Clytemnestra agreed to dispatch her at once to her husband-to-be. But upon setting her upon the sacrificial altar, just as he was about to plunge the knife down into her, Artemis felt pity and snatched her away, bringing her to Taurian lands where she became a priestess of Artemis. And it is said that in her place she was left a deer upon the altar.[224]

Or as Ovid relates it,

Stark political necessity now gained favor over sympathy
And a king's duties precedence over a father's affections
As Iphigenia waits by the altar, prepared for her offering
The virgin entourage erupts into copious unhappy weeping
But at the moment, when innocent blood is about to flow,
Then Diana yields to pity, enshrouding all in a deep mist
So at the dedication's peak, as all shouted prayerful cries
It is said that the goddess exchanged her then for a hind
As a substitute for this young maiden, the Mycenaean girl
This was deemed far more suitable, and once dispatched,
Both Diana and the waters declared the indignity stricken
So with wind now behind these thousand ships they went
And enduring a hard voyage at last came to Troy's shore[225]

And this is interesting in view of what we were speaking of earlier. Because when this substitution was made, Artemis then caused Iphigenia to be transfigured into the goddess Hekate.[226] And this is strikingly similar to what we said before concerning the sacrifice of Isaac, of him being snatched out of the path of the blade with a ram substituted so as to become the figure seen upon the moon. And is this not precisely what we viewed to be the image of the goddess on the moon, being that of Hekate?[*]

Epitheus: Yes.

Soleos: And it seems to me that her name meaning 'giving birth to powers' could likewise have something to do with her sacrifice. And this initial sacrifice is similar, I think, to that mentioned by Celsus.[†]

Epitheus: But what do you mean?

Soleos: I mean to say that the sacrifice of Iphigenia might itself represent the primordial sacrifice which set the universe into motion,

---

[*] See *The Eden Enigma: A Dialogue*
[†] Celsus mentions a living being whose sacrifice gave motion to the universe. (see Hoffman 1987: 97)

the very same which required the sacrifice to be repeated from time to time to keep it in motion.[*]

Epitheus: I see.

Thaeo: But then it occurs to me that this likewise has something to do with the 'thousand ships' launched by the Mycenaeans, if this was merely a recollection of the stars in the heavens. By which I mean that the sacrifice of Iphigeneia was made to set the stars in motion, as represented by the thousand Achaean (Greek) ships.[†]

Phaedo: And what you say makes sense, for recall that it is Isis who sacrificed her thigh so as to give the blood that caused the boat of Sekmet to run.[‡] Isis though is then also like Ishtar and the Bull of Heaven, whose own leg is severed and becomes the constellation of *Ursa Major*, which is likewise known to be the constellation which keeps the heavens turning in its circular motion. And this reminds me of something further, of what these passages might reveal, which say,

> He possessed unsurpassed knowledge of the Star's path
> And concerning the motion of the Sphere about the earth
> In circular rotation but also separately upon its own axis
> He travels as an apparition through air and flows of water
> This is known from the comet, having been mightily born
> Indeed, once he has done this he lives in the great heaven
> Set upon his golden throne, with the earth as his footstool[227]

---

[*] While most sacrifices to Artemis were conventional offerings, such as the bulls and virgins offered in Tauros, one unique sacrifice associated with Iphigeneia was practiced by the Spartans who did not sacrifice virgins but would place the victim before the statue of Artemis where he would be whipped to ejaculation. (Robert Graves, *The Greek Myths, London: Penguin*, 1955; Baltimore: Penguin pp. 73-75: "Iphigenia Among the Taurians")

[†] The ancients reckoned a thousand stars in the heavens as a round figure, merely representing an uncountable number. (see Krupp 1991: 205)

[‡] The boat by which the sun traverses the heavens

And although I ought not say more, this expression of being 'mightily born'[*] ('*iphi genethe*') is precisely the name of Iphigeneia.

Soleos: Indeed. Likewise, there are other sacrifices at the dawn of time, and Mimir likewise is associated with the moon, and the sacred mead which is located there. And some of these sacrifices were known to continue, such as the hanging of victims to Odin among the Norse, the sacrifice of the first-born to Cronos among the Cretans and Israelites,[†] the sacrifice of captives by the Aztecs and Maya, along with many others of like kind, done for the sake of propitiating the gods.[‡]

Thaeo: And let us not forget the Persians, for among them it is recorded that after the sun had been created it yet refused to move through the heavens. Thus was the 'triple-sacrifice' performed by the gods, consisting of Gayomard ('mortal life'), the *haoma* plant, and the sacred bull. And it was from the sacrifice of these three that the sun commenced its motion and likewise brought about the creation of new life; of plants, animals, and people. And this rotation from death through rebirth would continue so long as this triple-sacrifice was continued by man.[228]

Epitheus: And if we consider the fire god who represented the axis of the world, and who himself was believed to be buried beneath the ground, then in addition the sun and moon were seen to be revolving around this pole, as male and female, which is just as we find in dances around the May Pole. And when these celebrations involved the sacrifice of a human being or effigy, its purpose is surely explained in their representation of the motion of the heavens.

---

[*] Relating to an initiatory rebirth after traversing heaven (see Charlesworth 2009, Vol. 2: 799 footnote)

[†] Both Baal and Cronos received child sacrifices (Frazer 1998: 641), and Cronos (the Phoenician Israel), gave birth to a son Jeoud ('only-begotten') who was sacrificed (Frazer 1998: 265-266).

[‡] Or as it is said "*Sicut erat in principio, et nunc, et semper, et in saecula saeculorum,*" as the phrase that would be spoken at the human sacrifice; and what more appropriate times for sacrifices than at the summer and winter solstices.

Soleos: Quite so, Epitheus. And recall too that when Zeus is at the palace of King Lycaon ('wolf') that he grows angry and strikes the table so that it tips; while at the same time it is said that Rhea split Mount Lycaon so as to release the waters of a river. This I think is very similar to the river Van, meaning 'hope', which is said to run from the mouth of Fenrir, who is also a wolf.

Epitheus: Yes. But it occurs to me that if this river of 'hope' spills from the moon, it could thus in some way be related to the gift of 'hope' found in the Pandora story, which is a source of prophecy, or the divine mead.[*]

Soleos: Indeed. Though here is another possibility, for we learn that the river Lycaon merged with the water of the sea and that this became the source from which the sons of Arcus drink. And recall that Arcus is the son of Callisto, who was the daughter of this same King Lycaon of Arcadia; if Thaeo might be willing to relate their story.

Thaeo: Indeed,

> Callisto was very fond of the hunt, and thus she became a companion to the virgin huntress (Diana), who was quite fond of her because they were kindred spirits. However, it came about that Callisto was sought by Jupiter, who later took advantage of her, leaving her pregnant. Though she at first hid this fact from Diana, she eventually became aware of it when she saw her bathing in the river. And feeling betrayed from her failure to disclose this loss of her virginity, she punished Callisto by transforming her former statuesque shape into the crouching form of a bear ('*arktos*').
>
> Callisto then gave birth to Arcus, who was the son of Jupiter and thus the grandson of Lycaon, and this latter had the boy cut up and added to a meat dish which was served to the god when he visited his kingdom in disguise. Lycaon was determined to prove that his visitor was in fact a god, but Jupiter felt such revulsion for what the king had done that he pushed over the table and sent

---

[*] See *The Eden Enigma: A Dialogue*

thunderbolts hurling down to obliterate his palace. He then transformed Lycaon into a wolf, but the parts of Arcus he collected and assembled back together, handing him over to an Aetolian goat-herder to rear.

Once this boy had become a teenager he began to go out hunting in the forests, and there he came face to face with his own mother in her bear form. She fled but he pursued her all the way into the temple of Lycaean Jupiter, and Arcadian law required that anyone found within the sacred temple was to be put to death. But before the Arcadians could carry out the sentence, Jupiter felt sorrow and rescued them from their fate by whisking them away and setting them amongst the stars, where Callisto became the constellation of *Ursa Major* and Arcus became the constellation of *Bootes*, known as the 'bear's keeper' ('*arctophylax*'). [229]

This Arcus too is held to be the ancestor of the Arcadian people;[230] and that these constellations are known as the 'seven oxen' ('*septentriones*') and the ox driver ('*bootes*'), they are also the very constellation thought to drive the heavens around.

Soleos: Splendid. But then there is one further thing we might consider, in that Jupiter is said to have upset the table and thus it became permanently tipped. And this seems to be a reference to the discrepancy between the *ecliptic* and the *celestial equator.**

Thaeo: Very much. But I cannot help but think that there is something more to be known concerning Iphigeneia. And it might have something to do with what she is otherwise called, for she is referred to by Hesiod under the name of Iphimedea.[231†] And we can recognize that Iphimedea contains the component '*medea*' meaning 'members'.[232] And this too could relate back to the identity of the constellation of *Pegasus* as the body of the primordial being; at least in the sense that the sacrifice of this creature, as we were saying of the Chimera, might have given rise to the universe.

---

* See *The Zodiac Mysteries*
† A name meaning 'powerful members' or likewise 'strong mead'

Soleos: Truly. And what you are saying, Thaeo, has a distinct ring of truth about it, for we know too that Iphigeneia, after being rescued from her fate as the offering to Artemis, did henceforth become the companion of Achilles upon the Island of the Blessed, known as Orsilokhia ('midwife');[233] and that she is even to have become the mother of his son Neoptolemus.[234] But precisely the same is said of Medea, who is said to have become the husband of Achilles.[235*]

Thaeo: But then there is at least some reason to think that the original hermaphroditic form was that of a goat, as was the Gorgon, who then gave birth to twins, as goats are known to give birth to.

Epitheus: And I have also noticed that the Egyptian god Ptah, upon whom the earth was to have formed, was named Djed while '*al-jadi*' means 'he-goat', suggesting that there is a connection here between the origin of the world and the goat. And the great god Pan is a goat, as Loki is associated with goats, but there are various other references which suggest that the first being, the primeval giant, who gave birth to twin gods, as with Athena and Hephaistos, was of goat form. And thus we might presume it was this very being who was the source of the first gods, as we figured was so of the unified form represented by Zeus-Hera.[†]

Thaeo: And as we find in the case of the birth of Hephaistos and Athena, Hephaistos is born from Hera without Zeus and Athena is born from the head of Zeus without Hera, but with the assistance of Hephaistos. And we might deem this to be like the beheading of the Gorgon. And so the goat-god (Hephaistos, Pan, Dionysos) then falls to earth where he becomes lame and lures down his sister, the moon (Athena, Selene, Ariadne), who then form a child through his divine semen and her divine breath which becomes a living being.

And it could be that the crown of Ariadne (*Corona Borealis*) is the very crown by which Dionysos first entices her to him, for we find similar occurrences between the God (Bacchus/Dionysos) and Erigone, and likewise Pan and (the moon goddess) Selene.[236] In the

---

[*] The goddess Aphrodite also bore the name of Philommedea (Hesiod, '*Theogony*' 200), *supra*.
[†] See *The Zodiac Mysteries*

same way Hephaistos transfixed the goddess (Athena) with the weapons he had fashioned in his smithy.

Soleos: Yes, and recall that it is said that Hephaistos is lamed in three different ways: at birth, from falling to earth, and from being stabbed with a spear by Athena. But it is likely that the first defect was that he was deemed a mutation and so was thrown out of heaven, thus making him lame. Although being 'lame' also appears to mean that he was afflicted with mortality in his fall to earth, and the Egyptians took lameness to be an attribute of the dead.[237] But it rather seems that it is his child Erechthonios who is truly lame, which he indeed is; while Hephaistos finds himself punished for the rape of his sister by being bound and then covered with earth, thus providing a substrate for the ground we tread upon.

Thaeo: Very good. Poseidon too, called the wide-ruling one, is also known as a lord of wealth, just as is Pluto. But as we said, Poseidon is likewise comparable with Niord, who is comparable with the goddess Nerthus, whose name is akin to the Etruscan sea god Nethuns.[*] And this god too appears with the sun and the dawn, who might be the comparable with Niord's children Frey and Freyia.[†]

Soleos: But there is also a possibility, given the confusion between Poseidon and Prometheus that Poseidon is merely an epithet for Prometheus and Hephaistos. Essentially he is called the 'earth-shaker' and this role is also that of Loki and by extension Prometheus, both of which lie covered and chained, as does, we might add, Cronos. But this also suggests the reason why it is said that in Poseidon's place was left a goat, as we find too with Dionysos; since he was associated with the goat and appears to be equivalent to a large extent with Pan, Satan, Hephaistos, and Loki.

Epitheus: And that makes a great deal of sense, but ought we to equate the hermaphroditic progenitor giant with the fire giant? Or are they alike only because they share some similar traits which were then confused. For consider that Yama appears in the underworld

---

[*] The Etruscan equivalent of Neptune
[†] The gods Usil and Thesan, comparable to Eos and Aurora

beneath a tree drinking mead, which is similar to Mimir; while Prometheus and Cronos are bound in the underworld and known for their prophetic powers. But it seems to me that this beheaded god who prophesies is quite distinct from the goat-formed fire giant, who fell to earth and is now chained beneath a mountain. And recall too that Cronos is said to be on the 'Isle of the Blessed' but also to lie buried beneath the earth.

Soleos: Yes. Likewise, there initially appears to have been two distinct locations which were later confounded, for the underworld was thought either to lie to the north but also to the west, and this might be easily distinguished as two separate realms: the first being the location of the axis of the sky, and thus the great stem of the World Tree, while the other represents the location where the sun enters into the underworld.

Thaeo: Indeed. And Atlas too was thought to be to the west and to the north, and the Gorgons were to live both beyond the western Ocean but also in the land of Hyperborea.

Soleos: So could we then conjecture that the figure of Aegi-Pan arose simply because people in the past, when sacrificing a goat in an offertory cauldron, viewed this as a representative of the earth itself, and the sacrificed goat who gave rise to the world?[*] So if we go by this we would have to consider that the primordial being is actually a divine personification of the earth itself, in the form of a goat or goat-being. And too we find that Pan, Bacchus, and Faunus are all guardians of the earth, who likewise have the appearance of a goat. Though if the god Pan has something to do with the disk of the earth, it might explain why his name is also the same as the word 'pan'.

Thaeo: Yes, and this brings to mind what Homer says:

And Aries likewise suffered under Ephialtes and Otus,
Sons of Aloeus, who fettered him in merciless chains,
Who lay bound in a bronze cauldron, thirteen months[238]

---

[*] Aegi-Pan is sometimes Pan himself or his son by the goat Aega. (Hyginus, *Astronomica* 2.13; Condos 1997: 52)

227

A goat-man sits drinking wine, from an Etruscan mirror.[239]
The satyr is associated with Pan.

Soleos: But especially we might say so of Pan, whose name means 'all', and which we would have to associate with a god who encompasses the entire foundation of the world, the plate of the earth, and the firmament of the heavens.

Epitheus: However, the real meaning must be that Pan is the god who supports the world disk, like Atlas. And thus he is also like Loki, Hephaistos, and Ptah; and Ptah was likewise identified as the original mound around which the earth formed, as its hub or center.

Soleos: Quite true. And Pan likewise appears as *Capricornus*, which is the point of the end of the year and the start of the year, and too the winter *solstice* which was the birthday of the *sol invictus*, symbolized by a goat.[240*]

Thaeo: And I cannot help but think that everything we have been speaking of has something to do with the god Lupercus ('wolf'), who is a shepherd god like Pan, but associated both with the wolf and the goat. And his statue was graced with nothing more than a goatskin loin-cloth, to which dogs and goats were sacrificed in the chill of mid-February, and upon which they burned cakes made by the Vestal Virgins.[241]

Epitheus: That is interesting, Thaeo, because we likewise find it said of King David,

> David danced in front of Yahweh with all of his strength, and he was wearing a linen apron ('*ephod*'). Thus David and all the house of Israel carried up the ark of Yahweh accompanied by loud cries and the blaring of horns.
>
> And when the ark of Yahweh entered the city of David, Michal, daughter of Saul, looked out of her window and saw King David jumping and gesticulating in front of Yahweh, and there grew bitter feelings towards him within her heart.
>
> And they carried the ark of Yahweh and set it where it belonged, within the tent that David had had pitched for this purpose. And there he offered both burnt offerings and peace offerings before Yahweh. And when David had completed the burnt offerings and the peace offerings; he blessed all of the people in the name of Yahweh of Hosts, and there distributed to everyone, the entire population of Israel, both men and women, so that each received a biscuit, a morsel of meat, and cake of dried grapes. Then everyone left and returned to his home.
>
> David then returned to confer blessings upon his own household, but Michal, the daughter of Saul, came out to meet David, saying, "O how the king of Israel brought honor unto

---

[*] There might be some association here with the god Janus, as guardian of gateways. In West Africa they put the blood of a goat or sheep upon the gate to ward away evil. (Frazer 1988: 315)

229

himself upon this day, exposing himself today before the eyes of all of his maid-servants, just as a vulgar man will shamelessly expose himself!"

David replied to Michal, "But it was done in front of Yahweh, who selected me over your father, and before anyone in his house, to crown me the prince of Israel, who are the people of Yahweh. And so I will cavort in jubilation before Yahweh. And I will do things which are yet more disgraceful than this, so that I may be an object of scorn in your eyes; but by the maids of whom you spoke, by them I will be held in honor. And Michal, daughter of Saul, did not have a child unto the day of her death.[242]

And I cannot help but recognize that this resembles the Lupercalia, with the sacrifices made and the cakes distributed by David.[*] But too we had found that David himself was likened to the goat, both in the reference to him being replaced by a goat-skin pillow, as well as David and his men retreating from Saul into the caves of En-Gedi.[†]

But likewise the name of Solomon given by Nathan the prophet is Jedidiah,[‡] which means 'beloved of God', but also means 'goat god'. And relating to this, the Queen of Sheba was likewise known as a sorceress who had goat legs.[243] And there might be some connection here between the goatskins worn by the priests of Lupercus and the notorious *ephod* worn by David during his shameful dancing as he played upon his lyre.[244]

Thaeo: Truly. And we learn this of Pan during the Indian War between the sea armies of Poseidon and those of Dionysos,

There in the resounding uproar of the ocean did horned Pan; stepping lightly across the seldom travelled water, kicking up sea spray with his goat-hooves in such manner that he was left entirely dry; prance about rapidly; striking at the sea with his shepherd's crook and playing a war song upon his Pan-pipes (*syrinx*). Upon hearing a mimicking sound coming everywhere from the waves, one carried by the wind, he did traverse every which way over the sea's landscape upon his mountain-ready feet

---

[*] Raisin cakes are symbolic of paganism according to Hosea 3:1
[†] 1 Samuel 19:13, 24:1
[‡] 2 Samuel 12:25

in search of the source of those strange sounds; so that the echo of the ocean made by his pipes, and borne upon the wind, was itself being sought after.[245]

And then considering his mystic importance, we might recall too the mysterious herder encountered in the following episode,

Then from the roofs and a close hill the peasants started to throw at us a welter of stones, so that it was difficult for us to determine which threat was more severe: the dogs which were around us or the stones hurled from a distance. And one of these at that moment struck the woman who was riding upon me in the head. And her weeping and cries of agony caused her husband, the head herdsman, to quickly come to her assistance. And he in volumed tones called upon the gods, speaking aloud his complaint, as he cleansed the blood from her wound, "Why this savagery? For what purpose do you attack us and throw stones at helpless travelers, we who are human beings just as you are? What spoils do you hope to gain? What harm did we do that you seek revenge on us? You are neither savage men nor beasts who inhabit the cliff caves or scurry among the scree that you ought to delight in causing a man to flounder in his own blood."

No sooner had he finished speaking when the flurry of stones ceased and the ferocious dogs were called off, and then things again grew calm. And one of the men from the village yelled from out of a cypress tree, "We are not robbers and we do not wish to steal from you, but rather we concluded that you were; which is the threat which we'd hoped to avert through our efforts. So know that you may proceed on your journey in peace and security." And while this was welcome to their ears it was only with severe casualties amongst our number that we re-commenced our journey, for some had been bruised badly by stones or some displayed bite wounds; not one of us had emerged unscathed. But after we had travelled some while we arrived at a grove of tall trees and splendidly tinted grass, a tranquil location; there the chiefs sought to halt for a while for rest and recuperation, so that everyone might attend to his lesions. Initially they all fell down and lay upon the grass to recoup their strength before each then went about giving the proper care to his injuries. One washed blood from his with the water of a nearby stream, another pressed an acidic bandage to his contusion, while yet another bandaged a gaping gash. Thus each man was giving due attention to his own needs.

Then as this went on there was an ancient figure standing off and keeping a watchful eye on us from the height of a nearby rise. Clearly he was a shepherd, for there was a flock of goats grazing around him. One of our company enquired of him if he might have any goat's milk to offer for sale, either as fresh milk or new cheese. But for a time he only shook his head, before asking after an interval, "Would you think of food and drink or any other comestibles here? Have you any idea where you've chosen to rest yourselves?" Then with this he gathered his flock around him, about-faced, and went on his way. But what he said and how he suddenly withdrew caused a great deal of anxiety amongst our company. Left in a panic they were occupied with restless inquiries between themselves concerning what manner of place this might be, but found none who could satisfy them.[246]

And I mention this because Pan was known to be a goat herder and guardian of the forest, and as such could well represent the primal force locked within the very earth itself.

Phaedo: And I would like to tell you another well-known story, for here we have a situation where Pan rather resembles the god Baal, just as we find El seeking for himself a sign that Baal had been resurrected; here is the very same spoken of by Plutarch, when he writes about demigods, saying,

Regarding the death of these beings I once heard a man speak concerning them, and one who was neither a con nor a charlatan. It was Epitherses, the father of the lecturer Aemilianus, some of whom here have heard his oratory; and he lived at the same time I did and was my grammar instructor. And he told a story that once, when making a trip to Italy, he went upon a cargo vessel which also carried passengers. When evening had already come and they were close to the Echinades Islands, then the wind fell and the ship went adrift until it neared Paxi. At that time nearly everyone was still up and many had yet to finish their dessert wine, when suddenly there was heard from Paxi Island a human voice, someone shouting for Thamus. And everyone was quite astonished at this, as Thamus was the Egyptian pilot, not even known by name to many of the passengers. He was called two times and answered not, but upon the third call he answered, so that the one calling, raising his voice, yelled back to him, "When you are opposite Palodes, proclaim that 'Great Pan is dead.'" And, according to Epitherses, when he had heard this, everyone was baffled and discussed among themselves if it would be best to do as he had been told or to reject it and drop the entire matter. But given the situation, Thamus decided that if a wind arose he would continue by and say nothing, but if there came no breeze and the sea remained still all around them, he would proclaim what he had heard.

Thus, coming opposite of Palodes, they experienced no wind or waves; and Thamus at the stern, and facing the shore, repeated exactly the words, 'Great Pan is dead.' And even as the words were leaving his lips there arose such a tremendous lamenting, not of one voice but of many; and along with this were heard great cries of alarm. And as several people were onboard that ship this tale soon found its way all the way to Rome, and Tiberius Caesar had Thamus summoned to him. Tiberius was so sure of the veracity of this tale that he had some research done concerning this Pan; and the scholars, of which there were many within his entourage, concluded that he was the child of Hermes and Penelope.[247]

Read other books from the Paleoastronomy Series:

Volume 1: The Eden Enigma

Volume 2: Roar of the Tempests

Volume 3: The Death of King David

Volume 4: The Zodiac Mysteries

Volume 5: Blood & Incest

Visit: www.timothyjstephany.com

Bibliography

Adkins, Lesley and. Roy A. Adkins. <u>Dictionary of Roman Religion</u>. 1996. New York: Oxford, 2000.

Ananikian, Mardiros H. <u>Armenian Mythology</u>. 1922. Los Angeles: Indo-European, 2010.

Apollodorus. <u>The Library of Greek Mythology</u>. 1997. Trans. Robin Hard. New York: Oxford, 1998.

Apuleius. <u>The Golden Ass: A New Translation</u>. Trans. E. J. Kenney. London: Penguin, 1998.

Asimov, Isaac. <u>Asimov's Guide to the Bible: Two Volumes in One, Old and New Testaments</u>. 1968, 1969. Avenel, New Jersey: Wings, 1981.

Barnstone, Willis, ed. <u>The Other Bible</u>. San Francisco: Harper, 1984.

Bonfante, Larissa and. Judith Swaddling. <u>Etruscan Myths</u>. Austin: University of Texas, 2006.

Boyce, Mary, ed. trans. <u>Textual Sources for the Study of Religion: Zoroastrianism</u>. Ed. John Hinnells. Chicago: University of Chicago, 1984.

Budge, E. A. Wallis. <u>The Book of the Dead</u>. 1895. New York: Gramercy, 1999.

Budge, E. A. Wallis. <u>Egyptian Tales and Legends: Pagan, Christian, Muslim</u>. 1931. New York: Dover, 2002.

Budge, E. A. Wallis. <u>Legends of the Egyptian Gods: Hieroglyphic Texts and Translations</u>. 1912. New York: Dover, 1994.

Byock, Jesse L., trans. The Saga of King Hrolf Kraki. London: Penguin, 1998.

Carson, Ciaran. The Tain. London: Viking Penguin, 2008.

Cashford, Jules. Homeric Hymns. London: Penguin, 2003.

Celsus. On the True Doctrine: A Discourse Against the Christians. Trans. R. Joseph Hoffman. New York: Oxford, 1987.

Charlesworth, James H., ed. The Old Testament Pseudepigrapha Vol. 1: Apocalyptic Literature and Testaments. 1983. Peabody, Mass: Hendrickson, 2009.

Charlesworth, James H., ed. The Old Testament Pseudepigrapha Vol. 2: Expansions of the "Old Testament" and Legends, Wisdom and Philosophical Literature, Prayers, Psalms, and Odes, Fragments of Lost Judeo-Hellenistic Works. 1983. Peabody, Mass: Hendrickson, 2009.

Condos, Theony. Star Myths of the Greeks and Romans: A Sourcebook. Grand Rapids: Phanes, 1997.

Coogan, Michael David. Stories from Ancient Canaan. Louisville: Westminster, 1978.

Dalley, Stephanie, trans. Myths from Mesopotamia. 1989. New York: Oxford, 2000.

Deane, John Bathurst. Worship of the Serpent: Traced Throughout the World. 1833. n.l.: Forgotten Books, 2008.

de Boron, Robert. Merlin and the Grail. Trans. Nigel Bryant. Cambridge: D. S. Brewer, 2001.

de Santillana, Giorgio and. Hertha von Dechend. Hamlet's Mill: An Essay Investigating the Origins of Human Knowledge and its Transmission through Myth. 1969. Boston: Godine, 1977.

Fideler, David. Jesus Christ Son of God: Ancient Cosmology and Early Christian Symbolism. 1993. Wheaton, Illinois: Quest, 2007.

Frazer, James George. The Golden Bough: A New Abridgement. 1994. New York: Oxford, 1998.

Frazer, James George. Folklore in the Old Testament: Studies in Comparative Religion, Legend, and Law (Abridged Edition). New York: Avenel, 1988.

Gantz, Jeffrey. Early Irish Myths and Sagas. London: Penguin, 1981.

Gantz, Jeffrey. The Mabinogion. London: Penguin, 1976.

Grammaticus, Saxo. The History of the Danes: Books I-IX. Trans. Peter Fisher. Ed. Hilda Ellis Davidson. Cambridge: D. S. Brewer, 1979 and 1980.

Greenberg, Gary. Bible Myth: The African Origins of the Jewish People. Secaucus, New Jersey: Citadel Press, 1996.

Grimm, Jacob. Teutonic Mythology. 1883, 1888. Trans. Ed. James Steven Stallybrass. 4 vols. New York: Dover, 2004.

Guthrie, W. K. C. Orpheus and Greek Religion. 1952. Princeton: Princeton University Press, 1993.

Harley, Timothy. Moon Lore. 1885. Tokyo: Charles E. Tuttle, 1970.

Hesiod. The Works and Days, Theogony, The Shield of Herakles. 1959. Trans. Richmond Lattimore. Ann Arbor: University of Michigan, 1991.

Homer. The Iliad. Trans. Robert Fagles. New York: Viking, 1990.

Howey, M. Oldfield. The Encircled Serpent: A Study of Serpent Symbolism in All Countries and Ages. New York: Arthur Richmond, 1955.

Josephus. Josephus: The Complete Works. 1737. Trans. William Whiston. Nashville: Thomas Nelson, 1998.

Kramer, Samuel and. Diane Wolkstein. Inanna: Queen of Heaven and Earth. New York: Harper & Row, 1983.

Krupp, E. C. Beyond the Blue Horizon: Myths and Legends of the Sun, Moon, Stars, and Planets. New York: HarperCollins, 1991.

Larrington, Carolyne, trans. The Poetic Edda. 1996. New York: Oxford, 1999.

Leach, M., ed. Funk and Wagnall's Standard Dictionary of Folklore, Mythology and Legend. San Francisco: Harper Collins, 1984.

Lonnrot, Elias. The Kalevala. Trans. Keith Bosley. New York: Oxford, 1989.

Mair, A. W. and. G. R. Mair, trans. Callimachus, Lycophron, Aratus. 1921. Cambridge: Harvard, 1955.

Markman, Roberta H. and. Peter T. Markman. The Flayed God: The Mythology of Mesoamerica. San Francisco: Harper Collins, 1992.

Nilsson, Martin P. Greek Folk Religion. 1940. Philadelphia: University of Pennsylvania Press, 1972.

O'Flaherty, Wendy Doniger, trans. Rig Veda. London: Penguin, 1981.

Olcott, William Tyler. Star Lore: Myths, Legends, and Facts. 1911. New York: Dover, 2004.

Olivelle, Patrick. The Law Code of Manu. New York: Oxford, 2004.

Orpheus. The Hymns of Orpheus: With the Life and Theology of
Orpheus. 1792. Trans. Thomas Taylor. n.l.: Forgotten Books, 2008.

Otto, Walter F. Dionysus: Myth and Cult. 1960. Bloomington,
Indiana: Indiana University Press, 1965.

Ovid. The Metamorphoses of Ovid. Trans. Allen Mandelbaum. San
Diego: Harcourt, 1993.

Parke, H. W. Festivals of the Athenians: Aspects of Greek and
Roman Life. 1977. Ithaca, New York: Cornell University Press,
1990.

Pausanias. Guide to Greece: Vol. 1 Central Greece. Trans. Peter
Levi. 1971. London, Penguin, 1979.

Pausanias. Guide to Greece: Vol. 2 Southern Greece. Trans. Peter
Levi. 1971. London, Penguin, 1979.

Pindar. The Complete Odes. Trans. Anthony Verity. New York:
Oxford, 2007.

Plutarch. Moralia, Vol. V. Trans. Frank Cole Babbitt. Cambridge:
Harvard, 1936.

Simek, Rudolf. Dictionary of Northern Mythology. 1984. Trans.
Angela Hall. Cambridge: D. S. Brewer, 1993.

Staal, Julius D. W. The New Patterns in the Sky: Myths and
Legends of the Stars. Blacksburg, Virginia: McDonald &
Woodward, 1988.

St. Clair, George. Creation Records Discovered in Egypt. London:
Strand, 1898.

Storl, Wolf-Dieter. Shiva: The Wild God of Power and Ecstasy.
Rochester, Vermont: Inner Traditions, 2004.

Sturluson, Snorri. <u>Edda</u>. Trans. Ed. Anthony Faulkes. London: Everyman, 1987.

Temple, Olivia and. Robert Temple. <u>Aesop: The Complete Fables</u>. London: Penguin, 1998.

Ulansey, David. <u>The Origins of the Mithraic Mysteries: Cosmology & Salvation in the Ancient World</u>. 1989. New York: Oxford, 1991.

White, Gavin. <u>Babylonian Star-Lore</u>. 2007. London: Solaria, 2008.

ENDNOTES

[1] Hesiod, Theogony 104-115 (see Lattimore, 1987, pp. 129-130)

[2] Hesiod, Theogony 116-128 (see Lattimore, 1987, p. 130)

[3] 'Voluspa' 1-10, 17-18 (see Larrington 1999, pp. 4-6)

[4] Sturluson, Edda 4-7 (see Faulkes, 1987, pp. 9-11)

[5] Storl (2004), p. 125.

[6] Rig Veda 10.129 (see O'Flaherty, 1981, pp. 25-26)

[7] 'Greater Bundahishn' 1a. (see Boyce, 1990, p. 48)

[8] 'Greater Bundahishn' 14 (see Boyce, 1990, p. 51)

[9] 'The Sibylline Oracles' 6:19 (see Charlesworth, 2009, vol. 1, p. 407)

[10] 'Haggadah' (see Barnstone, 1984, p. 28)

[11] 'Jubilees' 4:29 (see Charlesworth, 2009, Vol. 2, p. 63), (Adam first buried) and 'The Life of Adam and Eve' 42:4 ff (see Charlesworth, 2009, Vol. 2, p. 293), (Abel not buried before Adam)

[12] 'Gylfaginning' 8 (see Faulkes, 1987, p. 12); 'Grimnismal' 40 (see Larrington, 1999, p. 57)

[13] 'The Epic of Creation' i (see Dalley, 2000, p. 235)

[14] 'Haggadah' (see Barnstone, 1984, p. 24)

[15] 'Gylfaginning' 14 (see Faulkes, 1987, p. 16)

[16] 'Jubilees' 2.2-16 (see Charlesworth, 2009, Vol. 2, pp. 55-57)

[17] 'The History of Creation' A & B (see Budge, 1994, pp. 3-13)

[18] Plutarch, 'Isis and Osiris' 32, Moralia V 363E (see Loeb 306, p. 79)

[19] Armenian source of the myth of Zurvan and his twin sons (see Boyce, 1990, p. 97)

[20] 'Creation', The Law Code of Manu 1.5-31 (see Olivelle, 2004, pp. 13-15)

[21] 'On the Origin of the World' (see Barnstone, 1984, pp. 63-64)

[22] Lonnrot, Kalevala 1:111-340 (see Bosley, 1999, pp. 4-10)

[23] 'The Fourth Book of Ezra' 12 (see Charlesworth, 2009, Vol. 1, p. 551); see also Daniel 7:13, I Enoch 62:7

[24] Hesiod, 'Theogony' 176-200 (see Lattimore, 1991, pp. 133-135)

[25] Hyginus, Fabulae 271

[26] Ovid, Metamorphoses iv 288 ff.

[27] 'On the Origin of the World' (see Barnstone, 1984, p. 69)

[28] Budge (1999), p. 186.

[29] White (2008), p. 125.

[30] Pausanias, Description of Greece i, 19.2 (see Levi, 1979, Vol. 1, p. 53)

[31] Sophocles, 'Oedipus Rex'

[32] See Apollosorus, Library 3.5 §§ 7-9, (see Hard, 1998, pp. 105-107)

[33] Sophocles, 'Oedipus Rex', 25 ff., 95 ff.

[34] 'The Wooing of Etain' (see Gantz, 1981, p. 59)

[35] Genesis 12:10-20; also Pseudo-Eupolemus, "Praeparatio Evangelica" 9.17.6-7 (see Charlesworth, 2009, Vol. 2, p. 881)

[36] Genesis 20:1-18
[37] Genesis 20:12
[38] Sturluson, 'Gylfaginning' 6-7 (see Faulkes, 1987, p. 11)
[39] Apollodorus, Library 3.4 § 3 (see Hard , 1998, p. 101)
[40] Callimachus, I, 'Hymn to Zeus' 30 ff. (see Loeb 129, p. 41); also Lycophron, Alexandra (see Loeb 129, p. 327)
[41] 'Jubilees' 4:33 (see Charlesworth, 2009, Vol. 2, p. 64)
[42] Hyginus, preface
[43] The Holy Bible Revealed: Genesis through Kings (2014)
[44] The Holy Bible Revealed: Genesis through Kings (2014)
[45] 'Jubilees' 4.33 (see Charlesworth, 2009, Vol. 2, p. 64)
[46] Genesis 19:27-38
[47] Ovid, Metamorphoses viii
[48] 'The Testament of Adam' 3.5 (see Cherlesworth, 2009, Vol. 1, p. 994)
[49] IV Ezra 16:19 (see Charlesworth, 2009, Vol. 1, p. 558); 'The Sybilline Oracles' 4:109 ff (see Charlesworth, 2009, Vol. 1, pp. 386-387)
[50] Enuma Elish: The Babylonian Creation Epic (2014), pp. 57-62, 67-69, 73-82; also 'Atrahasis' 1-2 (see Dalley, 2000, pp. 9-27)
[51] Enuma Elish: The Babylonian Creation Epic (2014), pp. 90-91, 93-95; also 'Atrahasis' 2 (see Dalley, 2000, pp. 27-29)
[52] Genesis 18:16-33
[53] Frazer (1988), pp. 82-83.
[54] Jubilees 3:32-4:15 (see Charlesworth, 2009, Vol. 2, pp. 60-62)
[55] Genesis 4:15-16
[56] Genesis 4:10-12
[57] Genesis 3:17-19
[58] Josephus, The Antiquities of the Jews 1.2.1 § 59
[59] 'The Life of Adam and Eve' 24:4 (see Charlesworth, 2009, Vol. 2, p. 283)
[60] III Baruch (Slavonic, Greek) 9:3, 9:7 (see Charlesworth, 2009, Vol. 1, p. 672); also 'Haggadah' (see Barnstone, 1984, p. 37)
[61] Harley (1970), p 86.
[62] 'The Life of Adam and Eve' 21.3 (see Charlesworth, 2009, Vol. 1, p. 264)
[63] Grimm 2004: p. 571.
[64] Beowulf 2435 ff.
[65] Pseudo-Eupolemus, 'Praeparatio Evangelica' 9.17.8-9 (see Charlesworth, 2009, Vol. 2, p. 881)
[66] Ovid, Metamorphoses i
[67] Frazer (1918), pp. 145, 275-6, also 107-110.
[68] Numbers 15:32-36
[69] Mabinogion, 'How Culhwch Won Olwen' (see Gantz, 1976, pp. 148)

[70] Genesis 13:5-9

[71] Genesis 36:6-8

[72] 'The Conflict of Horus and Set', Pyramid Texts, 4,500 B.P.

[73] 'The Tale of Two Brothers' (see Budge, 2002, pp. 104-105)

[74] See also Greenberg (1996), pp. 234-237.

[75] 2 Samuel 1:26

[76] Genesis 25:27

[77] The Gilgamesh Cycle (2014), pp. 5-14; also 'Gilgamesh' 1 (see Dalley, 2000, pp. 51-59)

[78] The Gilgamesh Cycle (2014), pp. 15-22; also 'Gilgamesh' 2 (see Dalley, 2000, pp. 59-61), 'Gilgamesh (OBV) 2,3 (see Dalley, 2000, pp. 136-142)

[79] The Tain vi (see Carson, 2008, pp. 77-78)

[80] Eratosthenes, Constellations 37 (see Condos, 1997, p. 105); Aratus, Phaenomena 360 ff. (see Loeb 129, p. 235)

[81] Staal (1988), p. 221.

[82] de Santillana (1977), p. 210.

[83] Poetic Edda, 'Grottasongr' 8-9 (see Larrington, 1999, p. 261)

[84] de Santillana (1977), pp. 210, 258

[85] Apollodorus, Library 1.9 § 26 (see Hard, 1998, p. 56)

[86] Ananikian (2010), pp. 49-50, 68-69.

[87] Apollodorus, Library Epit. 3.17 (see Hard, 1997, p. 149)

[88] 'Branwen Daughter of Llyr', Mabinogion (see Gantz, 1976, pp. 79-81)

[89] see Gantz (1976), pp. 141, 173, 190.

[90] 'The Book of the Dead', lxi (see Budge, 1999, p. 444); also Krupp (1991), p. 235

[91] The Gilgamesh Cycle (2014), p. 107.

[92] Ovid, Metamorphoses xi; Apollodorus, Library 3.13 § 5; Pindar 'Isthmian Ode' 8

[93] The Tain vi (see Carson, 2007, pp. 80-81)

[94] Gantz (1976), p. 117.

[95] Olcott (2004), p. 278.

[96] Aratus, Phaenomena 525-544 (see Loeb 129, p. 249)

[97] Olcott (2004), pp. 281-282; also Job 38:31

[98] Genesis 3:14-15

[99] see St. Clair (1898), p. 220.

[100] Hesiod, 'The Shield of Hercules' 364, 460 (see Lattimore, 1991, pp. 213, 219)

[101] Ovid, Metamorphoses ix

[102] Deane (2008), p. 177, also p. 167.

[103] Markman (1992), pp. 75-76 and Deane (2008), p. 173

[104] Howey (1955), p. 148; also Plutarch 'Isis and Osiris' 43

[105] Otten, H. 1958, 'Die erste Tafel des hethitschen Gilgamesh-Epos', Istanbuler Mitteilungen, 8, pp. 93-125 (Dalley, 2000, p. 127, note 32)

[106] Aratus, Phaenomena, 590 ff. (see Loeb 129, pp. 253, 255)

[107] Aelian, De Natura Animalium ('Of Nature of Animals') 12.21

[108] 2 Samuel 4:5-12

[109] 2 Samuel 21: 1-7

[110] 2 Samuel 21: 8-9

[111] 2 Samuel 21: 10-14

[112] Plutarch, 'Isis and Osiris' 13-19, Moralia V 356-358 (Loeb 306, pp. 35-49)

[113] Plutarch, 'Isis and Osiris' 27, 44-45, Moralia V 361D, 368F-369A (Loeb 306, pp. 65, 109)

[114] Genesis 16:12

[115] Diodorus iii 67; also Frazer (1998), p. 404

[116] Plutarch, 'Isis and Osiris' 69, Moralia V 378F (see Loeb 306, p. 161)

[117] Otto (1965), pp. 200, 203; Parke (1986), p. 98.

[118] Orphic Hymns (see Guthrie, 1993, p. 43); also Plutarch, ' The E at Delphi' 9, 'The Oracles at Delphi' 12, MoraliaV 388F-389A, 400C-D (see Loeb 306, pp. 223, 293)

[119] Otto (1965), pp. 77, 104.

[120] Plutarch 'Isis and Osiris' 34, Moralia V 364D (see Loeb 306, p. 83)

[121] Hesiod, Theogony 947-949 (see Lattimore, 1987, p. 181)

[122] Apollodorus, Library 3.1 §§ 1-2 (see Hard, 1998, pp. 96-97)

[123] Apollosorus, Library 3.1 § 3 (see Hard, 1998, pp. 97-98)

[124] Ovid, Metamorphoses viii

[125] Apollosorus, Library 3.15 §§ 5-7 (see Hard, 1998, p. 136)

[126] Apollodorus, Library 3.16 §§ 1-2, (see Hard, 1998, p. 138); also Pausanias, Description of Greece i 27.8 (see Levi, 1979, Vol. 1, p. 78)

[127] Apollodorus, Library 3.15 § 8 (see Hard, 1998, p. 137)

[128] Ovid, Metamorphoses viii

[129] Apollodorus, Library Epit. 1.7-10 (see Hard, 1991, p. 140), Pausanias, Description of Greece x 29.2 (see Levi, 1979, Vol. 1, p. 481)

[130] 'Saga of Hrolf Kraki' (see Byock, 1998, p. 44)

[131] 'Saga of Hrolf Kraki' (see Byock, 1998, pp. 38, 40)

[132] 'Saga of Hrolf Kraki' (see Byock, 1998, pp. 44-47)

[133] Robert de Boron, 'Merlin' (see Bryant, 2001, p. 107)

[134] Robert de Boron, 'Merlin' (see Bryant, 2001, p. 111)

[135] Robert de Boron, 'Perceval' (see Bryant, 2001, p. 171)

[136] Krupp (1991), pp. 230, 272; see Ovid Metamorphoses i, 169-175

[137] Mabinogion, 'How Culhwch Won Olwen' (see Gantz, 1976, p. 175)

[138] Hyginus, Poetic Astronomy 2.23 (see Condos, 1997, p. 62); also Otto (1965), p. 170

[139] Pausanias, Description of Greece ix 31.2 (see Levi, 1979, Vol. 1, p. 374)
[140] Pausanias, Description of Greece ix 31.2 (see Levi, 1979, Vol. 1, p. 374)
[141] 'The Book of Dead', xv (see Budge, 1999, p. 344)
[142] St. Clair (1898), pp. 402-403.
[143] Otto (1965), p. 203; Parke (1986), p. 103
[144] Phanodemus and Philochorus given in Otto (1965), p. 205
[145] Plutarch, 'The E at Delphi', Moralia V 394B (see Loeb 306, p. 253)
[146] Ulansey (1989), pp. 43-44.
[147] Otto (1965), p. 185 and Nonnus, Dionysiaca 47.665
[148] Grammaticus, History of the Danes Vol. 1, 67 (see Davidson, 1979, p. 73)
[149] Grammaticus, History of the Danes Vol. 1, 63 (see Davidson, 1979, p. 69)
[150] Grammaticus, History of the Danes Vol. 1, 67 (see Davidson, 1979, p. 73)
[151] Grammaticus, History of the Danes Vol. 1, 67-68 (see Davidson, 1979, pp. 73-74)
[152] Poetic Edda, 'Vafthudnismal' 47 (see Larrington, 1999, p. 47)
[153] Josephus, The Antiquities of the Jews 6.14.7 § 372 and 2 Samuel 1
[154] 'The Testament of the Patriarchs', 'Testament of Judah' 9:1 (see Charlesworth, 2009, Vol. 1, p. 797)
[155] 2 Samuel 21:20
[156] The Tain viii (see Carson, 2008, p. 112)
[157] see 2 Enoch 15:4 (see Charlesworth, 2009, Vol. 1, p. 126)
[158] 2 Kings 2:19-24
[159] Markman (1992), p. 271.
[160] Howey (1955), p. 93.
[161] Frazer (1998), p. 605.
[162] Howey (1955), pp. 93-94.
[163] Frazer (1998), p. 596.
[164] 'Sir Gawain and the Green Knight' 283
[165] Aratus, Phaenomena 160ff (see Loeb 129, p. 277); Olcott (2004), p. 89
[166] Apollodorus, Library 3.4 § 2 (see Hard, 1998, p. 100)
[167] Plutarch, 'The Obsolescence of Oracles' 15, Moralia V 418A-B (see Loeb 306, p. 395)
[168] Plutarch, 'The Obsolescence of Oracles' 21, Moralia V 421C (see Loeb 306, p. 411)
[169] Krupp (1991), pp. 152-153.
[170] Euripides fragment (see Colin Austin, Recherches de Papyrologie 4 (1967); Nova fragmenta Euripidea (1968) fragments 65.90-97.)
[171] Apollodorus, Library 3.14 § 6, 3.15 § 1 (see Hard, 1998, pp. 133, 134)
[172] Lycophron, Alexandra 110F (see Loeb 129, p. 329)

¹⁷³ see Olcott (2004), p. 65.
¹⁷⁴ Beowulf 87 f.
¹⁷⁵ Bonfante (2006), p. 45.
¹⁷⁶ Homer, Odyssey viii, 354 ff.
¹⁷⁷ 'The Tale of the Two Brothers' (see Budge, 2002, p. 99)
¹⁷⁸ 'The Book of the Dead', lxxxiii (see Budge, 1999, pp. 552-553)
¹⁷⁹ Apollodorus, Library 3.14 § 4 (see Hard, 1998, p. 131)
¹⁸⁰ Parke (1986), pp. 97-100.
¹⁸¹ Budge (1999), p. 184. (Thoth acted as judge between Horus and Set)
¹⁸² Leach (1984), p. 180.
¹⁸³ 'Coutrship of Inanna and Dumuzi' (see Kramer, 1983, pp. 30-36)
¹⁸⁴ Poetic Edda, 'Voluspa' 52-53 (see Larrington, 1999, p. 11); Sturluson, 'Gylfaginning' 51 (see Faulkes, 1987, p. 54)
¹⁸⁵ Mabinogion, 'Branwen Daughter of Llyr' (see Gantz, 1976, pp. 79-80)
¹⁸⁶ Robert de Boron, 'Perceval' (see Bryant, 2001, p. 154)
¹⁸⁷ Poetic Edda, 'Lokasenna' 17 (see Larrington, 1999, p. 87)
¹⁸⁸ 'Baal' iii-v (see Coogan, 1978, pp. 105-115)
¹⁸⁹ 'Baal' v (see Coogan, 1978, pp. 109-110)
¹⁹⁰ see Coogan (1978), p. 28.
¹⁹¹ 'Aqhat' iii, 'Baal' v, (see Coogan, 1978, pp. 41, 84, 114)
¹⁹² 'Baal' iii (see Coogan, 1978, p. 104)
¹⁹³ 'Aqhat' iii (see Coogan, 1978, pp. 40, 46)
¹⁹⁴ 'Aqhat' i (see Coogan, 1978, pp. 36-37)
¹⁹⁵ Otto (1965), pp. 184, 204.
¹⁹⁶ Orphic Hymns xlv 'To Liknitus Bacchus' and lii 'To Amphietus Bacchus' (see Taylor, 2007, pp. 108, 115)
¹⁹⁷ 'The Wooing of Etain' (see Gantz, 1981, pp. 39-40)
¹⁹⁸ Harley (1970), p. 94.
¹⁹⁹ White (2008), p. 65.
²⁰⁰ see White (2008), p. 68.
²⁰¹ 'Baal' iii (see Coogan, 1978, p. 101)
²⁰² Poetic Edda, 'Sigdrifurmal' 13-14, 18 (see Larrington, 1999, pp. 168-169)
²⁰³ Homer, Iliad iv, 117 (see Fagles, 1990, p. 148); Pausanias, Description of Greece viii 46.3 (see Levi, 1979, Vol. 2, p. 485)
²⁰⁴ Pausanias, Description of Greece viii 38.8 (see Levi, 1979, Vol. 2, p. 469)
²⁰⁵ Sturluson, 'Gylfaginning' 38 (see Faulkes, 2000, p. 32); 'Grimnismal' 18 (see Larrington, 1999, p. 54)
²⁰⁶ Frazer (1998), pp. 346-347.
²⁰⁷ Frazer (1998), pp. 400-401.
²⁰⁸ see Frazer (1998), p. 487.

[209] Pausanias, Description of Greece ii 10.4 (see Levi, 1979, Vol. 1, p. 155)

[210] see Frazer (1998), pp. 483-484.

[211] Aesop Fable 329 (see Temple, 1998, p. 242)

[212] 'The Sybylline Oracles' 5:518-519 (see Charlesworth, 2009, Vol. 1, p. 405)

[213] 'Gilgamesh' vi (see Dalley, 2000, p. 82)

[214] Lycophron, Alexandra 490f. (see Loeb 129, p. 361); Pausanias, Description of Greece viii 45

[215] Olcott (2004), p. 117 and Nilsson (1972), p. 47.

[216] Otto (1965), pp. 182-185.

[217] Homer, Odyssey xxiv, 74 f.

[218] Eratosthenes, Constellations 13 and Hyginus, Poetic Astronomy 2.13 (see Condos, 1997, pp. 49-52)

[219] See Apollodorus, Library 2.3 1-2; Pindar, Isthmian Ode 7; Hyginus, Poetic Astronomy 2.18; also Staal (1988), pp. 27-29.

[220] Plutarch, 'Isis and Osiris' 14, Moralia V 356F (see Loeb 306, p. 39); also St. Clair (1898), p. 220

[221] Apollodorus, Library 2.4 § 8 (see Hard, 1998, p. 70)

[222] Apollodorus, Library 3.10 § 7 (see Hard, 1998, p. 120)

[223] Antoninus Liberalis, Metamorphoses 27, etc.

[224] Apollodorus, Library Epit. 3.21-22 (see Hard, 1998, p. 150)

[225] Ovid, Metamorphoses xii

[226] Hesiod, Catalogue of Women (fragment 71) given in Pausanias, Description of Greece i. 43.1 (see Levi, 1979, Vol. 1, p. 119)

[227] Eusebius 13.13.5; also 'Orphica' long version E (see Charlesworth, 2009, Vol. 2, pp. 799, 840)

[228] Boyce (1990), p. 10.

[229] Hyginus, Poetic Astronomy 2.1, 2.4 (see Condos, 1997, pp. 56, 198); Apollodorus, Library 3.8 § 2 (see Hard, 1998, p. 115)

[230] Hyginus, Poetic Astronomy 2.1 (see Condos, 1997, p. 198)

[231] Hesiod, Catalogue of Women given in Pausanias, Description of Greece i. 43.1 and fragment 23(a) 17–26, Oxyrhynchus Papyri

[232] Hesiod, Theogony 200 (see Lattimore, 1991, p. 135)

[233] Antoninus Liberalis, Metamorphoses 27

[234] Lycophron, Alexandra 183f. (see Loeb 129, p. 337)

[235] Apollodorus, Library Epit. 5.5 (see Hard, 1998, p. 155)

[236] Virgil, Georgics 3.390 ff. and Ovid, Metamorphoses vi

[237] 'The Book of the Dead' plate xviii, chapter lxxiv (see Budge, 1988, p. 292)

[238] Homer, Iliad v, 337-439 (see Fagles, 1990, pp. 176-177)

[239] see Bonfante (2006), p. 13.

[240] Staal (1988), p. 217.

[241] Justin Martyr, Epitome of the Philippic History of Pompeius Trogus 43.1.7.

[242] 2 Samuel 6:14-23

[243] Arabic folk tale (the Queen of Sheba has legs like a goat); also 'The Testament of Solomon' 19:3 (see Charlesworth, 2009, Vol. 1, p. 982) (the Queen of Sheba is a witch)

[244] Josephus, The Antiquities of the Jews 7.4.2 § 85

[245] Nonnus, Dionysiaca 43.214 ff.

[246] Apuleius, The Golden Ass, viii (see Kenney, 1998, pp. 138-139)

[247] Plutarch, 'The Obsolescence of Oracles' 419B-D (see Loeb 306, pp. 401, 403)

www.ingramcontent.com/pod-product-compliance
Lightning Source LLC
Chambersburg PA
CBHW071032290526
45795CB00004B/1185